FISHING
WITH THE
FLY

Sketches by Lovers of the Art, with
Illustrations of Standard Flies. Collected by
Charles F. Orvis
&
A. Nelson Cheney

The Wellfleet Press

FOREWORD

Charles Frederick Orvis, born in 1831 in Manchester, Vermont, "a pleasant land among the mountains," made his mark by founding in 1856, the fishing-tackle company that bears his name. He was a pragmatic man with combined talents for mechanical engineering and business—a quintessential New Englander, in other words. Had he lived in Connecticut, there might today be a famous arms company called Orvis; in New Bedford he might have founded a seafaring dynasty. But the Green Mountains made him a trout fisherman, and his yankee practicality drove him to make a living from it. Few have ever combined the both so well.

Millions of people now know Charle's Orvis Company for its "lifestyle" clothing and gifts. The anglers among them recognize the initials C.F.O. as the name long given to the company's top line of trout reels. Well-read fly fishermen know Charles vaguely as the father of Mary Orvis Marbury, who became famous for one of the best-selling angling books in America, *Favorite Flies and Their Histories*. Today, Charles himself has effectively been eclipsed by his own commercial success and his daughter's historical presence. It ain't fair.

In 1874 Orvis earned a patent for a ventilated fly reel that established seemingly forever how a fly reel should look, feel and perform. He made high-quality bamboo rods for the many, instead of for the few who'd wait for custom-builts. Later on, with Mary's help, he was pivotal in establishing standards for fine flies. The power of the printed word was not lost on Orvis; he began a company dialogue about his products, fly-fishing, conservation and fisheries with the outdoor press that continues to this day. He established himself nationally as a fisherman—not "merely" a fishing businessman—in 1883, when Houghton Mifflin published this book, compiled by Charles and fellow angler Nelson Cheney. It's a collection of two dozen fly-fishing articles, spanning Maine to Alaska, by the premier outdoor writers and fish culturists of the age—"Nessmuk," Robert Barnwell Roosevelt, Seth Green, and Dr. Henshall among them. Included are 149 color reproductions of the appropriate flies, with quotations from the literature. From the first line of the first chapter—Charles Hallock's "I suppose that all can be instructively written of the salmon has already been said." to the last article, where Ned Buntline avers that "Fishermen are *born* such—not made!"—this book could nearly have been written today.

At $2.50, it sold so well that it stayed in print through four editions, yet this volume is the first reprint since 1889. Charles Orvis's personality shines distinctly through it; he concludes his own chapter this way: "More than half the intense enjoyment of fly-fishing is derived from the beautiful surroundings, the satisfaction felt from being in the open air, the new lease on life secured thereby, and the many, many pleasant recollections of all one has seen, heard and done."

—*Silvio Calabi*

CONTENTS.

INDEX TO PLATES AND FLIES.

INDEX.

"Together let us beat this ample field,
Try what the open, what the covert yield."

—Pope.

"Gentlemen, let not prejudice prepossess you. I confess my discourse is like to prove suitable to my recreation, calm and quiet. So much for the prologue of what I mean to say."*—Izaak Walton.*

FISHING WITH THE FLY.

ETCHINGS ON A SALMON STREAM.

BY

CHARLES HALLOCK.

I suppose that all that can be instructively written
of the salmon has already been said. The processes of
natural and artificial propagation have become familiar
to all who desire to learn; the secrets of their periodical migrations—their advents and their absences—have
been fathomed from the depths of ocean; their form
and beauty have been lined by the artist's brush, and
their flavor (in cans) is known to all the world where
commerce spreads her wings. And yet, the subject always carries with it a perennial freshness and piquancy,
which is renewed with each recurring spring, and en-
livened by every utterance which attempts to make it
vocal; just as the heavenly choirs repeat the anthem of
the constructed universe intoned to the music of the
assenting spheres! The enthusiasm which constantly
invests it like a halo has not been dissipated or abated
by the persistent pursuit of many centuries, albeit the
sentiments of to-day are but the rehearsal of the orig

1

inal inspiration, and present knowledge the hereditary
outcome of ancient germs.

All down the ages echo has answered echo, and the
resounding rocks have transmitted orally the accented
annals wherever the lordly salmon swims.

Now, hold rhapsody, and let us look to the river!
Do you mark the regal presence in yonder glinting
pool, upon which the sun flashes with an intensity
which reveals the smallest pebble on the bottom?
Nay? You cannot see that salmon, just there at the
curl of the rapid? Nor his knightly retinue drawn up
there abreast just behind him in supporting position?
Then, my friend, you are indeed a novice on the river,
and the refraction of the solar rays upon its surface
blinds your unaccustomed eyes. Well, they do certainly look but shadows in the quiet pool, so motionless
and inanimate, or but counterfeiting the swaying of the
pensile rock-weeds of the middle stream. What comfortable satisfaction or foreboding premonitions do you
imagine possess the noble lord while he is taking his
recuperative rest in the middle chamber, after passing
from his matriculation in the sea? Faith! you can
almost read his emotions in the slow pulsations of his
pectoral fins, and the inflection of his throbbing tail!
Perhaps he shrinks from the barricade of rock and foam
before him; or hesitates to essay the royal arch above
the gorge, which reflects in prismatic hues of emblem-
atic glory the mist and mysteries of the unattempted
passage.

And his doughty squires around him ; do they share his misgivings, or are they all royal bloods together, *sans peur sans reproche*, in scaled armiture of blue and silver, eager to attain the land of promise and the ultimate degree of revelation ? Ah ! the way is indeed beset with difficulties and crucial tests, but its end is joy and the fulness of knowledge : and "knowledge is the beginning of life."

Let us go nearer, and with caution. Ha ! what flash was that across the pool, so swift and sudden that it seemed to begin and end at once ? It sped like a silver arrow across the line of sight, but it was not a silver arrow ; only *the salmon* on his route up stream, at the rate of 90 miles per hour. Were it not for the obstructions of the cascades and the long rapids, and perchance the wicked set-nets of the fishermen, it would not take him long to accomplish his journey to the head of the stream, and there prepare for the spawning-beds. But were the way to procreation made thus easy, and should all the salmon of a season's hatching survive, they would stock their native rivers so full in a couple of years that there would be no room for them. So the sacrifice of life is necessary that life may continue. Strange the paradox !

I love to see the salmon leap in the sunlight on the first flood of a "June rise," and I love to hear his splash in the darkness of the still night, when the place where he jumped can be determined only by the sound, unless perchance his break in the water disturbed the reflection of a star. I have stood on heights afar off at the opening of the season, ere my unconsecrated rod had chance to exercise its magic, or my lips and feet to kiss the river, and with the combined exhilaration of impatience, desire, and joy, watched the incessant spurts of silvery spray until my chained and chafed spirit almost broke at the strain; and I have lain on my couch at midnight sleepless and kept awake by the constant splash of the salmon leaps. More interesting, if not so stimulating, is the leap of the salmon at obstructing falls, with the air filled with dozens of darting, tumbling, and falling fish—the foam dashing and sparkling in the sun, the air resonant with roar, and damp with the ever-tossing spray. Nay, more : I have seen a fall whose breast was an unbroken sheet thirty feet perpendicular, inclosed by lateral abutments of shelving crags which had been honey-combed by the churning of the water in time of flood ; and over these crags the side-flow of the falls ran in struggling rivulets, filling up the holes and providing little reservoirs of temporary rest and refreshment for the running salmon ; and I have actually seen and caught with my hands a twelve-pound salmon which had worked its way nearly to the counterscarp of the topmost ledge in its almost successful effort to surmount a barrier so insuperable ! Surely, the example of such consummate pertinacity should teach men to laugh at average obstacles which stand in the pathway of their ambition !

I always become enthusiastic over the rugged grandeur of some Canadian rivers with which I am familiar.

We have no such rivers in our own domain, except on the Pacific slope; and except in parts of Scotland and Norway, the streams of Europe must be tame in comparison. It is because so few of our own anglers have the experience to enable them to draw contrasts, that they do not more appreciate the charm of salmon fishing. Even a vivid description fails to enforce the reality upon their comprehension, and they remain listless and content with smaller game. Beyond the circumscribed horizon of grass-meadows and the mountain trout streams of New England and the Blue Ridge their vision does not reach. There is a higher plane both of eminence and art.

Opportunely for man's periodical proclivities, nature has given to salmon and green peas a vernal flavor and adaptation to each other, as well as to his desires, so that, when the spring comes around they act directly on his liver, expelling all the effete accumulations of winter, stimulating the action of the nerves and brain, and imparting an irresistible desire to go a-fishing. They oil the hinges of the tongue and keep it wagging until June. When that auspicious, leafy month arrives, not all the cares of State will hold a President, Vice-President, or even a Vice-Regent, from taking his annual outing on the salmon streams. Representatives of royalty and representatives of republicanism join sympathies and hands. The Governor-General of Canada

sails to his favorite river in a government vessel with
her officers in full panoply of brass buttons and navy-
blue. The President of the United States abandons
the well-worn star routes for more congenial by-paths.
Wealthy Americans in private yachts steam away to the
tributaries of the St. Lawrence, and clubs cross lines
on their exclusive casting grounds. The humbler citizen, with more limited purse, betakes his solitary way
to the rehabilitated streams of Maine, enjoys fair sport,
and while he fishes, thanks the indefatigable Fish Com-
missioners of the State for the good work which they
have accomplished.

So everybody is happy, and nobody left out; and
therefore so long as the season lasts—Hurrah for Salmon and Green Peas, and vive la Salmo Salar !

" I may, peradventure, give you some instructions that may be of use even in your own rivers ; and shall bring you acquainted with more flies than Father Walton has taken notice of in his Complete Angler."—*Charles Cotton.*

" Eh, man ! what a conceit it is when ye reach a fine run on a warm spring mornin', the wuds hatchin' wi' birds, an' dauds o' licht noos and thans glintin' on the water ; an' the water itsel' in trim order, a wee doon, after a nicht's spate, and wi' a drap o' porter in't, an' rowin' and bubblin' ower the big stanes, curlin' into the linn and oot o't ; and you up tae the henches in a dark neuk whaur the fish canna see ye ; an' than to get a lang cast in the breeze that soughs in the bushes, an' see yer flee licht in the verra place ye want, quiet as a midge lichts on yer nose, or a bumbee on a flower o' clover."—*Norman McLeod, D.D.*

" Salmon fishing is confessedly the highest department in the school of angling."—*George Dawson.*

1. **Prince Wm. of Orange.**   2. **Butcher.**
3. **Jock Scott.**   4. **Silver Doctor.**
6. **Silver Gray.**   7. **Curtis.**

5. **Fairy:**

" The noblest of fish, the mighty salmon, refuses bait utterly, and only with the most artistic tackle and the greatest skill can he be taken ; the trout, which ranks second to the salmon, demands an almost equal perfection of bait, and in his true season, the genial days of spring and summer, scorns every allurement but the tempting fly. The black bass prefers the fly, but will take the trolling spoon, and even bait, at all seasons ; whereas the fish of lesser station give a preference to bait, or accept it alone. This order of precedence sufficiently proves what every thorough sportsman will endorse—that bait fishing, although an art of intricacy and difficulty, is altogether inferior to the science of **fly** fishing."—*Robert B. Roosevelt.*

"Sometimes a body may keep threshin' the water for a week without seein' a snout—and sometimes a body hyucks a fish at the very first thraw !"—*Christopher North.*

"Salmon fishing is, to all other kinds of angling, as buck shooting to shooting of any meaner description. The salmon is in this particular the king of fish. It requires a dexterous hand and an accurate eye to raise and strike him ; and when this is achieved, the sport is only begun, where, even in trout angling, unless in case of an unusually lively and strong fish, it is at once commenced and ended. Indeed the most sprightly trout that ever was hooked, shows mere child's play in comparison to a fresh run salmon."—*Sir Walter Scott.*

" 'I chose the largest fly I could find,' said the captain, ' because the water here is very deep and strong ; and as the salmon lies near the bottom I must have a large fly to attract his attention ; but I must not have a gaudy fly, because the water is so clear that the sparkle of the tinsel would be more glittering than anything in nature ; and the fish, when he had risen and come near enough to distinguish it, would be very apt to turn short.'

" 'You have it now, precisely,' said the parson ; ' the depth of the water regulates the size of the fly, and the clearness of the water its colors. This rule, of course, is not without exceptions ; if it were there would be no science in fishing. The sun, the wind, the season, the state of the atmosphere, must also be taken into consideration ; for instance, this rapid we are going to fish now, is the very same water we have been fishing in below, and therefore just as clear, but it is rough, and overhung by rocks and trees. I mean therefore to put on a gayer fly than any we have used hitherto.' "—*Rev. Henry Newland.*

" I unhesitatingly assert that there is no single moment with horse or gun into which is concentrated such a thrill of hope, fear, expectation, and exultation, as that of the rise and successful striking of a heavy salmon. I have seen men literally unable to stand, or to hold their rod, from sheer excitement."—*H. Cholmondeley-Pennell.*

FLY CASTING FOR SALMON.

BY

GEORGE DAWSON.

THERE is no essential difference between trout and salmon casting. The same general principles apply to both, and it only requires the careful application of the skill attained in the one to become equally expert in the other. The difference is simply the difference in weight. A twelve-foot trout rod weighs, say, eight ounces, and an eighteen-foot salmon rod, with reel, weighs two or three times as much. The one can be manipulated with one hand; the other requires both. With the one you ordinarily cast forty or fifty feet; with the other sixty or eighty; and with rods equally approximating perfection, it is as easy to cast the eighty feet with the one as the forty feet with the other. I do not mean to say that no more muscular exertion is required in the one case than in the other, but simply that with such slight effort as is necessary with either, it is as easy to place your fly where you wish it with the one rod as with the other. No great muscular exertion is necessary to cast with either. Indeed, the chief difficulty in casting is to get rid of the idea that a great deal of muscular effort is necessary to get out a

long line.   That coveted result is not to be attained by
mere muscle.   If you have a giant's strength you
mustn't use it like a giant.   If you do you will never
make a long or a graceful cast with either trout or
salmon rod.   With both there must be only such
strength used as is necessary to give the line a quick
but not a snappy back movement—keeping up the
motion evenly until the fly is placed where you desire it.

The most difficult attainment, in both salmon and
trout casting, is to be able, with instinctive accuracy, to
measure the distance traversed by the backward movement of your line.   If you begin the return too soon
your line will snap and thereby endanger your fly ; if
you are too tardy it will droop and thereby lose the
continuity of tension indispensable to a graceful and
effective forward movement.   This essential art can
only be attained by practice.   Some attain it readily ;
others never ;—just as some measure time in music
with unerring accuracy, without a teacher ; some only
acquire the art after protracted drilling, and others
never acquire it at all.

There is almost as perfect rhythm in fly-casting as in
music.   Given a definite length of line and the expert
can measure his cast by his one, two, three, four, as accurately as a teacher can regulate the time of his orches-
tra by the movement of his *baton*.   While this is true
in casting with either rod it is most noticeable in casting
for salmon.   The heavy line, the massive springy rod,

and the great distance to be traversed, render each movement—the lift from the water, the backward flight of the line, the return motion, and the drop at the point desired—as distinct to a quick perception as the beat of a bar in music.

But there are occasions when it would not do to cast by count. If the wind is strong in any direction the movement of the line is perceptibly effected; and if the wind happens to be at your back, it requires great skill and care to counteract its influence and secure satisfactory results. With such a wind, unless you are perfect master of the situation, you will be apt to snap off more flies in an hour than you will be likely to lose legitimately in a fortnight. Nine-tenths of all the flies I ever lost took their departure before I learned how to cast safely with a high wind at my back.

In many salmon rivers the pools are so placed and the general body of water is of such depth that you can always cast from your anchored canoe. As, under such circumstances, there are no obstructions behind you, less care is required in keeping your fly well up in its backward flight than when casting from the shore—as in some rivers you always have to do.

In the salmon season the water is usually well down in the banks, and in many rivers the slope from high water mark to the summer channel is considerable. In casting, as a rule, you stand near the water; unless, therefore, you cast high—that is, unless you keep your fly well up in its backward flight it will almost certainly

come in contact with a stone or boulder of some sort
and be broken.   To avoid this mishap requires great
care.   You must keep the point of your rod well up
always—several degrees higher than when casting on
the water.   My first experience in shore-casting where
the banks had a precipitous slope cost me a great many
pet flies ; and I never got to feel really "at home" in
casting under such circumstances.   It detracts from the
sport when your mind is occupied with the proper swing
of the line.   But enough of ecstacy remains to enable
one to overlook this inconsiderable drawback.   Only
give the angler an opportunity to cast from any sort
of standpoint and he will speedily discover the proper
lift and swing to overcome any obstacle, and be happy.

Salmon casting—especially the frequency of the cast
—depends largely upon the character of the water you
are fishing.   If the pool is straight and narrow and the
current strong, and you are casting from a canoe, you
can so manipulate your fly as to render frequent casts
unnecessary—the important thing being not to let
your fly sink, as it is not likely to do in such a current.
In large pools where the current is sluggish, as is sometimes the case, frequent casts are necessary in order to
touch it at every point with your fly on the surface.
Where you are able to cast across a pool, if the current
moves with a moderate force, you can sweep it at each
cast by giving your rod the proper motion.   This latter
class of pools are those most coveted, because you can
cover a great deal of ground with very little effort.   If

you fall in with a pool—as you sometimes will—where the current is so sluggish as to be almost imperceptible, frequent casts are unavoidable. Without them, not only will your fly sink, but your line will soon acquire a slack which not only gives one an uncomfortable feeling but is unsafe in case of a rise. The very first requisite in salmon fishing is a taut line. It is not only requisite for safety, but without it it is impossible to promptly and properly recover your line for a new cast.

But there is nothing so tests a salmon angler's skill and patience as to cast in an eddy or whirl. No matter how carefully or at what distance one casts, the moment the fly touches the water it begins to come back upon you, compelling constant casting if you cast at all. The result is a great deal of hard work with very little effect, because to keep a straight line your fly must be lifted almost the very moment it finds a lodgment on the surface. In such a pool one soon becomes weary with his efforts to place and hold his fly in the desired position, for it is not often that he is rewarded by a rise. Since my first experience in such a pool I have never hankered after its counterpart. And yet it was a sort of success in this way : Having become tired casting I allowed my fly to go as it pleased. It was soon out of sight, having been drawn down by one of the whirls, and in reeling up to prevent its being twisted around the rock I presumed to be the primary cause of the whirl, I found myself hooked to a fish which had taken my fly at least ten or twelve feet below the sur-

face. When I first felt him he came up as easily as a
six-ounce chub, and I supposed I had nothing heavier
than a medium sized trout. But as soon as he felt the
hook and saw my canoe he showed his mettle, and gave
me just such a fight as I might have expected from a
twenty-pound salmon, as he proved to be. That was
the first and last salmon I ever took with the fly so far
under water. The rule with some anglers is " to let
the fly sink a little " ; my rule is never to let it sink at
all. When a fish strikes I want to see him. There is
no movement that so thrills and delights me as the rush
of the salmon for the fly. To me, half the pleasure of
a rise is lost if I don't see the head and shoulders of
the kingly fish when he leaps for the lure.

The manner of casting is almost as varied as the
casters themselves. You will seldom see two salmon
anglers cast precisely alike. Some cast with a straight
backward and forward movement, without the diver-
gence of a hair. Others secure a half sweep to the line
by giving the backward movement over the left shoulder and the return over the right, or *vice versa*. Still
others almost invariably cast sideways, or "under" as
it is called, seldom lifting their rod perpendicularly.
Some stand as erect and motionless as a statue when
they cast. Others sway to and fro as if they made their
body rather than their arms do the work ; and others
still push themselves forward as they cast, as if they
were not sure their fly would reach its destination unless they followed it. These, however, are simple man-

nerisms. Each may be equally expert—that is, equally successful in placing his fly just where he wants it and just at such distance as he please. My own preference and practice is, a slight sway of the body and a nearly straight backward and forward movement of the line. There are, of course, occasions when a semicircle sweep of the line, or a lateral movement, or an under cast is necessary to reach some desired objective point. All these movements, when they are deemed necessary, will come from experience ; but for unobstructed waters I prefer a straight cast, and only such slight motion of the body as will give occasional respite to the arms ; for it is no boy's play to so handle a ponderous salmon rod for hours in succession as to give the needed sweep to an eighty-foot line.

The flies used for salmon are more numerous and varied than those used for trout, and quite as uncertain and puzzling to those who use them. I have taken salmon, as I have taken trout, out of the same water within the same hour with flies of directly opposite hues, and of shapes and sizes which were the counterpart of nothing "in the heavens above, in the earth beneath, or in the waters under the earth." There are, however, standard flies which experience has shown to be generally more "taking" than others, and for this sufficient reason are always found in salmon anglers' fly books. But no expert deems any fly or any dozen flies invariably adapted to all waters and all conditions of wind and weather. It is superlative nonsense, therefore, to multiply varieties indefinitely. It is only necessary to have an " assortment," gaudy and sombre, large and small, but plenty of them. It is very unpleasant to run short when you are two or three hundred miles away from "the shop." Those who have had any considerable experience know just what they want, and the only safe thing for the novice to do, when ready to lay in his stock, is to seek advice of someone who knows something of what may be required in the waters to be visited.

And then let him go to the quiet and roaring rivers where salmon congregate, experiment with such flies as he has, lure the fish by his skilful casts, strike quick, fight hard, and be happy.

Albany, Dec. 7th, 1882.

THE SALMON AND TROUT OF ALASKA.

BY

L. A. BEARDSLEE,

Captain U. S. Navy.

FROM the great salmon of the Yukon, to the tiny fingerlings, which in innumerable quantities throng in the various creeks of Alaska, and are as ambitious to seize a single salmon egg as are their larger brethren to appropriate great masses of the same, however illy the bait may cover and disguise the hook which impales it, there is not, I am convinced, an Alaskan fish, which through any merit of its own, is entitled to an introduction to the angling fraternity through the medium of this volume, and to the companionship of the beautiful fac-similes of the flies, which in life they scorned.

From personal observation and collected information, I am prepared to accuse all of the salmon family which are found in Alaska, of the grave offence of utterly ignoring the fly, either as food or plaything, and of depending upon more gross and substantial resources.

They are odd fish, and require peculiar treatment both in catching and discussing. And it is to this cause alone that they are indebted for the honor of being made honorary members of the gallant band of game-fishes of which this volume treats.

2

I have selected them as the subject of my contribution, because a single glance at the array of well-known names of those who are to be my co-contributors, convinced me that if I wished to present any new, interesting, or valuable facts upon any icthyological subjects within my range, I would have to travel well out of the ordinary tracks, and go prospecting in some "far countree."

This I have done, and I feel confident that I alone of the contributors have been "forced by circumstances over which I had no control," into a situation where the obtaining of my notes became pleasure instead of toil.

The notes which will be woven into this paper are not all of them entirely new. Some have entered into a series of letters, which over the signature "Piseco" have appeared in the columns of the *Forest and Stream,* during 1879–80–81. Through the courtesy of the editor of that journal, I am permitted to again make use of them.

I have preferred a grave charge against the salmon and trout of Alaska ; it is but just that I should explain the basis upon which it is founded, and endeavor to establish my claim to be somewhat of an authority on the subject.

From the middle of June, 1879, to the latter part of September, 1880, I, as the commander of the U. S. ship of war *Jamestown,* was stationed in the Territory of Alaska, with general instructions to restore and preserve order among the incongruous collections of Whites, Creoles, and Indians of which the inhabitants of that forsaken country was composed.

My command was moored in Sitka Harbor, but during the two summers and autumns of my sojourn, my duties called upon me to make frequent trips of from ten to two hundred miles, to various portions of the Territory.

These trips were made in small steamers which I hired, steam launches and boats of the ship, and Indian canoes, and in them I explored many of the straits and sounds which separate the islands of the Alexander Archipelago.

Naturally fond of fishing and gunning, my Orvis rods, with full assortment of flies, all gear necessary for salt-water fishing, and my rifle and shot-gun, were my inseparable companions; and after days spent in explorations, sometimes of bays and sounds never before entered by white men, and in one case of a large bay forty miles deep by fifteen broad, existing where the latest charts showed solid land only, my evenings were spent poring over works on natural history, icthyology, and ornithology, and jotting down in my note-book descriptions of my finds. Such jolly times! One day a mineral lode, another great flocks of ptarmigan, another a bear, a mountain sheep, or some new fish—gave me something to dream of.

The Alexander Archipelago, of which Baranoff, Kruzoff, and Tchitagoff Islands are the principal, is separated from the coast by Chatham Strait, which, beginning at the southward as a continuation of Puget Sound reaches to above 60° north at Chilkhat ; it is from three to ten miles wide, deep and steep, too, throughout, bordered on the coast side by high, heavily timbered, snow-clad mountains, and on the other by high wooded islands. On both sides, many of the ravines are occupied by immense glaciers, from which flow icy streams, the birthplace of salmon.

Running nearly east and west there are several straits and sounds connecting Chatham Strait with the Pacific Ocean, of which Peril Strait, Icy Strait, and Cross Sound, are the principal. These, too, are bordered, as is Chatham Straits, and are the homes of glaciers and glacial streams.

Many of these streams I have personally fished, and among those under my command were several with kindred tastes, and I became possessed of the results of their experience.

I have read all that I could find of works on Alaska, and since my return have naturally conversed much with every one whom I have met who had also an Alaskan episode in his life, and have collected testimony on the point at issue. One and all affirm that my experience has been theirs, and the most strenuous efforts with well selected flies have failed to record a single capture of trout or salmon. The first bit of evidence I collected is worth recording. When the news that the Yankees had purchased Alaska, and thus become own

ers of the land north as well as south of British Columbia, was communicated to the Scotch Admiral of
the English squadron at Victoria, Vancouver's Island,
he ejaculated, *" Dom the country ! let 'em have it ; the
blausted saumon won't rise to a floi."* Such was our
united experience and verdict.

Of course, as we caught no end of them (trout and
salmon) there were baits which would seduce them, and
these were, for the trout, salmon roe, and for the salmon,
live herrings.

There was no poetry in our trout fishing, for compared
with salmon roe in slippery, sticky, slimy chunks, fish
worms are æsthetically dainty.

There are several little lakes and more streams in the
vicinity of Sitka ; some within reach for a day's fishing, and some within an hour's. The principal of these
are *Piseco Lake* and stream, back of and running
through the town ; *Indian River* and pond, *Saw-Mill*
creek and lakes, from one to five miles to the eastward ;
the *Redoubt* river, lake, and fall, seven miles to the
southward ; and a nameless lake and outlet on Kruzoff
Island, the lake embedded in a deep valley, one side of
which is formed by the foot-hills of Mount Edgecomb,
a noble, eternally snow-clad extinct volcano. In all of
these trout or salmon are abundant in the season ; in
some both, and in some are found species which do not
exist in others.

At the *"Redoubt"* I believe that all varieties and
species are found. The place is named from a huge

dam which the Russians built across the mouth of a
deep and wide ravine, thus forming a large lake of the
river which here empties into the sea. The dam is
provided with a number of salmon gates and traps.
From the first run to the last, every passing school leaves
here its tribute, seduced by the proximity of the beautiful lake; which tribute, duly smoked or salted, is
barrelled for the San Francisco market by a very " lone
fisherman," a Russian who for many years, without
other companionship than his klootchman (Indian wife)
and dogs, has devoted his life to the business.

If in this paper I make an occasional blunder, by
transposition, or misapplication of the terms " specie "
and " variety," or fail on a scientific nomenclature, I beg
that it will be remembered that my claim is not to be
an authority on icthyology, when such names are necessary, but on Alaska fish, which get along very well
with their English, Indian, or Russian names.

I find in my note-book memoranda of the capture of
bathymaster-signatus, chirus deccagramus, and even a
cotlus-polyacanthocephalous, but had not Professor
Bean instructed me, I should have continued (and I
believe I did) to call the first two after the fish they
most resembled, viz., rock cod and sea bass; and of
the last named I have lost and forgotten the description. But we can spare him; the salmon and trout
will, I feel sure, furnish all the material needed, and I
will confine myself to them.

THE SALMON.

Five species of salmon have been identified as found in Alaska ; these are :

The Oncorhynchus Chouicha,
The Oncorhynchus Keta,
The Oncorhynchus Nerka,
The Oncorhynchus Kisutch,
The Oncorhynchus Garbosha.

I am indebted to Professor Bean for the above list. In it I recognize some familiar Russian names, and I will supplement the nomenclature. The *"Keta"* is the big hump-backed salmon of the Yukon, sometimes attaining a weight of sixty pounds ; the *Nerka* is also called by the Russians *Crassna-rebia,* or red-fleshed ; and the distinction is well made, for compared with it, the flesh of the other species seems to fade into pink ; the *"Kisutch"* or "black throat" is so called on account of the intense blackness of the roof of the mouth and throat ; the flesh is lighter red than the *Nerkas,* but more so than any other species, and as a table fish it excels all others, bringing twice the price at retail ; the *Garbosha* is the small hump-back, and strikingly resembles the " red fish " of Idaho. This is the only salmon that I am sure ascends any of the streams near Sitka, except at the Redoubt, where the *Kisutch* and *Crassna-rebia* are taken in late August and early September. The common name for the *garbosha* is the "dog salmon," and a more hideous object than one of them as found swimming listlessly or dying in one of the pools, it is hard to conceive. I find this note of description : "Aug. 26th.—In a shallow pool I saw a fish some two feet long, feebly struggling as though he were trying to push himself ashore. I picked him up and laid him on the grass. A sicker fish never continued to wag his tail ; his skin was yellow, picked out with green and blue spots, from an inch to three in diameter ; and one on his side was about an inch wide and six inches long, bleeding and raw as though gnawed by mice. One eye was gone, one gill cover eaten through, and every fin and the tail were but ragged bristles, all web between the rays having disappeared."

The first run of the salmon is well worth description. About the middle of May, varying from year to year by a few days only, the inhabitants of dull, sleepy old Sitka experience a sensation, and are aroused from the lethargy in which they have existed through the long winter. The word spreads like wildfire, *the salmon are coming!* Everybody rushes to the heights which furnish prospect, and strain their eyes for confirmation.

One of our sailors, musically inclined, paraphrased very neatly the old song, "*The Campbells are Coming! huzza! huzza!*" and achieved fame by portraying the emotions nightly under the lee of the forecastle.

So good an outlook has been kept by the keen-eyed

Indians, and the Creole boy in the belfry of the Greek church, that when first the glad tidings are announced, the fish are many miles away, and no signs of their advent visible to the unpracticed eye. Far away to the southward, there hangs all winter a dense black bank, the accumulation of the constant uprising of vapor from the warm surface of the Kuro-siwo, or Japanese Gulf Stream, which washes the shores of this archipelago ; condensed by the cold winds sweeping over the snow-clad mountains to the northward, it is swept by them, and piled up as far as the eye can reach, covering and hiding the southern horizon as with a pall.

Presently our glasses reveal bright flashes upon the face of this curtain ; and soon, to the naked eye, it appears as though the whole horizon had been encircled with a coral reef, against which the dashing waves were being shattered into foamy breakers. The breakers advance, and soon among them we discern black, rapidly-moving forms, and here our previous nautical experience comes into play, and, "Holy mither, d'ye mind the say pigs !" as shouted by Paddy Sullivan, the captain of the afterguard, explains most graphically the phenomenon.

The salmon *are* coming, and with them, among, and after them, a host of porpoises ; an army so great, that an attempt to estimate in numbers would be futile.

The Bay and Sound of Sitka are dotted with many beautiful, well-wooded islands ; between them, the channels are deep and blue, and these are soon thronged by the fleeing salmon and their pursuers ; the harbor is soon reached ; but it does not prove one of safety, for although there are immense flats covered only at half to whole tide, where the salmon could, and the porpoises could not go, the former avoid them, and, clinging to the deep water, seek vainly the protection of our ship and boats, which do not deter the porpoises in the slightest degree.   For two or three days, our eyes, and at night, our ears, tell us that the warfare, or rather massacre, is unceasing ; then there comes an interval of several days, during which there are no salmon nor porpoises.

I had formed an idea, a wrong one, that the presence of salmon would be made manifest by the leaping of the fish ; on the contrary, were we to judge by this sign alone, but very few had visited us.

The first school had hardly gotten fairly into the harbor, before I, with others, was in pursuit.

The cannery boats, and Indians, with their seines, and I with a trolling line and fly-rod.

A single fish apparently, was at intervals of perhaps a minute, leaping near a point.   Indian Dick, one of my staff, excitedly pointed that way, and urged me to go. *"There! there! sawmo sugataheen"* (plenty).   I was inclined to look elsewhere, or wait for a larger school: but Dick remonstrated, *" Man see one fish jump, sir, may be got thousand don't jump, he under."*   And Dick was right ; but a very small percentage leap from the water, of which I became more fully convinced when I went with Tom McCauley, head fisherman of the cannery, on seining trips, or rather on a seining trip, for the affair disgusted me ; and, as with my experience of Spanish bull-fighting, one trial was enough. Imagine so many fish that *tons* were the units used in estimating, penned up by the walls of the seines, into an enclosure, massed so solidly that five Indians, striking rapidly at random into the mass, with short-handled gaff hooks, at such rate that, upon one day's fishing, this boat, manned by eight Indians and one white man, secured *thirteen tons* of marketable fish. It was bloody, nasty butchery, and sickened me. Not a fish attempted to leap out of the net.

McCauley supplied me with some data, from his point of view.

"About the middle of June, the fish are plentiful enough to start the cannery, and the season lasts from ten to twelve weeks." He has observed *" Seven different kinds of salmon, all of which are good for canning and for the table; but two species which come latest are the most valuable, the flesh being very red and rich with oil"* (Kisutch and Crassna Rebia) ; that *" all of the salmon ' dog' more or less, and that the dogging begins immediately after they have attempted to enter the streams, not before August; that after this process has begun* (and he discovered it in fish which, to my inexperienced eyes showed no signs of it) *the value for canning was depreciated,"* and all such he rejected, and gave to the flock of poor Indians, who, in their canoes, followed us to secure them. If McCauley's ideas are correct, the Alaska salmon caught in salt water, should be superior

to those of the Columbia River and elsewhere, caught in
brackish water.   During the season of 1879 there were
packed at this cannery, 144,000 lbs. of fish ; the
largest catch of any one day was 36,000 lbs. (over 16
tons) ; the greatest quantity canned, 9,000 lbs. ; the
largest fish obtained, 51 lbs. ; and the average weight
12 lbs.   The cost of the fish can be estimated at
less than one cent per pound.   Just what "dogging"
is, I don't know.   McCauley's opinion, which was
shared by many others familiar with the fishing, is that
it is a sickness indicated by a change of form and
color, produced by contact with fresh water, and that
the most hideously hump-backed, hook-jawed, red and
purple garbosha, was once a straight-backed, comely
fish ; which, if true, upsets some theories.   All I
know about it is, that previous to the advent of the
garboshas, in August, no change of form and color is
observable in any of the fish, none of which enter the
streams.   During August, at the same time and place
in the creeks, there can be seen garbosha salmon in all
stages of the transformation, and the change in form
and color is coincident.   Some are silvery and nearly
straight ; others tarnished, and with slight elevation
of back ; others red, with greater protuberance ; and
finally, some purple-red, with fully developed humps,
which more than double their height above the median
line ; and these monsters the Indians like best, and say
that they are better for smoking than any other.

Another idea which I had imbibed in regard to salmon,

became greatly modified by my experience. I thought, and I believe many do, that the instinct which prompts the salmon to run in from the sea, is to reach, by the shortest route, the place of birth ; and that they make a straight wake from the ocean to the mouth of their native creeks ; and that while impelled by this instinct, they refrain altogether from food. In all of this, I think that I was mistaken ; and that the fish which begin to swarm in Sitka Harbor in May, and continue coming and going for nearly three months before any enter the stream, are simply visitors, which, on their way north, are driven in to seek shelter from the porpoises and other enemies.

That they feed at this time, I have plenty of evidence. We caught small ones, on hand-lines baited with venison. Numbers were taken trolling, using any ordinary spoon. I had with me pickerel, bass, and lake trout spoons, of brass and silvery surface. All were successful, the silvery ones the most so.

And I had many good strikes upon *spectabilis* or salmon trout, of six to eight inches, spun on a gang and trolled. The Indians in Chatham Strait catch a great many upon hooks baited with live herring ; these are attached to short lines, which are fastened to duck-shaped wooden buoys, and allowed to float away from the canoe. I have myself been present at the capture of a number in this manner.

The Greek Priest, and companies of the least poor of the Creoles, own seine boats, which go out daily ; and after every fair day's seining the sandy beach in front of Russian town presents a picturesque appearance, dotted as it is with heaps of from one to three tons of salmon, whose silvery sheen reflects the light of the bonfires, around which, knives in hand, squat all the old squaws and children, cleaning on shares. Nearly all of the fish taken by them are smoked for winter's use.

Every glacial stream in Alaska is, in its season, full of salmon, alive and dead. One, which for want of a better, was given my name, and appears on the charts as *Beardslee River*, I will describe ; for in it I saw, for the first time, that which had been described to me, but which I had doubted ; a stream so crowded with fish that one could hardly wade it and not step on them ; this and other as interesting sights fell to me that pleasant August day.

As we, in our little steamer, neared *William Henry Bay*, situated on the west side of *Chatham Strait*, and an indentation of *Baranoff Island*, we found ourselves in a pea-green sea, dotted here and there with the backs of garbosha salmon ; the fish, which were of the few that had survived the crisis of reproduction, having drifted out of the bay, and with their huge humps projecting, were swimming aimlessly, and apparently blindly (for after anchoring, they would run against our boats, and directly into hands held out to catch them), in the brackish surface water ; made so and given its peculiar color by the water of Beardslee River, which arising at the foot of a glacier, had been fed by rivulets from others on its course to the sea, and through its lower specific gravity, rested upon the salt water. These sick salmon were so plentiful that I thought that a large per. centage had lived and escaped the danger, but upon landing at the mouth of the river, saw that I was mistaken. For several miles the river meanders through an alluvial flat, the moraine of receded glaciers. The moraine was covered with a thick growth of timothy and wild barley, some standing six feet in height; much more pressed flat by layers, three and four deep, of dead salmon, which had been left by the waters falling. Thousands of gulls and fish crows were feeding upon the eyes and entrails of these fish, and in the soft mud innumerable tracks of bears and other animals were interspersed with bodiless heads of salmon, showing that they, too, had attended the feast. I waded the river for over two miles, and the scene was always the same. That wade was one to be remembered. In advance of me generally, but checked at times by shoal water, there rushed a struggling and splashing mass of salmon, and when through the shoaling, or by turning a short corner, I got among them, progress was almost impossible ; they were around me, under me, and once when, through stepping on one I fell, I fancy over me. All were headed up stream, and I presumed, ascending, until, while resting on a dry rock, I noticed that many, although *headed up*, were actually slowly *drifting down stream*.

In many pools that I passed, the gravel bottom was

hollowed out into great wallows, from which, as I approached, crowds of salmon would dart; and I could see that the bottom was thickly covered with eggs, and feasting on them were numbers of immense salmon trout.

I saw frequently the act of spawning; and I saw once, a greedy trout rush at a female salmon, seize the exuding ova, and tear it away, and I thought that perhaps in some such rushes, lay the explanation of the wounds which so frequently are found on the female salmon's belly after spawning.

At first, I thought there were two species of salmon in the creek; one unmistakably the hideous garbosha, the other a dark straight-backed fish; but upon examining quite a number of each variety which I had picked up, I found that all the hump-backed fish were males, and the others all females; that is, all that I examined; but as they were all spent fish, I could not be sure. I therefore shot quite a number of livelier ones, and found confirmation.

I saw one female that was just finishing spawning. She lay quiet, as though faint, for a couple of minutes, then began to topple slowly over on to her side, recovered herself, and then, as though suddenly startled from a deep sleep, darted forward, and thrust herself half of her length out of the water, upon a gravel bar, and continued to work her way until she was completely out of water, and there I left her to die.

A very large proportion of the fish were more or less bruised and discolored; and upon nearly all there extended over the belly a fungoid growth resembling rough yellow blotting paper.

The size of the fish was quite uniform, ranging from two feet to thirty inches.

But that I had seen the living spent fish in the bay, I could have readily believed the truth of the impression of many, that the act of spawning terminates the life of the salmon of the Pacific coast.

One more point on the salmon, and I will leave them.

Upon our first arrival, we all indulged very heartily upon them, and in two or three days, a new disease made its appearance among us. A number of us were seized with very severe gripes and cramps, and these lasted, in all cases, for several days, and in some for a much longer period, two of the men becoming so reduced that it was necessary to send them to hospital. The direct cause, our doctor ascertained, was the diet of salmon to which we had taken ; and by regulating and reducing the consumption, the difficulties were checked.

In conclusion, I would say that I have made every effort that would naturally occur to a fisherman to take Alaska salmon with flies, of which I had good assortment, and never got a rise.

ALASKA TROUT.

I am indebted to Professor Tarleton H. Bean for a classification of the various trout, of which specimens had been duly bottled and labelled, during our stay in Alaska. I had fancied, from differences in the mark-

3

ings, that I had *five* species at the least, but Bean ruth-
lessly cut the number down to three, viz. :

   Salvelina Malma, or *Spectabilis,* or *Bairdii.*

   Salmo Gardneri, and

   Salmo Purpuratus, or Clark's trout.

The first named, called commonly by us the salmon
trout, was abundant in all of the streams, from about
middle of June until middle of September, evidently
timing their arrival and departure by the movements of
the salmon, upon whose eggs they live. I have noted,
on June 1st, "No salmon trout yet in any of the
streams. Several fine, large ones captured by the Indians in nets set in sea." Ten days after, the streams
were full of them, and in the earlier part of the interim
many would run into the pools of the lower parts with
the flooding tide, and out again on the ebb.

When they left us in September, it is probable that
they migrated south, for in a letter to *Forest and
Stream,* dated Portland, Oregon, September 28, a correspondent states that, in that month, "there begins to
appear in the streams near the Columbia river, a trout,"
whose description tallies exactly with that of the *spectabilis,* except that the correspondent speaks of their
affording *fine sport with the fly ;* this the trout while in
Alaska fails to do. At first, the *spectabilis* affect the
rapids, but after a few days seek the deep pools, where
they gather in great numbers, and bite ravenously on
hooks covered with spawn and sunk to the bottom.
Occasionally, when spawn was out, we used a bit of fresh

venison ; but at the best they cared little for it, and
when the blood became soaked out, the bait was useless.
Although fairly gamy when hooked, fishing for these
trout was but a poor substitute, for one who had felt and
remembered the thrills caused by sudden strikes of our
Adirondack fish.   I have often when pool-fishing, seen
them leisurely approach the bait, and nibble at it as
a dainty, full-fed kitten will at a bit of meat, and when
one did get the hook, we found it out only by a slight
resistance to the series of light twitches which it was necessary to give it.   They have evidently been taught by
experience that salmon roe is not apt to attempt escape.
The usual size of the fish ranged from six to twelve
inches—now and then one larger.   The largest taken by
any of us, near Sitka, fell victim to my " salmon spawn
fly," and gave my little Orvis rod half an hour's good
work.   It measured twenty-one inches, but was very
light for the length, weighing but two and three-quar-
ter pounds.   At the Redoubt river, much larger ones
were taken ; and two which I shot in Beardslee river
were over two feet in length ; how much they weighed
I never found out, for their surroundings of sick and
dying salmon, upon whose eggs they were feeding, prej-
udiced me against them and I left them.

In shape and color the *spectabilis* vary greatly, both
factors depending upon the length of time they have
been in fresh water.   When fresh run, they are long and
lean, shaped somewhat like the lake trout of Adirondack lakes.   The colors are dark lustrous olive-green

back, growing lighter as the median line is approached, and blending into a silvery gray tint, which pales to a pure white on the belly ; the green portion is sprinkled with golden specks ; the flesh is hard, and very good for the table. After a very short sojourn in the creek, bright crimson specks appear among the golden, which, however, fade to a pale yellow ; the lustre of the green disappears, they become heavier, but the flesh becomes soft and uneatable, and the skin is covered with slime. Salmon trout taken late in August and early in September, were full of ripe ova.

Professor Bean placed some fish, that had been taken in salt water, into a bucket of fresh, and the crimson spots made their appearance in less than a day.

When fully decked with these, and fattened, they resembled our *fontinalis* greatly—the head, however, being somewhat larger, and the tail less square.

Salmo Gardneri. My acquaintance with this species is very limited. The first one that I saw I took in Sawmill Creek, well up to the head, in September, 1879. Seeing that it differed greatly from the *spectabilis*, I preserved it in alcohol, and it was subsequently identified by Professor Bean. It measured a trifle over ten inches, and was very plump, weighing seven and a quarter ounces. In my notes, I describe it thus : " Body, dark green on back, but in general colors very much like a steel head or quinnat salmon ; covered with round, black spots, from one-sixteenth to one-eighth inch in diameter ; these extend considerably below the

median line, and the tail and dorsal fins are covered
with them ; the second dorsal adipose, but less so than
that of the *fontinalis*, having a slight show of membrane, on which there are four spots ; ventral and anal
fins, yellowish in centre, bordered with red ; belly, dull
white ; tail, nearly square ; scales, quite large, about
the size of those of a fingerling chub ; flesh, firm ; and
skin, not slimy. No signs of ova or milt."

On the 28th of April, 1880, I made note : "The
first salmon of the season made their début to-day—
that is, if they are salmon, which I doubt.

"Five beauties, from thirty to forty inches long, were
brought alongside, in a canoe paddled by a wild-looking
and awe-struck Siwash, who, with his crouching Klootchman and papoose, gazed upon our ship, guns, and us
with an expression that showed them to be unfamiliar
sights. He was evidently a stranger, and was taken in,
for he took willingly two bits (25 cents) each for the
fish, and no Sitka Siwash but would have charged treble
the price. Through an interpreter, I learned that he-had
spent the last seven months in a shanty on the western
side of Kruzoff Island, and that well up, among the
foot-hills of Mount Edgecomb, there was a little lake,
from which there flowed a small stream into the Pacific,
and that in the headwaters of this stream he had speared
these fish, which run up the stream in the fall, remain
all winter in the lake, and in early spring spawn in the
head of the outlet."

All of this militated strongly against the theory that

they were salmon, and when, on being dressed, the females were found to be full of ripe ova, said theory was upset completely. My ten-inch specimen of last September supplied us with a clue, and it was soon decided that these magnificent fish were indeed trout; for in every respect except size, and size of spots, some of which were a quarter of an inch in diameter, the fish were identical. Whitford, the oldest inhabitant, confirmed the Indian's story, and gave me in addition the Indian name for the fish—" *Quot*," and that of the Russians, which I forget, but it meant " Mountain Trout," and said that they are found only in the lakes, high up in the mountains, and that in winter the Indians spear and catch them through holes in the ice.

We found the flesh to be very delicious—far more so than the best of the salmon. The processes of cooking, both by broiling and boiling, had a curious effect, for the flesh, which, when uncooked, was of a very bright red, blanched to pure white.

The trip to Mount Edgecomb, in the early spring, involved hardship and danger; and although several of us resolved that we would undertake it, for the sake of such fish, somehow we never did, and I have thus described all of the *gardneri* that I ever saw.

Salmo purpuratus (*Clarkii*). The most beautiful of the trout family, although in no way equal to our Eastern trout in any other respect.

The *purpuratus* is a lake trout, and found only in low-lying lakes. Just back of Sitka, at the foot of the mountains, and elevated perhaps twenty feet above the sea, is a little lake dubbed by me *"Piseco."*

Handy to get at, and its outlet running through the centre of the town, it became, in early spring, our first resort for fishing. Arriving in June, 1879, many of us had, through days of fruitless endeavor, during the summer and autumn, grown to disbelieve the tales of the inhabitants, that this lake abounded in trout ; but on the 20th of May, 1880, from somewhere, there thronged the shallow edges, among the lily pads, great schools of these trout, and for about two weeks there was no limit to the number one could take of them. Salmon spawn was the best bait, but a bit of venison would answer. A fly they would not rise to. In size, they ranged from six to twelve inches—the latter size being, however, very exceptional ; their average was about eight inches. The description in my notes is : "Specimen, May 27th. Length, nine and one-half inches ; depth, two and three-eighth inches ; weight, five ounces ; colors—back, rich, dark brown, growing lighter toward median line ; at which, covering it for a space of half an inch, there is a longitudinal stripe of rich purple, extending from opercle nearly to tail ; below the median line, bright olive-green, lightening to silvery white on belly. All of the tinted portion is profusely sprinkled with oval black spots, which mark also the dorsal, caudal, and adipose fins ; the ventral and anal fins are yellowish bordered with crimson ; tail, nearly square.

" The entire tinted portion has a beautiful golden iridescence, so that when held in the sunlight, and looked at from the rear, it seems to be gilded." It may be noticed that, with the exception of the purple stripe and the golden iridescence, the description of this fish is almost identical with that of the *gardneri*. I think it quite possible that they are the same at different ages, and that later in life these Clarkii may become ambitious and seek more lofty lakes. None that were taken contained ova.

Where they came from, unless they run up the inlet at night, no one found out, for although closely watched in the daytime, none were ever seen in it.

After about two weeks the greater portion disappeared, and although sought in the deep waters of the lake, could not be found. Major William Governeur Morris, the Collector of Customs of Alaska, assures me, however, that during the summer of 1882, he found certain places in the lake where he caught them until August. On July 4th he with a friend caught four hundred and three in three hours, baiting with a single salmon egg.

I am not sure that we could not have again found them, but the fishing having grown slack in the lake, and growing daily better in the creeks, we spent most of our time on the latter.

COMPARISON OF ALASKA WITH EASTERN TROUT.

The principal differences between the Alaska and

Plate I. Description on page 7.

SALMON FLIES.

Plate II. Description on page 45.

 LAKE FLIES.

Made by C.F.ORVIS, Manchester,Vt
COPYRIGHTED

Eastern trout are, first, all Alaskans have hyoid teeth, the eastern trout have not.

No Alaskan trout will take a fly. All Alaskan trout, I think, spend a portion of their lives in salt water. Length being equal, the Alaska trout, with the exception of the Gardneri, or mountain trout, are lighter than those of our eastern streams.

Using as a standard the average weight of a number of ten-inch Adirondack trout, the following table will show this :

Fontinalis-Adirondack, length 10 inches, weight 6 oz.

Fresh-run Spectabilis,	"	10	"	"	5 oz. 20 grains.
Crimson-specked "	"	10.3 "		"	5 oz. 106 "
Salmo Clarkii,	"	9.6 "		"	5 oz.
Salmo Gardneri,	"	10.1 "		"	7¼ oz.

In conclusion, I must again request that this contribution shall not be considered and judged as an attempt to scientifically describe the fish treated upon, but rather as what it really is, a condensation of the field-notes of an amateur angler.

I have, in giving the sizes, weights, and other data in regard to the Alaska salmon and trout, depended almost entirely upon my personal knowledge and experience ; it may not be out of place to add to them some data gathered from reliable authorities.

In his report on the resources of Alaska, Major Wm. Governeur Morris writes : " Sixty thousand Indians and several thousand Aleuts and Esquimaux depend for the

most part upon dried salmon for their winter sustenance."

The Hon. Wm. S. Dodge, formerly Mayor of Sitka,
states in an official report : " And additional testimony
comes to us from numerous persons, that at Cook's Inlet the salmon average in weight sixty pounds, and some
of them reach a weight of one hundred and twenty
pounds, and Mr. T. G. Murphy only last week brought
down from there on the *Newbern* a barrel full, con-
taining only *four* fish." Surgeon Thomas T. Minor,
who some years ago visited Cook's Inlet, in connection
with business of the Smithsonian Institution, makes
statements which confirm the foregoing.

In the vicinity of Klawack a cannery is established.
A catch of seven thousand fish at one haul of the seines
is not unusual, many weighing over forty pounds.

Mr. Frederick Whymper, artist to the Russian Over-
land Telegraph Expedition, says in his well-written
and interesting account of his adventures : " The
Yukon salmon is by no means to be despised. One
large variety is so rich that there is no necessity when
frying it to put fat in the pan. The fish sometimes
measure five feet in length, and I have seen boats whose
sides were made of the tough skin."

And a writer who, if disposed to strain the truth
would not do so to say anything in favor of Alaska,
says in an article in *Harper's Magazine,* Vol. LV.
page 815 : "The number of spawning fish that ascend the Yukon every June or July is something

fabulous. . . . It would appear reasonable to anticipate, therefore, the adoption by our fishermen of some machinery by which they can visit the Yukon when the salmon begin to run, and while they ascend the river catch a million pounds a day, for the raw material is there, of the largest size, the finest flavor, and the greatest number known to any stream in the world."

My general views about Alaska differ widely from those of the writer, but on the salmon question, I indorse all I have quoted, excepting only the word flavor.

I do not think the Alaska salmon equal in this respect to those of the Atlantic coast, and far behind those of the Rhine ; they are, however, superior to those of the Columbia River.

In speaking of the salmon, I find I have omitted to mention that in early spring, before the arrival of the salmon trout, and after their departure in fall, great quantities of fingerling salmon pervaded the streams, and bit eagerly at any kind of meat bait.

While the *spectabilis* were present, these little fellows kept out of sight and notice.

Since the body of this paper was written there has been on exhibition by Mr. Blackford, of Fulton Market, New York, a number of trout, pronounced to be the *salmo irideus*, one of which, weighing fifteen pounds, was sent to the Smithsonian Institution, and there identified by Professor Bean as being " *Salmo gardneri, the great trout of Edgecomb Lake.*"

I, studying these fish in their glass tank, did not form this opinion, for Blackford's trout had a broad red band extening from just back of the eye to the tail, covering the operculum, a marking not existing on any of the Edgecomb trout I have seen. But the Professor assures me that "*color on the lateral line is not a specific character.*" On comparing my notes of description of these fish, I find that in all other respects they did appear identical, hence that the conclusion arrived at by Prof. Bean, that "the *gardneri* and the *irideus* (or rainbow trout of McCloud River), are identical seems well founded. If so, and my crude supposition that the *Clarkii*, obtained in Piscco Lake near Sitka are also identical with the *gardneri* turns out to be correct, there can be a condensation of nomenclature, which will lead to at least one valuable result from this paper.

"No sooner had the barbed hook fastened in its insidious hold, and the impaled monarch learned that he was captive, than every effort of his lithe and agile frame was brought into play to recover freedom. In every struggle, in every effort to burst the bonds that made him captive, there was an utter recklessness of consequences, a disregard for life that was previously unknown, as from side to side of the pool he rushed, or headlong stemmed the sweeping current. Nor did the hero confine himself to his own element ; again and again he burst from its surface to fall back fatigued, but not conquered. The battle was a severe one, a struggle to the death ; and when the landing net placed the victim at my feet, I felt that he had died the death of a hero. Such was my first sea-trout, no gamer, truly, than hundreds I have captured since ; but what can be expected of a race of which every member is a hero ?"—*Parker Gilmore.*

1. **Silver Doctor.** 2. **Scarlet Ibis.**
3. **Black June.** 4. **Gray Drake.**
5. **Captain.** 6. **Academy.**

"If, indeed, you be an angler, join us and welcome, for then it is known to you that no man is in perfect condition to enjoy scenery unless he have a fly-rod in his hand and a fly-book in his pocket."—*Wm. C. Prime.*

"It was something more than a splendid trout that he brought to our view as we met him at the landing. The young heart in the old body—the genuine enthusiasm of the veteran angler—the glorification of the gentle art which has soothed and comforted many an aged philosopher—all this he revealed to us, and we wanted to lift the grand old man to our shoulders and bear him in reverent triumph up the ascent."—*A. Judd Northrup.*

"From the fisherman's point of view, the sea trout is equal to the finest grilse that ever ascended Tay or Tweed, exceeding, as

he does, for gameness and pertinacity every other British fish."
—*David Foster.*

"As to flies, the indifference of sea-trout about kind, when they are in the humor to take any, almost warrants the belief of some anglers that they leap in mere sport at whatever chances to be floating. It is true they will take incredible combinations, as if color-blind and blind to form. But experiments on their caprice are not safe. If their desire is to be tempted, that may most surely be done with three insects, adapted to proper places and seasons. One need not go beyond the range of a red-bodied fly with blue tip and wood-duck wings for ordinary use, a small all gray fly for low water in bright light, and a yellowish fly, green striped and winged with curlew feathers, for a fine cast under the alders for the patriarchs."—*A. R. Macdonough.*

"His tackle, for bricht airless days, is o' gossamere ; and at a wee distance aff, you think he's fishin' without ony line ava, till whirr gangs the pirn, and up springs the sea-trout, silver-bricht, twa yards out o' the water, by a delicate jerk o' the wrist, hyucked inextricablv by the tongue clean ower the barb o' the kirby-bend. Midge-flees!"—*The Ettrick Shepherd.*

"O, sir, doubt not but that Angling is an art ; is it not an art to deceive a trout with an artificial fly ?"—*Izaak Walton.*

"Sea-trout show themselves wherever salmon are found, but not always simultaneously with them. In rivers where the salmon run begins in May or early June, you need not look for sea-trout in any considerable numbers before well on into July. Intermediately they are found in tide-water at the mouths of the salmon rivers, and often in such numbers and of such weight as give the angler superb sport."—*George Dawson.*

"What I maintain is, that the brook trout perpetually preserve their autonomy, and that the armies of sea trout are never reinforced from the brooks."—*Charles Hallock.*

SEA-TROUT.

BY

FITZ JAMES FITCH.

SUNDAY morning, August 2, 1874, found us, Mr. A. R. Macdonough and me, at Tadousac, a French Canadian village, very small for its age, situated on the northeast shore of the Saguenay River, one and a half miles from the junction of its dark and mighty waters with the turbid and mightier St. Lawrence. This day was the beginning of the culmination of four months of preparation for a month's release from the business world, its toil, care and worry. The preparations began with the payment of $150 in gold—$171.20 currency—the rent named in a lease securing to us the exclusive right to fish a river on the north shore of, and emptying into, the St. Lawrence many miles below the Saguenay. We left New York sweltering in a temperature that sent the mercury up to the nineties ; were fanned by the cool evening breeze of the Hudson, and later by the cooler breath of the old Catskills, around which cluster the recollections and associations of thirty years of my life. We had travelled by rail to Montreal, 412 miles, and spent a day there ; by steamboat to Quebec, 180 miles, where we passed twenty-four hours. We had left this, the most interesting city of English-speaking North America, in the morning by steamboat, and, after a day of delights upon this majestic river, the St. Lawrence, reached L'Anse à l'Eau, the landing for Tadousac, 130 miles, in the evening of August 1st.

We felt as we walked out upon the wide piazza of the Tadousac Hotel that

"——simmer Sunday morn
When Nature's face was fair,"

and looked up that mysterious river, the Saguenay, and upon its castellated mountains of granite, that indeed " the lines had fallen to us in pleasant places."

We had reached the end, as our course lay, of railroads and steamboat lines, and must finish our journey in *chaloupe* and birch-bark canoe. We were there to leave civilization and its conveniences for nature and primitive modes of life. In the story I am relating my progress up to this point has been as rapid as was our transit. From this point on it must correspond with our slower mode of progression ; and hence there must be more of detail in what follows. I hope, but cannot expect, that the reader will find the change as agreeable and free from irksomeness as we found our *chaloupe,* canoe, tent, and life in the woods.

After an excellent breakfast, we lighted cigars and walked down to the humble cottage of my guide, David, on the beach of the little bay of Tadousac, who had in charge our tents, stores, camp equipments, and three new birch-bark canoes, ordered months before.

and for which we paid $75 in gold. David paddled us
out to our *chaloupe,* anchored in the bay, and introduced me to Captain Edward Ovington, master, and
his nephew, Fabian, a lad of sixteen or seventeen
years, his mate. The *chaloupe* was thirty feet "fore
and aft;" beam, 9½ feet. Six or eight feet aft we
called the quarter-deck. A comfortable seat surrounded
three sides of it, affording sittings for eight or ten persons. Next forward of this, and separated from it by a
bulkhead, was a space of six or eight feet for freight.
Next came our cabin, eight by nine feet, and just high
enough to enable us to sit upright on the low shelf
which was to serve as a seat by day and bed at night.
Then came the forecastle, in which was a very small
cooking stove. The vessel was rigged with main and
topmast, strengthened by iron shrouds, with a large
mainsail, topsail, jib and "jigger," as it is called by
Canadian boatmen. It was in respect to the jigger that
the craft differed from a sloop-rigged yacht or boat.
Clear aft, and back of the rudder-post, was a mast about
fifteen feet high; running from the stern of the vessel
was a stationary jigger boom, something like the jib-
boom, except that it was horizontal; on these was
rigged a sail in shape like the mainsail. The boat was
a fair sailer, strong, well built, and from four to six
tons burden. In returning to the hotel we stopped at
and entered the little French Roman Catholic Church.
It is not known when it was erected. Jacques Cartier,
in his second visit to America, in 1535, explored the

4

Saguenay; and Father Marquette made Tadousac his residence for a short time. When he first came to this country in 1665, tradition tells us, he established a mission there and built a log chapel on the site where the church we entered stands. The latter is a wooden building, about twenty-five by thirty feet, with a handsome altar placed in a recess chancel, the rear wall of which is adorned with three oil paintings. The centre one, over the altar, was the Crucifixion. A small porch, or vestibule, of rough boards, had been added in modern times. A little antique bell swung in the belfry on the east gable, which was surmounted by an iron floriated cross. The church was filled with devout *habitans*, mainly—there was a sprinkling of summer boarders and anglers—who listened with apparent interest to the extempore sermon of a young French priest of prepossessing appearance and manner. In the afternoon I attended the English Episcopal Church, about a mile from the hotel, and midway between Tadousac and L'Anse à l'Eau. Here I felt quite at home, enjoyed the services, and joined heartily in the prayer for the "Queen, the Royal Family, and all who are in authority." I was compelled to put a U. S. greenback, to represent my contribution of one dollar, upon the plate. I have been sorry ever since that I did not secure a reputation for honesty and fair dealing by adding a dime to pay the premium on gold, and thus make good our (then) depreciated currency.

August 3d.—A gray flannel suit and shirt were

donned this morning. Our fishing clothes and paraphernalia were packed in large canvas bags, toilet articles, etc., in grip sacks, and all else left in our Saratoga
trunks, and in charge of the hotel manager until our
return. At 11 o'clock we walked down to the beach
where David and the Captain met us with our respective canoes. I asked "Dah-veede" (he was very
particular about the pronunciation of his name), "how
shall I dispose of myself in this cranky thing?" "Sit
down on the bottom, sir." The latter part of the sitting process was rather emphatic. I wondered how I
was to get up! All being on board the good *chaloupe*
Quebec, the sails were spread to the breeze, and by one
o'clock we had beat out of the bay, down the Saguenay, and were on the St. Lawrence. As we sailed,
the canoes which had been in tow were hoisted on
deck; one, turned upon its side, was lashed to the
shrouds of the vessel on either side, and the third,
turned bottom up, was laid upon the cabin deck. The
wind was N. W., and favorable, so that we made about
eight knots an hour. We landed at Escomains, to take
on board Pierre Jacques, a full-blooded Indian, pos-
sessing the usual characteristics of his race—laziness
and love of whiskey. He was Mr. Macdonough's guide;
and, despite the weaknesses mentioned, proved a good
guide and a most skilful canoeist. We continued to
sail until ten o'clock at night, when we dropped anchor.
The night was dark and rainy, the wind fresh, and the
river very rough, causing our little craft to dance, roll,

and pitch in a most disgusting manner. We had no
seasickness on board, but much wakefulness on my side
of the cabin. Being thus " Rocked in the cradle of
the deep," was not a success as a soporific, in my case,
at least.

August 4th.—Seven o'clock, A. M. We have been
sailing since daylight this morning, and are now at
anchor near the Sault au Cochon. Mr. Macdonough
had occasion to visit a country store near the falls, and
suggested that I try to catch a trout for breakfast.
The stream which empties into the St. Lawrence here
is of considerable size—say forty feet wide—and pours
over a ledge of rocks, or precipice, about fifty feet in
height, into the head of a small bay. The water under
and near the fall is very rough and swift. My guide
launched my canoe, paddled me out, and placed me in
such a position that I could cast in the eddy formed
by the swift waters from the fall. With a hornbeam
rod, of ten ounces in weight, and twelve feet in length,
armed with two flies, I whipped the waters. A few
casts brought up a trout. I saw its head as it rose for
my dropper, struck, and hooked the fish. It ran down
with the current, my click reel singing the tune so delightful to anglers' ears, until near one hundred feet of
line was out. Placing my gloved thumb upon the
barrel of the reel, I checked its progress. The trout
dashed right and left, from and towards me, at times
putting my tackle to a severe test. It kept below the
surface of the water ; therefore, I could only judge of

the size of my captive by the strength it exerted in its efforts to escape. My enthusiastic guide was much excited, and cheered me by such remarks as, "Juge he big trout. He weigh three, *four*, FIVE pounds ! He very big trout !" I concurred in his opinion, as it often required the utmost strength of my right hand and wrist to hold my rod at the proper angle. After playing the fish fifteen or twenty minutes, without its showing any signs of exhaustion, I slowly, and by sheer force, reeled the fish to the canoe, and my guide scooped it out with the landing net. I then discovered it was not the monster we had supposed it to be, but that it was hooked by the tail fly at the roots of the caudal fin. The fish was killed, by a blow upon the head, and weighed. The scales showed two pounds two ounces. The guide paddled ashore, and upon the rocks near the falls built a fire and prepared our breakfast. The fish was split open on the back, spread out upon a plank, to which it was secured by wooden pegs, set up before the fire, and thus broiled, or more properly, roasted. A more delicious trout I never tasted.

Up to this point, what has been written has been abstracted from the prolix journal that I kept of this bout.

As I have taken my first sea-trout from Canadian waters it is fitting that I turn to the subject of this article,

SEA-TROUT.

Like all anadromous fishes its " ways are dark and

past finding out." Hence scientists, naturalists, anglers
and guides differ widely and materially in regard to its
proper name, its species, and its habits.   Scarcely any
two writers upon the subject have agreed in all these
points.   Sea-trout (*Salmo Trutta*) abound in northern
Europe.   As stated by Foster in his "Scientific Angler," in "nearly every beck and burn, loch and river
of Scotland and Ireland ; and are readily taken with a
fly."   These sea-trout have been mentioned and described by many eminent writers—Sir Humphry Davy,
Yarrel, Foster, and others.   The description given of
this fish, the number of rays in its fins, its coloring
and markings, and lastly the absence of all red or ver-
milion spots render it absolutely certain that they are
not in species identical with the sea trout of the Domin-
ion of Canada.

As is shown by Thaddeus Norris, in his admirable
work, "The American Angler's Book," conclusively I
think, the supposed identity of the two kinds of
sea-trout mentioned have led many writers astray
when speaking of the sea-trout found in American
waters.

Norris has applied to the latter fish the name *Salmo
Canadensis*, given, I believe, by Col. Hamilton Smith,
in 1834.   Whether icthyologists can find a better or
more appropriate one matters not.   It is desirable that
there be a name to distinguish this fish from all others,
and this one, if generally adopted, will serve all necessary purposes.

In describing the fish Norris writes thus : "A Canadian trout, fresh from the sea, as compared with the brook trout, has larger and more distinct scales ; the form is not so much compressed ; the markings on the back are lighter and not so vermiculated in form, but resemble more the broken segments of a circle ; it has fewer red spots, which are also less distinct." He also thinks the sea-trout, until they attain the weight of two pounds, more slender in form. Again I quote *verbatim :* "In color, when fresh run from the sea, this fish is a light, bluish green on the back, light silvery gray on the sides, and brilliant white on the belly ; the ventral and anal fins entirely white; the pectorals brownish blue in front and the posterior rays rosy white. The tail is quite forked in the young fish, as in all the salmonidæ, but when fully grown is slightly lunate."

Genio C. Scott, who laid no claim to being a scientist, but who was a close observer, also compares the same fish, which he calls the Silver-trout or sea-trout, *Trutta Argentina,* or *Trutta Marina,* with the brook trout. He says, "The sea-trout is similar to the brook-trout in all facial peculiarities. It is shaped like the brook-trout. The vermicular marks on the back, and above the lateral line, are like those of the brook-trout; its vermicular white and amber dots are like the brook-trout's ; its fins are like the brook-trout's, even to the square or slightly lunate end of the tail. It has the amber back and silver sides of such brook-trout as have access to the estuary food of the eggs of different fishes, the young herring," etc.

These descriptions differ but little, and are, I believe, as accurate in the main as can be given. Both these writers, as will be seen, are discussing, and have taken opposite sides upon the question, whether the Canadian sea-trout is an anadromous brook-trout. This question was very well presented by Mr. Macdonough (my companion) in an article entitled " Sea-Trout Fishing," published in *Scribner's Monthly Magazine* for May, 1877. He begins thus : " What is a sea-trout ? A problem to begin with, though quite a minor one, since naturalists have for some time past kept specimens waiting their leisure to decide whether he is a cadet of the noble salmon race, or merely the chief of the familiar brook-trout tribe. Science inclines to the former view upon certain slight but sure indications noted in spines and gill covers. The witness of guides and gaffers leads the same way ; and the Indians all say that the habits of the sea-trout and brook-trout differ, and that the contrast between the markings of the two kinds of fish taken from the same pool, forbids the idea of their identity. Yet the testimony of many accomplished sportsmen affirms it. The gradual change of color in the same fish as he ascends the stream from plain silvery gray to deepest dotted bronze ; his haunts at the lower end of pools, behind rocks, and among roots ; his action in taking the fly with an upward leap, not downwards from above—all these resemblances

Plate III. Description on page 79.

LAKE FLIES.

Made by C.F.ORVIS, Manchester,Vt.
COPYRIGHTED.

Plate IV. Description on page 101.

LAKE FLIES.

support the theory that the sea-trout is only an anadromous brook-trout. . . . Indeed the difference in color between the brook-trout and sea-trout ranges within a far narrower scale than that between parr, grilse, and salmon." The reader who has not read the paper would doubtless thank me for quoting it entire.

As will have been seen, the conscientious and lamented Thad. Norris, when he wrote as above quoted, thought that the Canadian sea-trout were not the English *Salmo Trutta,* nor the *Salmo Fontinalis,* and as proof gave this table showing the number of rays in the fins of the following fish :

	D.	P.	V.	A.	C.
Sea-trout (*S. Trutta*)	12	13	9	10	19
Canadian Tront (*S. Canadensis*)	10	13	8	9	19
Brook or River Trout (*S. Fontinalis*)	10	12	8	9	19

He adds, speaking of the last two fish—" there being only a difference of one ray in the pectorals, which may be accidental." I am credibly informed that some years after his book was written, and after a more familiar acquaintance with the *S. Canadensis,* his views underwent an entire change, and that he wrote "the *S. Canadensis* is the *S. Fontinalis gone to sea.*"

The space allowed me for this paper will not admit of my quoting further from the writings of those above mentioned or of others upon this subject.

I will now state, as briefly as I can, my own views re-

sulting from long familiarity with brook-trout, gained
by thirty-five years of angling for them, my acquaintance with the sea-trout of Long Island, and those found
in Canadian waters.   In regard to the markings of the
fish *immediately after migrating from salt to fresh water*
it is unnecessary to say more, except that the vermicular marks differ somewhat in different fish.   Some that
I caught and examined closely had, as Scott says, "ver-
miculate marks on the back very plain and distinct."
And on others, as Norris writes, "the markings on the
back were lighter and not so vermiculated in form, but
resembling more the broken segments of a circle." The
fish in this respect differ from each other far less than
often do brook trout, taken from the same pool.   Norris thinks the sea-trout more slender in form than the
brook-trout until the former attains the weight of two
pounds.   I have not been able to discover this difference between sea-trout and the brook-trout taken from
the waters of this State.   The trout of Rangeley Lake,
and waters adjacent in Maine (I assume, as I believe,
they are genuine brook trout), are thicker and shorter
than trout of the same weight caught in the State of
New York, or the Canadian sea-trout.   I have two
careful and accurate drawings—one of a sea-trout which
weighed four and one-quarter pounds, and measured
twenty-two and one-half inches in length, and five and
one-eighth inches in depth—the other of a Rangeley
trout that weighed eight pounds, and measured twenty-
six inches in length, and eight and a half inches in

depth. I have seen and measured several Rangeley trout—two of seven pounds each, one of four and one-half pounds, etc., and in all I think there was a similar disproportion as compared with the other trout above mentioned.

As regards the number of rays in the fins of sea-trout I can only say that while fishing for them I counted the rays and found them to compare in number with those of the brook-trout as given by Norris in the table inserted *ante*.

All the writers from whom I have quoted, and all persons with whom I have conversed who have fished for these sea-trout, concur in the opinion that soon after the sea-trout enters fresh water, a change in color and appearance begins, which ends in assimilating, as nearly as may be, the fish in question to the brook trout. On the first day's fishing, when my guide accompanied me, he opened the mouth of a trout and called my attention to small parasites—"Sea-lice," he called them—in the mouth and throat of the fish. He said that the presence of these parasites was a sure indication that the fish had just left the salt water ; that they would soon disappear in fresh water. As a matter of curiosity I examined the mouths of several fish, and invariably found that if they presented the appearance described by Norris and Scott, the parasites were present ; but if they had assumed a gayer livery none were to be found. The change in color, which begins with the trout's advent to fresh water, is progressive, and ceases only when the object of its mission, the deposit and impregnation of the spawn, is accomplished. In proof of this I will state that during the last days of our stay on the stream, and notably in fish taken fifteen or twenty miles from tide water, it was not infrequent that we caught trout as gorgeous and brilliant in color as the male brook trout at the spawning season. Whether this change of color is attributable to the character of the water in which it "lives, moves, and has its being," to the food it eats, or other causes, it is impossible to say. I often caught from the same or adjacent pools, trout fresh from the sea and dull in color, and those showing in a greater or less degree the brilliancy of the mountain brook trout. Of course they differ widely in appearance, and therefore it is not surprising that the "Indians all say," as expressed by Mr. Macdonough, "that the contrast between the markings of the two kinds of fish forbids the idea of their identity."

As mentioned by Mr. Macdonough the sea-trout have their "haunts at the lower end of pools" [and upper end he might have added with truth], "behind rocks, among roots," in short, in the same parts of a stream that an experienced angler expects to find and does find the brook trout.

The sea trout will take the same bait, rise at the same fly, and rest at the same hours of the day, as brook trout. The flies that I ordered, made from samples furnished by Mr. Macdonough, who had had some years' experience on the stream before I accompanied him, were much larger and more gaudy than the usual trout flies, and ordinarily were sufficiently *taking* in character ; but, on very bright days, when the water was low and clear, we found that the flies used by us on the Beaver Kill, and Neversink, in Sullivan County, New York, were better. The largest trout taken by us on this bout—four and one-quarter pounds—was hooked with a stone fly made by Pritchard Brothers, of New York, for use on those streams. On one occasion, I took at one cast, and landed safely, two trout, weighing three pounds and one-quarter, and one and three-quarters pounds, respectively, upon one of the said stone flies and a medium-sized gray hackle.

In conclusion of this part of my article, I will say that, for the reasons above given, I have no doubt but that the Canada sea-trout are anadromous brook trout, and that they should be classed with the *salmo fontinalis,* or, if preferred, *salvelinus fontinalis.*

The trout in question come up the St. Lawrence from the ocean in large numbers, and file off, probably in accordance with the instinct of anadromous fishes, to the streams in which they were severally hatched. The detachment for our stream reaches it invariably in the first days of August. "When once fairly in the current" (I quote from Mr. Macdonough's paper), "their movements up-stream are very rapid. Passionless and almost sexless, as the mode of the nuptials they are on their way to complete may seem to more highly organized beings, they drive with headlong eagerness through tor-

rent and foam, toward the shining reaches and gravelly
beds far up the river, where their ova are to be deposited."
They stop for but a short time for rest in certain pools;
one of these resting places was directly in front of our
tents. Two, three, or more, could be taken from it in
the morning; sometimes, not always, in the evening;
but assuredly the ensuing morning; and so on, until
the beginning of September.

When these fish return to "the ocean, that great re-
ceptacle of fishes," as Goldsmith styles it, is a problem
not yet solved. Some think they remain until winter,
or spring. I incline to the opinion that they go back to
the sea in the fall soon after their procreative duty is
performed. It is well known that the *salmo fontinalis*
gives no care or thought to its offspring; and evinces
no love or affection for it after it passes the embryotic
or ova-otic stage; and that during that stage their pa-
rental fondness is akin to that of the cannibal for the
conventional "fat missionary." The voraciousness that
prompts the parent trout to eat all the eggs they can
find as soon as deposited and fertilized, would also
prompt them to return to the estuaries so well stocked
with food suited to their taste and wants.

What becomes of the young fry during early *fishhood*
is another problem. From the fact that no small trout
are caught or seen in the rivers, at the source and in
the tributaries of which millions are hatched, it is fair
to assume that the young remain where they were incu-
bated until they attain age, size, and strength that ena-

ble them to evade, if not defend themselves against, the attack of their many enemies. When this time arrives, they doubtless accompany their parents, or the parents of other troutlings (it is, indeed, a wise fish "that knows its own father"—or mother), on their migration to the sea. During our stay upon the stream I caught but two trout as small as one-fourth of a pound, but one of six ounces, and few as small as half a pound. The average size of our whole catch was one pound four ounces.

Since writing the foregoing, I have received from Dr. J. A. Henshall, an answer to a letter that I addressed to him, before I began this article, in which I asked him to give me the nomenclature of the sea trout of the lower St. Lawrence, and also to inform me whether he thought these fish anadromous brook trout.

I here record my thanks to the Doctor for his courteous compliance with my request, and give a copy of so much of his letter as relates to the fish under consideration, which, to my mind, settles the question of the *status* of the sea-trout of Canada.

"CYNTHIANA, KY., Jan. 29, 1883.

"DEAR SIR,—The so-called 'sea-trout' or 'salmon-trout' of the lower St. Lawrence, is the brook trout (*S. fontinalis*), but having access to the sea, becomes anadromous, and like all anadromous and marine fishes, becomes of a silvery appearance, losing, somewhat, its characteristic colors. The brook trout has a wide range (from northern Georgia to the Arctic regions), and of course presents some geographical variations in appearance, habits, etc., but does not vary in its specific relations. Mr. ——" (naming an American author to whom I referred), "was wrong in calling this fish *Salmo trutta*   *S. trutta* is a European species; and if he applied the name to the Canadian brook trout it is a misnomer. I cannot say, not having read ——" (a work by said author mentioned by me). "Trusting this may meet your wants, I am,

" Yours very sincerely,

"J. A. HENSHALL.

" *P.S.*—On next page please find nomenclature of the sea-trout of the lower St. Lawrence.

" CANADIAN SEA-TROUT.

"*Salvelinus fontinalis*, (Mitchill), Gill & Jordan.

"SYNONOMY.—*Salmo canadensis*, Ham. Smith, in Griffith's *Cuvier*, x, 474, 1834.   *Salmo immaculatus*, H. R. Storer, in *Bost. Jour. Nat. Hist.*, vi, 364, 1850.

" VERNACULAR NAMES.—Canadian brook trout, sea-trout, salmon trout, unspotted salmon, white sea-trout, etc.

"SPECIFIC DESCRIPTION. —Body oblong or ovate, moderately compressed; depth of body one-fourth to one-fifth of length; back broad and rounded.

" Head large, not very long, sloping symmetrically above and below; head contained four or five times in length of body. Nostrils double; vomer boat-shaped; jaws with minute teeth; no teeth on hyoid bone; mouth large, the maxillary reaching to the eye; eye large.

"Scales very small, in two hundred and twenty-five transverse rows; caudal fin slightly lunate in adult, forked in young; adipose fin small.

" Fin rays: D. 10; A. 9; P. 13; V. 8; C. 19.

" Color: back mottled with dark markings; sides lighter; belly silvery white; red and yellow spots on body, mostly on sides.

" Coloration often plain and silvery in sea-run individuals."

The so-called "sea-trout of Long Island, as stated

by Mr. Charles Hallock, in his "Fishing Tourist," and of certain streams in Connecticut, as mentioned by Mr. W. C. Prime in "I go a-Fishing," are genuine brook trout. Although they have access to the salt water, and go there for food—and hence are fat and delicious in flavor—they *are not anadromous brook trout.* They do not "pass from the sea into fresh waters, at *stated seasons*" (Webster's Dic.). They are caught at all times from February or March until the following autumn in fresh water, and, as Hallock expresses it, "they run in and out with the tide."

When this article was commenced it was my intention to write not only of the sea-trout, but to give an account of our excursion in 1874; and in doing so to speak of the events of each day succeeding those of which I have written. It has already exceeded in length the measure that was fixed upon, hence I can give the reader only a casual glance at us as we proceed to our destination; and a look now and then into our camp.

I left our party—breakfast over—at the Sault au Cochon, at about eight A. M. of August 4th. Soon thereafter we set sail and made such progress that a few hours brought us to the mouth of our river. It was low tide when we reached it—low tide means something here, as the tide has a rise and fall of fifteen feet—and hence the anchor was dropped near the river's mouth, canoes launched, our personal baggage transferred to our respective canoes—Macdonough's was named *Com-*

5

modore, in honor of his father, who made an imperishable name on Lake Champlain in the war of 1812, and mine *La Dame*, in honor of some one who lived in my imagination ; I never met her elsewhere. In the third canoe were placed the tents, camp utensils, and stores for twenty-four hours. When all was in readiness I lighted my pipe, seated myself on the bottom of my canoe, leaned back against one of the *bords* or cross bars ; then David, sitting upon the V formed by the sides of the canoe at the stern, with paddle in hand, sent the birch bark flying up our river. Like most Canadian trout streams it consists of a series of still, deep pools, and swift, rocky rapids, alternating. Often the rapids have a fall of one foot in ten, and are from one to five, and sometimes ten or more rods in length. It is marvellous how these canoeists will force a loaded canoe up them. In doing so they stand near the back end and use a long, iron-pointed " setting pole." Before sunset we reached our camping place, five or six miles from the St. Lawrence. The guides built a fire to dispel the mosquitoes, which were fearfully numerous and bloodthirsty, and then set about pitching our tents. M. and I lighted cigars, put our rods together, and in ten minutes' time had taken from the pool in front of us, each two trout, weighing from one pound two, to one pound eight ounces each. Having caught enough for dinner we busied ourselves in arranging our tents, preparing our beds, etc. My journal for the day ends with the following brief entry : Nine P. M.—We are now settled in camp, have eaten a good dinner, smoked our cigars, and are going to bed.

Aug. 5th.—Having had a good night's sleep I rose at five A. M., made a hasty toilet, took my rod and threw into the pool, within forty feet of my tent, and took during a few minutes three trout weighing three-quarters, one and a-quarter, and one and a-quarter pounds respectively. M. soon followed and caught two of one and a-quarter pounds each. Breakfast over we sent our guides with the canoes down to the *chaloupe* for the rest of our tents, stores, etc., and consequently we can only fish the home pool to-day. With a hatchet I cut out a path through the laurel thicket to the head of the pool, six or eight rods distant ; returned to camp, put on my India rubber wading pants and rubber shoes (having a leather sole filled with Hungarian nails), took my rod, walked to the head of the pool, and cast my flies on the swift waters. In an instant a pair of capacious jaws emerged from the water. I struck, and as the head disappeared, saw the tail and half the body of an enormous trout. . . . In twenty minutes the fish was in my landing net. I walked proudly and in a most contented frame of mind back to camp. "That," said Mr. Macdonough, "looks like old times." The scales were hooked in his jaw, the index showed three pounds, eight ounces. . . . Our camp is on a sandy point of land around which curves the pool, and from which, for the space of about one-eighth of an acre, all trees were cut and the land cleared off, under the direction, tradition states, of Sir Gore Ouseley, who first encamped here about twenty years ago, with eighteen servants, retainers, and guides, of whom my guide was one, and the cook. The stumps have rotted away, and the clearing is covered with timothy and red-top grasses. We have cut much of this with our knives, and intend to finish haying to-day. The grass when cured is to be used in making our beds more luxurious. The pool in front is nearly two hundred feet across at one point, and in places ten or fifteen feet deep. In the centre and near the foot is a rock island about seventy-five feet long. In the foot of the pool between this rock and our camp large trout have been seen at all hours of the day.

Opposite our camp is quite a hill covered with spruce, larch, and white birch. We have canvas beds, supported by crotched sticks about eighteen inches high, upon which poles are laid and the canvas stretched. 5 P. M.—I have filled two canvas sacks with hay for a bed, and a pillow-case with the same, for a bolster. These, with my small feather pillow, sheets, blankets, and night-shirts, will render sleeping in the "bush" Christian-like and endurable. 7 P. M.—I have just cast into the pool and caught a pound and a-half trout, making for the day six trout, weighing nine pounds four ounces, and have not fished in the aggregate one hour. The guides, Captain and Fabian, have arrived with the three canoes and all stores.

Aug. 6th, 7.30 A. M.—We have just finished break-

fast. It consisted of coffee, trout fish-balls, broiled
ham, rice and wheat *crêpes* (pancakes) with butter and
maple sugar. My guide is an excellent cook and our
stores abundant and of good quality. We purchased
them in Quebec at a cost of $73.59 in gold. A tub of
butter, barrel of bread, and sack of coarse salt, to preserve the trout, were purchased at Tadousac, and cost
$11.34 in gold.

5 P. M.—I have just come in from my first day's
fishing. Began at 10 A. M., quit at 4 P. M. I fished
below and Macdonough above the camp.

> M. killed 15 fish, weight 26 lbs., 4 oz.
> F.   "   25 "   "   31 lbs., 4 oz. = 57 lbs., 8 oz.

Aug. 7th.— . . . Dinner is a great institution
with us. Next to catching a trout of three pounds or
over it is the event of the day. Ours of this evening
was as follows :

> Soup: bean with extract of beef.
> Fish: boiled trout.
> Vegetables: potatoes and boiled onions.
> Pastry: rice cakes and maple sugar.
> Dessert: crackers, cheese, and orange marmalade.
> Wines: claret and sherry.
> Tea: English breakfast.

Our canoes are beauties. They are eighteen feet long,
three feet three inches wide in the centre, and fifteen
inches in depth. With two men in they draw but
three or four inches of water.

Aug. 9th.—We left our camp with one tent, two canoes, and provisions for four days ; walked through the woods three miles to a lake, through which our river runs, which is eight miles above us by the stream.

. . . It is a lovely sheet of water about three and a-half miles long and one and a-half wide, surrounded, except at the inlet and outlet, by rocky cliffs, in many places five to eight hundred feet high. . . .

Aug. 10th.—To our usual breakfast was added this morning a broiled partridge (ruffed grouse) which Fabian killed with a stick or stone yesterday, in making the portage. While at breakfast a gray or silver fox ran past us within twenty feet of where we sat. The woods are filled with squirrels ; their chattering is heard constantly. Large and very tame fish-hawks abound—reminding one of the beach from Sandy Hook to Long Branch. . . . We have tickled the lake with a spinner, trolled with a long hand line, for pickerel. We fished but an hour with two lines. We caught fourteen, weighing thirty-four pounds.

Aug. 11th.—We fished down from the Middle Camp (as our present one is called). M. had the morning's fishing in the " spring hole," and took six fish averaging two pounds each. In the Magdalen pool I took three one pound trout immediately upon throwing in. Suddenly not ten feet from where I stood (I was in the water up nearly to my waist), and directly in front of me, a monster fish from three to four feet long, and of thirty or thirty-five pounds weight, shot up from the water, stood seemingly upon its tail for an instant, and with a heavy splash fell over into the pool. "My God ! what is that ?" I asked my guide. "It's a *saumon*, sir," he calmly replied. I was all excitement and began whipping vigorously where it rose. Failing to get it up, I put on a salmon fly. By this time salmon were leaping above me, below me, and at my very feet. I whipped diligently, letting my fly fall like thistle-down upon the water, and then with a splash to attract attention, and now letting it sink and float with the current. It was all in vain ; three hours of my most skilful fishing failed to entice one of the wily monsters. Neither could I get up a trout; they had all been driven away by the salmon. I caused my guide to paddle me over the still pool just above, and saw in the pellucid water, three or four feet beneath the surface, ten or fifteen large salmon. They lay perfectly still for a time, and then darted through and around the pool in every direction, as if in play. Suddenly they would congregate in the centre of the pool and lay with their heads up stream, the largest slightly in advance of the rest, as motionless as if the water had become ice, encasing the fish.

Aug. 12th.—At Main Camp. . . . The canoeing down from the Middle Camp—five miles—was delightful, and at times very exciting ; that is, in running the rapids, which are numerous. In making a portage around the " Little Falls " we started up a cock partridge. It alighted upon the limb of a dead tree no

higher than my head.   We approached within six feet
of it, and stood for a minute or two gazing at the graceful bird.   It returned our gaze with head turned aside,
and a look of curious inquiry which said, as plainly as
if it had spoken, "What kind of animals are you?"
I could easily have hit it with my landing-net handle
but would not make it "a victim of misplaced confidence."   This incident reminded me of the lines of
Alexander Selkirk, in the English Reader, which was
in use in my early school-boy days :

> "They are so unacquainted with man,
> Their tameness is shocking to me."

I may add that squirrels were constantly running about
our camp, exhibiting no more fear than those in the
parks of Philadelphia.

  Aug. 14*th.*—" David build a fire between our tents,
it is cold," I called out about five o'clock this morning.   "Yes, sir," he replied ; "a black frost this
morning, had to thaw out my boots before I could get
them on."   Our little encampment consists of two
wall tents, ten feet square, for the use of Mr. Macdonough and myself.   They are about fifteen feet apart,
opening towards each other, upon a line twenty feet
from the pool, upon ground five or six feet above it.
Back of our tents is our dining-table, made of planks
split from the spruce, and sheltered with a tent fly.   In
rear of this is the kitchen fire ; and still farther back,
two "A tents," one for the use of our men, and the
other for the protection of our stores.

I do not often look into our kitchen: Seeing Fabian wipe my silver-plated fork upon his pantaloons, between courses, cured me of this. "Where ignorance is bliss 'tis folly to be wise." I did, however, look into the kitchen to-day to see how our excellent bread was baked. It was properly made with "raising powder," kneaded and formed into loaves. A trench was dug in the ashes and sand, forming the bed of our camp fire, wide and long enough to admit of three loaves. They were put into the trench, without any covering except the hot sand and ashes, with which they were surrounded on all sides, top and bottom. Live coals were raked over the mound, and it was left for time and heat to do the rest. An hour or so after I saw the bread taken from the ashes. It was brushed slightly with a wisp broom, which removed the little of ashes and sand adhering; and the bread was as clean as if it had just left the baker's oven, and was of a uniform rich brown color. Lamb and green peas (French canned) formed one course at dinner to-day. The flavor of fresh mutton is much improved by non-intercourse with the butcher for two weeks.

Sunday, Aug. 16.—Another bright and beautiful day. It would be pleasant to hear "the sound of the church-going bell, which these rocks and these valleys ne'er heard," It is now near two weeks since we entered upon our camp life, and we have seen no signs of civilization, save in our camp; nothing but forest, rock, water and sky, all as they came from their Great

Creator's hand. No sounds have been heard to carry us back in thought to the world of life and labor, save the occasional booming of the fog cannon at a government station on the south side of the St. Lawrence. How strangely did the warning voice of this gun, telling us of danger to the mariner, break upon the silence of the hour as we sat watching the fairy forms and fantastic shapes in our first evening's camp-fire !

Pleasant as it is to the writer to live over again the days of which he has written—to dwell upon the scenes in which he was an actor, so vividly presented to his mind's eye as he writes of them—pity for the too-long suffering reader has prompted him to close the lids of his journal and restore it to its place in the book-case.

It only remains to write somewhat of our success in fishing. The season was a very dry one, our river very low, and no rain sufficient to affect it fell during our stay, consequently the trout did not come up in as large numbers as usual, and the clearness of the water rendered successful fly-fishing more difficult. We caught on this occasion but two hundred and forty-three trout, of the aggregate weight of three hundred and four pounds. All these fish were taken with a fly, save one: thereby hangs a tale heretofore untold. At Tadousac, on our way out, I saw a gentleman, to whom I had been introduced, making something in the construction of which he used three snelled hooks and about three inches in length of thin white rubber tubing. I asked

"What is it?" "A devil," he replied. He gave me
materials, and while sailing down the river I made
one. One day at the Home Pool I saw ten or a dozen
large trout. They paid no heed to my flies. "Try the
devil," my guide whispered. In a moment of weakness
I yielded to the tempter and put it on. The first cast
caused commotion in the watery camp. At the second
I struck and soon drew out on the beach a pound and
a half trout. I looked upon the beautiful fish with
compassion, cursed myself for resorting to such unfair
means, removed the cruel hooks as tenderly as I could
from the mangled and bleeding mouth, and taking off
the *devilish* invention threw it as far as possible into
the woods.

> . . . . "The beasts of game
> The privilege of chase may claim."

I have not since used, and shall not in the future
use, this rightly named instrument, and hope no angler
will. I have narrated this only unpleasant feature of
my bout to illustrate the *devilish* ingenuity of "pot
fishermen" and the curiosity of sea-trout. I wonder
what was the gender of the fish !

With a view of showing the capabilities of our river
in the production of fish, I have aggregated the scores
from 1872 to 1882 inclusive. In one of these years
three rods were in use, in three others two, and in the
other years but one. The average time of fishing in
each year was about three weeks.

Number of trout taken, 5,525; aggregate weight,

6,625¼ pounds ; average about one pound three ounces. In the year 1881 the average size of two hundred and thirteen trout taken with a single rod in eight days' fishing was one pound fourteen ounces. Not one of these fish was wasted. A few were eaten upon the stream, but most of them were given to the guides, who salted and packed them in barrels for future use. A sack of coarse salt and empty fish barrels were always included in the anglers' stores.

Three days after the last date mentioned we were again on board our *chaloupe* " homeward bound." The loss in weight in our stores was made good by the barrel of salted *anadromous salvelinus-fontinalis* which were to supplement and eke out the pork barrel of our honest and worthy guides during the long ice-bound winter before them.

Tadousac was reached about sunrise on a bright morning. At nine o'clock we were in citizen's dress and seated at the hotel breakfast table. A glance around the room showed that summer birds and Cook's tourists had mainly migrated to more southern latitudes. Our trunks were re-packed, our guides paid $1.50 each per day, and the captain $2.00, gold, and bade adieu. We took the Saguenay steamboat for Quebec, the Grand Trunk Railroad from Point Levi to Montreal, where we passed the night. The next morning we travelled by rail to Rouse's Point and by boat down that charming Lake, Champlain. At the various landings many persons, including several friends, came on board.

Nearly all carried snugly-cased fishing rods, whose summer work was ended. The Chateaugay, the Saranacs, Paul Smith's, Baker's, Martin's, and various other familiar names met our ears. We envied none of them. Our cup of joy, happiness and contentment was full to the brim. There was no room for "envy, hatred and malice," but a feeling of gratitude and thankfulness to the Author of every "good and perfect gift," welled up from our hearts.

"To one escaping but seldom from the weary routine of office work, to swing even a seven-ounce rod all day may become a burden; while to him whose muscles are braced by abundant exercise and robust health it seems but as a feather's weight. The truth is, that there is in this matter no hard and fast line where dogmatism may take its stand and say, *this is right and that is wrong.* Let each use that rod which to him affords the most pleasure, and for him that rod is the best, whether it be forty feet long or only two."—*Henry P. Wells.*

"There is certainly something in angling that tends to produce a gentleness of spirit, and a pure sincerity of mind."— *Washington Irving.*

"The flies used in lake fishing are larger than those for rivers ; and I have frequently observed that the winged flies answer better than palmers. Perhaps the cause of this may be, that many rivers and small trout streams are bordered with trees, which overhang them, and from which drop the insects that the palmers imitate." —*T. C. Hofland.*

"When a trout cnooses to prey upon what he thinks is weaker than himself, the angler ought not to be blamed for it."—*G. W. Bethune, D.D.*

"I said anglers were born, not made ; but when born they can be improved, and wish to learn as well as teach."—*Fitz James Fitch.*

"Imitate never so closely the form and general character of the fly at which the fish are rising—if the *color be wanting* you will have no sport."—*Hewett Wheatley.*

"Always strike from the reel by leaving the line free from pressure of the fingers, and then you don't strike too hard."—*Fred Mather.*

"It is of record that when the Pilgrims went to King James for their charter they said to him that they desired to go to the new world to worship God and catch fish."—*Samuel S. Cox.*

" Every angler has his own peculiar notion in regard to the best fly; and the difficulty of presenting a perfect catalogue will be very apparent, when it is considered that the *name* of the fly of one writer bears a different name and description from that of another, and it is more than probable that the name and description of some of the flies in my list may not be in accordance with the views and opinions of many old and experienced anglers."— *"Frank Forester."*

" After staying in a village parlor till the family had all retired, I have returned to the woods, and partly with a view to the next day's dinner, spent the hours of midnight fishing from a boat by moonlight, serenaded by owls and foxes, and hearing, from time to time, the croaking note of some unknown bird close at hand." —*Henry D. Thoreau.*

7. **Ferguson.**	8. **Abbey.**
9. **Royal Coachman.**	10. **Seth Green.**
11. **Professor.**	12. **Montreal.**

" He sat down on a lump of granite, and took out his fly-book. It is a sport, he added, as he was selecting the flies, that there is less to be said against than shooting, I imagine. I don't like the idea of shooting birds, especially after I have missed one or two. Birds are such harmless creatures. But the fish is different—the fish is making a murderous snap at an innocent fly, when a little bit of steel catches him in the very act. It serves him right, from the moral point of view."— *William Black.*

" There is much diversity of opinion about the manner of fishing, whether up or down the stream ; the great majority of anglers, both in Europe and this country, favor the latter method, and very few the former."—*John J. Brown.*

" ' Beautiful ! ' Well you may say so, for what is more beautiful than a well-developed pound trout ? "—*Charles W. Stevens.*

"Reader, did you ever throw the fly to tempt the silvery denizen of the lake, or river, to his destruction? Have you watched him, as it skimmed like a living insect along the surface, dart from his hiding-place, and rush upon the tempting but deceitful morsel; and have you noticed his astonishment when he found the hook was in his jaw? Have you watched him as he bent your slender rod 'like a reed shaken by the wind,' in his efforts to free himself, and then have you reeled him to your hand and deposited him in your basket, as the spoil of your good right arm? If you have *not*, leave the dull, monotonous, every-day things around you, and flee to the Chazy Lake."—*S. H. Hammond.*

"I now come to not only the most sportsman-like, but the most delightful method of trout-fishing. One not only endeared by a thousand delightful memories, but by the devotion of many of our wisest and best men for ages past; and, next to my thanks for existence, health, and daily bread, I thank God for the good gift of fly-fishing. If the fishes are to be killed for our use, there is no way in which they are put to so little pain as in fly-fishing. The fish rises, takes your fly as though it were his ordinary food; the hook fixes in the hard gristly jaw, where there is little or no sensation. After a few struggles he is hauled on shore, and a tap on the head terminates his life; and so slight is the pain or alarm that he feels from the hook, that I have over and over caught a trout, with the fly still in his mouth which he has broken off in his struggles an hour or even half an hour previously. I have seen fish that have thus broken off swim away with my fly in their mouths and begin to rise at the natural fly again almost directly."—*Francis Francis.*

"That is the sport, to throw the fly, and in half a minute take it quickly out. Though the whole earth is given to the children of men, none but we jolly fishers get the plums and raisins of it by the rivers which run along the hills."—*Charles Kingsley.*

RANGELEY BROOK TROUT.

BY

JAMES A. WILLIAMSON,

Sec. Oquossoc Angling Association.

ABOUT twelve summers ago, when spending a delightful vacation at Manchester, Vermont, under the shadow
of Mt. Equinox, my attention was called to a little book
which gave a description of the exceptionally large
brook trout inhabiting the waters of the Rangeley
Lakes.

Never having heard, heretofore, of a fish of that species that weighed more than three pounds, and never
having caught any over a pound and a half (although
I had dropped a line in many waters and exerted my
utmost muscle in casting a line for fingerlings), I could
not bring my mind to believe that such fish as were
described really existed, and at once pronounced it another fish story. Although much interested in the
narrative I finally threw down the book in disgust, and
as I did so, observed for the first time that the author
was Robert G. Allerton, a very old friend, whom I had
always esteemed a man of veracity. I at once took a
new interest in the subject and determined to investigate the matter personally. I came to New York, had

an interview with **Mr.** Allerton, who was the Treasurer
of the Oquossoc Angling Association, and by his advice
joined the club, and in due time started for the promised land of mountains, lakes, and large trout, and after
the usual vicissitudes of travel reached my destination
at Camp Kennebago about the middle of September.

The forests were just developing their autumnal
hues, the air was fresh and bracing, and all nature
seemed to conspire to make one realize that there was
health in every breath inhaled, and beauty in every
phase of land and water. Having secured a first-rate
guide and boat, and partaken of a trout breakfast,
which was relished immensely, such as can only be
appreciated by one who has left the haunts of civilization and gone into the wilderness for recuperation, I considered my first duty was to pay my respects
to Mr. Allerton, who was in camp at Bugle Cove.
From this location Lake Mooselemeguntic lies spread
out before you, while Mt. Washington in the distance
rears its snowy peak, overtopping Jefferson, Monroe,
and the other giants of the White Hills of New Hampshire.

The crystal waters of the lake tempt us to cast a fly,
and a suitable place having been secured, we proceed to
business. After making several casts in a manner
more or less scientific but without success, my former
unbelief came creeping over me, and, as my arm became
tired and almost refused to do its duty, a sense of
despondency overcame me, which I am sure sensibly

affected the beauty if not the efficacy of my casts. But suddenly I am awakened to the realization of the fact that a big fish has seized the fly and is making the reel hum in its frantic endeavors to secure its liberty. Fathom after fathom of the dainty line disappears beneath the water, and at last prudence dictates a gentle snub, which finally terminates in a decided check to the mad career of the quarry. Having succeeded in turning his head in a different direction, another rush is made across stream, making the line whiz as it cuts through the water ; then suddenly he takes a downward course and ceases from all apparent effort to free himself. He now sulks for a long time, and impatience begins to take the place of the excitement with which the fight began. The guide, who, during the fray had hoisted his anchor, got ready his landing-net, and was now holding his boat in position with the oars, suggested that I had better send him a telegraphic message, which was accordingly done by striking the rod with a key. The first few strokes seemed to make little or no impression, but presently he convinced us that he was still there, although we had some forebodings that he had escaped by winding the line around a log or some other object at the bottom of the stream. He was up and alive in every sense, and performed the same tactics for liberty with apparently more vigor than at first. These were kept up for about half an hour, when he again took a turn of sulking, but this time of shorter duration, and when he again began his rushes it was with

an evident loss of strength, but no diminution of determination and pluck.

A friend who was watching and timing me from his
boat came over to inquire how the battle was progressing, and pertinently asked, "Whether the fish was
going to take me or I the fish." At last the strength
of the tackle, the pliability of the rod, and the determination of the rodster overcame the pluck and strength
of the fish, and he was brought to the boat turned upon
his side and was beautifully landed by the guide. The
scales were at once applied, with a result of eight
pounds full weight.

My inquiring and interested friend informed me that
I had been two hours and twenty minutes in the fight,
and as I sat down in the boat I, for the first time, realized that I was tired.

Now, my dear reader, do not think that this kind of
sport is of common occurrence, for from that time to
this, I have taken but two fish of equal weight; the
average, however, has been much larger than trout
from any other locality in which I have fished. Any
fish under half a pound is considered unfit to land,
and is again committed to the water to grow larger.
The number of trout does not seem to be falling off;
but this can be accounted for by the annual plant of
fry from the Hatching House of the Oquossoc Angling
Association, who have for years past turned about one
million fish into these waters, and now contemplate increasing the amount to five million ; still I think there

is a sensible diminution of the size of the catch, which now run from one-half to four pounds, and anything over that weight is the exception. This would seem to confirm the supposition of Professor Agassiz, made many years ago, that these large fish possibly may have reached an age of from 100 to 200 years, as they were evidently very old.

Any one who has been thrilled with the vigorous strike of one of the ordinary sized fish would be almost beside himself when one from three to five pounds rose to his fly, and if his tackle was good, the sport derived therefrom would serve him a lifetime ; and when the shades of night had fallen upon the camp, and he with his fellow-fishermen collected around the great fire, point and vigor would be given to his recital of how he caught and played the monster he that day had brought to his creel.

"Athenæus—called by Suidas 'a literary man '—who wrote in the middle of the third century, cites in his writings no less than 1,200 separate works and 800 authors, and of the latter the names of a very large number are given in his 'Banquet of the Learned' as those of authors who had written on fish and fishing."—*Rev. J. J. Manley.*

"A huge fish takes the bait *fallacious*, suspended from the rod."—*Theocritus* (270 B.C.).

"I have heard of a Macedonian way of catching fish, and it is this: *They fasten red wool round a hook and fit on to the wool two feathers which grow under a cock's wattles, and which in color are like wax.* Their rod is six feet long and the line is of the same length. Then they throw their snare, and the fish, attracted and maddened by the color, comes up, thinking from the pretty sight to get a dainty mouthful ; when, however, it opens its jaws, it is caught by the hook and enjoys a bitter repast, a captive."—*Ælian* (second century).

"While the other, stooping over the rocks toward the waters below, lowers the bending top of his limber rod, casting his hooks laden with killing baits. Upon these the vagrant crowd of fishes, unskilled in snares, rush, and their gaping jaws feel too late the wounds inflicted by the hidden steel."—*Ausonius* (fourth century).

"Nor shall I leave thee unhonored in my discourse, O Thymallus (grayling), whose name is given thee by a flower ; whether the waters of the Ticino produce thee or those of the pleasant Atesis, a flower thou art. In fine, the common saying attests it ; for it is pleasantly said of one who gives out an agreeable sweetness, he smells either of fish or flower : thus the fragrance of the fish is asserted to be the same as that of the flowers. What is more pleasing than thy form ? More delightful than thy sweetness ? More fragrant than thy smell ? "—*St. Ambrose, Bishop of Milan.*

FLY-FISHING FOR TROUT IN THE RANGELY REGION.

BY

HENRY P. WELLS.

THE cosmopolitan angler, he who wets his line in many waters in many localities, recognizes and is governed by one truth, of the existence of which the experience of him who confines his fly-fishing to a single restricted locality, gives no intimation.

The conservative Englishman differs from the more progressive American, and the phlegmatic Dutchman from the vivacious Frenchman. All may be gentlemen in the highest sense of the term, yet each has his local whims and peculiarities, a due deference to which is one of the conditions of successful and profitable intercourse with him.

The widely experienced angler recognizes these local differences in trout, as in men. He therefore stocks his fly-book with many sizes of many-colored flies ; while the other contents himself with half a dozen varieties, possibly of two slightly different sizes, and smiles with scarcely disguised pity and contempt at the, in his opinion, quantity of useless lumber which fills the former's fly-book.

As trout prefer different flies in different waters, so have they also a preference as to the manner in which they shall be served to them.

The Turk curls his legs under him and attacks his food with the implements which nature has provided him, while the European insists on a plate, knife, and fork.

Fishing for trout in the Rangely region is a case in point.

Every angler who visits that home of large trout, aspires to the biggest. The following remarks apply solely to the method of taking such, and with the fly only. Small fish up to two, or two and a half pounds, can readily be taken there in the usual manner, and by the exercise of a very moderate degree of skill.

In ten quite protracted trips to those waters, I have never seen nor heard of a trout exceeding two pounds in weight rising to a natural fly. Rise the large ones do, rolling up to the surface with a swirl like that made by the blade of an eighteen-foot oar, showing a breadth of tail and side that causes the heart of the unaccustomed angler to bound into his throat, and nearly choke him with mingled wonder and desire. But unless dashing through a school of minnows on some still evening, why these giants thus disport themselves has eluded observation. It seems certain that they then take no food, and that its pursuit cannot be the object they have in view. At such times, large flies and small flies, as well as every other wile known to the fisherman (except a shot-gun), has been tried, and tried in vain. Many regard it as an un-lucky omen, and such has been my own experience. The most careful observation has suggested but one pos-sible explanation—that it is done to aggravate the an-gler. If so, it is phenomenally successful in result.

Assuming it to be true that these large trout are not surface feeders, it might be supposed that those com-binations of form and color which were most successful in taking them, would bear little or no resemblance to the local insects ; and such is the fact.

As in most other localities, a half-dozen varieties are sufficient. But these should be tied on large hooks ; those shown in the illustrations of " Lake Flies " in this book being none too large—indeed, hooks even as large as numbers 1, 2, and 5 of the first plate of " Salmon Flies " are at times not at all amiss.

The most taking flies are as follows :

Before all others in my esteem ranks the " Parma-cheene Belle."

We generally cease fishing in the middle of the day. After dinner the fly-box is apt to appear, and the word to be, " Well, John, what shall we tease them with this afternoon ? " Thus, some seven years ago, this fly was born. Of a very large family, it, on the grand general principle of the survival of the fittest, alone outlived its youth.

That the large trout looked upon the artificial fly not as an insect, but as some form of live bait, we agreed was probably the fact. Upon this theory, that combination should be most successful which most closely reproduced the colors of some favorite trout-food. Why, I cannot now recollect, but the belly-fin of the trout itself was selected as the type.

It would seem also to follow that some combination was possible, which, if sufficiently conspicuous to be readily seen under all circumstances, would be all-sufficient in itself, and preclude the necessity of any change. So far, nothing has occurred to lead me to doubt that the "Parmacheene Belle" complies with these conditions, and has these merits.

Place all the other known flies on the one hand, and that single fly on the other. Then force me to elect between them and to abide by the choice, and I should take the "Parmacheene Belle" every time for fishing in those waters. In sunshine and in rain, at high noon and in the gloaming, I have tried it under all circumstances and conditions for years, and every season it has gained in my esteem.

This fly somewhat resembles the "No Name," figured as No. 15 of "Lake Flies" in this book. As I tie it, the tail is two strands of white and two of scarlet ; the body of yellow mohair, with silver tinsel ; the hackle double ; first white, with a scarlet hackle wound over this—capping the former, so to speak ; the wing white, striped with scarlet. By scarlet, the color of the red ibis is to be understood.

Next in value, and of equal merit one with the other, come the "Montreal," numbered 12 of "Lake Flies," and the "Silver Doctor," numbered 4 of "Salmon Flies." The "Silver Doctor," numbered 1 of "Lake Flies," in which brown is the predominant color of the wing, is there inferior to the other.

The "Grizzly King," 23 of "Bass-Flies," and the "Yellow Professor," No. 11 of "Lake Flies," are both also very taking ; but they are improved if the wing is made of two separate mallard feathers, set with the concave side of each feather outward. The wing then opens and shuts when the fly is drawn through the water—a performance which seems amazingly to tickle the fancy of large trout.

The "Brown Hackle" is here, as elsewhere, a good fly. It should be plump in body and heavily hackled.

All these flies should have the former characteristic.

The next question is, how should the fly be managed. "I tell the tale as 'twas told to me."

During the first of a companionship—one of the pleasantest of my life—I was fishing under the tutelage of that prince of guides, my esteemed friend John S. Danforth—a man, though unexcelled as a hunter, trapper, woodsman, and angler, still not unknown in the literary world.

I then knew I had much to learn of fly-fishing and the habits of trout, as I have still. In pursuit of knowledge I asked, "John, who catches the most big fish of all those who visit these waters ? " He replied that a Mr. S——, of Boston, was the happy man, and explained and illustrated his system, rod in hand.

But a single large fly was used. It was cast, neither line nor leader having a suspicion of a kink, allowed to rest where it fell until it had sunk a foot or so below the surface, then slowly moved about three feet, another pause of five or six seconds followed, then the fly was slowly drawn to within the proper distance, and at last, smoothly and quietly taken off the water, preparatory to another cast. A marked change in the size of the fish taken attended the adoption of this method.

I have never known or heard of a trout of over three and one-half pounds being taken in those waters upon a fly moving on the surface. It may happen, but it is surely rare. I have not unfrequently known large trout to take the fly of an angler who habitually so fished, but upon investigation it has, without exception, appeared that the rise occurred when the fisherman was discouraged, or attending to something beside his flies, and at that moment they were idly sinking beneath the surface.

I have talked with many Rangely guides on this subject, and I have yet to hear one of them advocate any other method of handling the fly.

One fly is better than a larger number, since these large fish are difficult to control when first fastened. They then naturally make for cover, and a second fly increases the danger of a foul. Sometimes, it is true, a small fish on the drop-fly will tow the stretcher through the water, and thus entice a large one, when every other means has been tried in vain. Still, take it all in all, a single fly will prove the most profitable.

In this fishing more than any other, a straight line and leader is essential. The fish will not hook themselves. The eye, and the eye alone, tells when to strike. The slightest disturbance of the water where the fly is, or where it is supposed to be, must be followed by a demonstration on the part of the angler without the loss of a fraction of a second. Then no " turn of the wrist " will serve the purpose. While with small fish, this is the proper and artistic thing, with the large ones there, it is a delusion. You must "sock it to them," but always with a free reel that undue vigor may be harmless. Therefore, to use a fly which can readily be seen is advantageous, a merit which that first-named possesses above every other. The first pause, or the first of the succeeding movement of the fly, is the critical time. Not unfrequently I have then seen large trout slowly swim up to the fly, and take it in. The only indication that he had it would be its eclipse. As far as feeling him was concerned, he might as well have been in the next county. Then a delay of over a single wink's duration is fatal ; for before "you can say " not "Jack Robinson," but even "Jack," the fly will have been ejected ; and though you charm thereafter never so wisely, as far as that fish is concerned you will labor in vain. One taste of that to him he thinks far better than a feast.

During the first week, of June, 1883, I divided my fishing between the Magalloway River, above Parmacheene Lake, in Maine, and the Lake itself. In a lovelier sheet of water than the latter never did angler wet a line. There in the extreme northwestern corner of Maine it nestles in the bosom of the wilderness, a perfect gem in its matchless setting of forest-clad hills. Not even a ripple from the storm of life breaks on its pebbly shores, or mars the perfect reflection of the heaven above in its mirror-like surface. As the mariner struggling in the grasp of winter's icy blast, his very life trembling in the balance, looks to the distant port; as the pious Mussulman, lost in the immensity of the desert, turns toward Mecca as the last hope of his fainting soul, so from the worry and turmoil of city life turns my heart to thee, beloved Lake!

Seldom has it been my good fortune to have such fishing, for the trout were not only superabundant, but of good size and appetite, and with every muscle beneath their iridescent skins braced with the vigor of perfect health.

No true angler kills fish to waste, and such John and I aspire to be. So it has been our practice for years, where circumstances permit, to make a small pond into which we place all the sizeable fish we take. In the quiet noonday hour on its margin we build our little fire and eat our frugal lunch, and then while away an hour or two in perfect idleness and content, admiring the matchless beauty of our captives in their crystal prison. When, brother Angler, it is within your power, try this; and if the love of nature inspires you, as it must if you are worthy the name, the hours passed upon the margin of your little preserve will be a bright spot in your memory for many a year.

We had stocked our pool and returned its denizens to liberty many times, when we happened to remember a pond fed by springs and discharging by exfiltration, where minnows were abundant, but which contained no trout. We determined to colonize it. Water transportation was available for the greater part of the distance, but the last hundred yards was land carriage. Over this John took the trout in a large tin pail, his broad felt hat floating on the surface of the water it contained, to keep them in ; for had their veins circulated quicksilver they could not have been more lively. These fish ran from two and a half to one and a quarter pounds ; and, as I recollect, there were fifty of them. Therefore considerable time was consumed in the portage. When the trout were placed in their new home, they were so exhausted by their struggles, as to be quite content merely to rest and breathe. I watched them lying motionless at my feet, in about a foot of water. Occasionally a leaf would drift into the mouth of some one of them, borne by the current of water circulating through its gills. It seemed an instant before the presence of the intruding matter was realized, then it was shot out with sufficient force to project it some inches through the water. I use the word shot out advisedly, for no other conveys a just idea of the suddenness of the operation. I then thought how very, very brief is the time in which the angler must strike to a rise, if he hopes to save his fish.

June, and the last twenty days of September are the

best parts of the season, and only then can it be hoped to take large trout with the fly.

Little fly-fishing is done on the Rangely Lakes in June, trolling being then the customary method by which the large fish are taken. A six-inch chub on a single hook makes up the lure, triple hooks or gangs being prohibited by a rigidly enforced law. My own experience there in that month is limited to three days in 1883. I was then fairly successful in numbers but failed in size, nothing over two and a half pounds being taken. The common report is that the large trout will not then take the fly ; but some of the guides with whom I conversed thought the prevalence of this opinion was due to the fact that so little fly-fishing was then practised—in other words, that its merits had never been fairly tested at that season. If a fly is properly presented to a large trout, I cannot believe that it would be more likely to be ignored then than in September, since a few days before the large trout in neighboring waters took it fully as well, if not better, than in the month last named. But it may be they do not bunch in June as they do in September, or perhaps not in the same places, though even this was not the case in the waters before referred to. Therefore, though it is believed the chance of taking large trout in the Rangely Lakes is as good in the one month as in the other, still this opinion has not been sufficiently subjected to the crucial test of actual trial, to warrant its acceptance as an established fact.

By trolling more ground is covered, and, of course,

with increased chance of success. But to my mind, taking a trout other than with the fly is akin to sacrilege,
and unworthy an angler. Though forced to admit it
would be difficult to defend this opinion—perhaps prejudice would more accurately describe it—on strictly
logical grounds, it remains all the same a fixed canon of
my angling morality.

A guide is requisite to one unfamiliar with these waters·
As far as surface indications are concerned, to a stranger
one place looks about as promising as another ; and the
water area is so great, that only by the utmost good fortune could the best places be found. These it is the
guide's business to know thoroughly, as well as which of
them promises most under the then conditions of time
and weather. The Rangely guides are, as a general rule,
a very superior class of men—quiet, gentlemanly, oblig-
ing, and thoroughly conscientious in their endeavor to
give their employers the best possible sport. Not the
slightest apprehension need be felt on the latter score.
The stranger is strongly recommended to place himself
absolutely in his guide's hands, and to tell him in language and in a manner, the sincerity of which cannot be
doubted, that you propose to fish where, and in such manner, and with such flies as he may recommend ; and that
if he thinks any change in the manner of fishing would
improve the chances of success, that he is to mention it
at once. Otherwise, even though you fasten your fly to
the butt of your rod and whale the water with that, he
will be silent, and to all outside appearance will act as

though that was the usual and only proper way to fish with the fly. Anxious as they all are to please their employer, experience has taught them that it is unadvisable to make any comment whatever which may be construed into disparagement of his angling skill. Wisdom is the child of experience, and no matter how great that of the angler may have been elsewhere, there at least his guide can instruct him to advantage ; for he has seen almost every conceivable method of fly-fishing, and has heard his comrades describe the very few which have not come under his personal observation. The merits and demerits of each have been appraised in his mind by the infallible touchstone of actual trial, and if his advice can be had, it cannot but prove valuable to any one.

Though these recommendations are strictly followed, and though the guide exerts himself to the utmost, still as long as trout are capricious, so long will success, though probable, be uncertain.

Remember that only exceptional luck is chronicled in fishing, and that as to failure therein a discreet silence is ever in order.

From some printed accounts of that region, it might be inferred that an eight pounder occupied every superficial yard of those waters, clamoring to be caught. This is not strictly true. Indeed, if you cast seven consecutive days from morning till night, with perhaps a couple of hours rest in the middle of each day, and during that time get one single rise from a fish of seven pounds or over, your luck will then be fully up to the average.

Fish you will take with the fly and plenty of them, but of the large ones, but few at best.

But it is wortn a year of common fishing to fasten one long, slim, limber five pounder. For from a half to three quarters of an hour or so, he will make music which to the anglers' ear has a charm, compared to which the sweetest strains of Patti or Nilsson are but discordant sounds.

This may be your good fortune at the first cast,—may be, though probably it will not. But at all events, repeat to yourself the wise saying of the Philosopher of the Magalloway, "If you want to catch any fish, you must keep your line wet," and hammer away at them. In time, if you follow the method herein before set forth, your turn will surely come ; and then you will forget all the weary waiting that has gone before, and will rest that night a happy man, even though you have the toothache.

" There is no genuine enjoyment in the easy achievement of any purpose ; there is no bread so sweet as the hard-earned loaf of the man who works for it. The rule holds good in the school of the sportsman."—" *Bourgeois.*"

" Happily, fishermen, like hunters, do not always agree, nor in many of the details of the fly-fishing art do they think and act alike."—*D. W. Cross.*

" To the angler the value of even a moderate acquaintance with ichthyology cannot be exaggerated. Not only is it of the greatest practical use, by the insight which it gives him into the habits, food, spawning-seasons, etc., of the several fish—and consequently into the best means of taking them—but it also doubles the pleasure of success."—*H. Cholmondeley Pennell.*

" The moment the trout seizes the artificial fly it is as far in his mouth or throat as it will ever be, therefore it is sound to say you cannot "strike" too quick, after you have *seen* or *felt* the trout."—*D. W. Cross.*

" When the fly is thrown on the stream some little resemblance of life must be attempted to be given to it."—*Alfred Ronalds.*

" It is astonishing how many there are calling themselves sportsmen, who are content to remain all their lives simply killers of fish—of the habits, idiosyncrasies, and even of the very names of which they are too often ignorant.—*H. Cholmondeley Pennell.*

" The materials for an artificial fly should be compared and matched with the natural one, by the eye and judgment of the fly-fisher."—*Michael Theakston.*

" There is nothing like the thrill of expectation over the first cast in unfamiliar waters. Fishing is like gambling, in that failure only excites hope of a fortunate throw next time."—*Charles Dudley Warner.*

" Let it be seen that a love of the 'gentle art' openeth first the heart, then the fly-book, and soon the stores of experience and knowledge garnered up through long years, wheresoever we meet a 'Brother of the Angle'; and that to us 'angling is an employment of our idle time, which is not then idly spent'; that therein we find ' a rest to the mind, a cheerer of the spirits, a diverter of sadness, a calmer of unquiet thoughts, a moderator of the passions, a procurer of contentedness, and that it begets habits of peace and patience in those that possess and practice it.'"—*Thaddeus Norris.*

" Fly-fishing holds the same relation to bait-fishing that poetry does to prose. Not only the fly, but every implement of the fly-fisher's outfit is a materialized poem."—*James A. Henshall, M.D.*

13. Bee.	14. Tomah Jo.
15. "No Name."	16. Blue Bottle.
17. Grasshopper.	18. Canada.

" Between the tyro and the proficient grayling fisher there exists a wider gulf than is the case with the experienced and inexperienced in any other branch in the whole art of fishing. Practical skill and general artistic bearing are more fully exemplified in fishing for grayling, than for trout and salmon, whilst upon the same ground the unskilled efforts of the bungler stand at a yet more glaring contrast."—*David Foster.*

" Hooking a large grayling, I had good evidences of his plucky qualities ; the pliant rod bent as he struggled against the line, curling his body around columns of water that failed to sustain his grasp, and setting his great dorsal fin like an oar backing water, while we cautiously worked him in, his tender mouth requiring rather more careful handling than would be necessary for a trout ; making a spurt up stream, he requires a yielding line, but after a time he submits to be brought in, rallying for a dart under the boat, or beneath a log, as an attempt is made to place the landing net under·him."—*Professor Milner.*

" Do not despair. There was—alas ! that I must say there was —an illustrious philosopher, who was nearly of the age of fifty before he made angling a pursuit, yet he became a distinguished fly-fisher."—*Sir Humphry Davy.*

" Fly-fishing for grayling and trout are not altogether identical. Both are frequently found in the same water, and are to be taken with the same cast of flies. Finer tackle, as a rule, is required in the case of the former, as also smaller and brighter flies." —*David Foster.*

" The grayling generally springs entirely out of the water when first struck by the hook, and tugs strongly at the line, requiring as much dexterity to land it safely as it would to secure a trout of six times the size."—*Dr. Richardson.*

" Grayling will often take the fly under water, rising so quietly that you will scarcely see any rise or break of the water at all. It is desirable, therefore, to watch the line narrowly, and to strike whenever you think it stops or checks, and you will now and then be surprised, although there is no break in the water, to find a good grayling on the hook. For, as is often the case with trout, the big ones are very quiet risers."—*Francis Francis.*

" To be a perfect fisherman you require more excellencies than are usually to be found in such a small space as is allotted to a man's carcass."—*Parker Gilmore.*

"The trout has, so to speak, a Herculean cast of beauty; the grayling rather that of an Apollo—light, delicate, and gracefully symmetrical."—*H. Cholmondely-Pennell.*

" The ways of the grayling differ according to his locality."— *E. Sterling, M.D.*

"The angler who cares *nothing* for his score, is as little a true angler as one who cares *only* for his score."—*Frank. S. Pinckney.*

THE GRAYLING.

BY

FRED MATHER.

THE very name of my beloved fish calls up a host of recollections that form themselves into a picture that, above all others, is the most cheerful one adorning memory's wall. We old fellows live largely in the past, and can afford to let younger men revel in the future ; and in my own case, I can say that, having filled Shakespeare's apothegm of " one man in his time plays many parts," there are often retrospects of life as a boyish angler, an older hunter, trapper, and general vagabond on the frontiers ; a soldier ; and a later return to a first love. Of these glances over the shoulder of time, a few trips to Northern Michigan and its grayling streams mark the journey of life with a white stone.

When Prof. Cope announced, in 1865, that he had received specimens from Michigan, the English anglers in America were incredulous, and there was some spicy correspondence, in the sportsmen's papers of those days, concerning the identity of the fishes. As usual, the scientist discomfited the angler, and proved his position. The fish had long been known to the raftsmen and natives of Michigan by local names, but had never been identified as the historic grayling.   Some eight years after the discovery of Prof. Cope that we had the grayling in American waters, Mr. D. H. Fitzhugh, Jr., sent some of them to Mr. Charles Hallock, then editor of *Forest and Stream*, and they were shown in New York to the doubters, who even then were not convinced.

Mr. Fitzhugh took great interest in the new fish, which, as a lumberman and an angler, he had long known as a "Michigan trout," but had never recognized as the gentle grayling, and he has since done more than any other man to popularize it and introduce it to anglers.

He invited Mr. Hallock, Prof. Milner, and myself to come up and fish for it, and we each extolled its attractions in the press.   As a consequence, the fish has been nearly exterminated by vandals who fish for count, and the waters where we fished at first are nearly barren.

Of all game fishes the grayling is my favorite.   It is gamy but not savage ; one does not feel the savage instinct to kill that the black bass or the pike raises in him, but rather a feeling of love for a vigorous fighter for its life who is handicapped with a tender mouth. To me the fish is always thought of as the "gentle grayling," and the "golden-eyed grayling," although the latter epithet is not always a correct one, owing to the changes in the iris.

In fishing for grayling it is well to use a medium-sized fly of a subdued color ; a yellow body and a brown wing is the fly that should be used if only one is

Plate V. Description on page 109.

TROUT FLIES.

Made by C.F. ORVIS, Manchester, Vt.
COPYRIGHTED.

Plate VI. Description on page 143.

TR·O·U·T FLIES.

recommended ; it is a most killing combination. Brown Hackles, Red Ibis, Professor, Queen of the Water, and other trout flies are also killing ; but the first-mentioned fly, whose name I do not know, owing to a defective memory and the vagaries of fly nomenclature, is the most killing, and a cast into the upper edge of a pool below a rapid is usually most successful.*

The beauty of the grayling is of a kind that is better appreciated after some acquaintance. The bright colors of its " magnificent dorsal," as the phrase went a few years ago, are not its chief claim to admiration. Its shapely contour, striped ventrals, iridescent caudal, and its beatific countenance win the heart of the angler and make him love the grayling, and feel that it is a fish to respect for the higher qualities expressed in its physiognomy, and not one that it is merely a satisfaction to kill as he would a savage pike. True, we kill the grayling, but we do it in a different spirit from that in which we kill some other thing. It was not only my good fortune to know " Uncle Thad " Norris, but to have fished with him. The dear lovable old man, who long since paid his fare to the grim ferryman, once said : " When I look into a grayling's eye I am sorry I killed it ; but that feeling never prevents me from making another cast just to see if another will rise."

In another century Norris will be more read and appreciated than he is to-day. Of all American angling

---

* Oak-fly.

writers of this century he will stand foremost, and
yet he never wrote as fully as he intended of the
fish that he told me had afforded him more pleasure than any other.   He had not revised his "American Angler's Book" for some time before his
death, and so his remarks on Back's grayling must
stand as he wrote them before the era of the Michigan
grayling.   He there says of the Arctic grayling :
"The grayling being a fish in the capture of which
the American angler cannot participate, we give no
account of the manner of angling for them, but refer the reader who may have interest or curiosity on
that score to English authors."   He intended to re-
vise that sentence and give his own experience, but the
Reaper judged him ripe for the harvest before he did
it.   In my opinion he was one of those who should
never have been ripe for that harvest, and his loss to
our angling literature was a severe one.

That the grayling will take bait, truth requires the
admission ; would that it were not so.   I would prefer
that its food was the soaring insect, or even the floating thistledown, with an occasional feather from an
angel's wing dropped in the moonlit flood ; but science
has laid bare its interior with the searching scalpel, and
the Cæsarian operation has brought forth the lowly
caddis-worm and other larvæ, and the bait-fisher has
taken advantage of the knowledge and pandered to the
baser appetite of the fish.

That the grayling does not eat other fish is proved

by its small mouth, as well as by its known habits. It is not a leaper, like the trout, but takes the fly from the surface with merely an exposure of a portion of its head. When struck, it makes a vigorous rush, and, if it does not fight as long as the trout does, it gives much resistance at the last moment by the sidelong movement it makes when being reeled in, which is due to the size and curvature of its dorsal fin. It inhabits only the coldest of streams, and while the grayling of Europe is found in the trout streams, it is not to be found there in Michigan.

We have several species of grayling in America. Two of these only are accessible to anglers, the Michigan grayling, *Thymallus tricolor,* and one at the head waters of the Yellowstone, the *T. Montanus.* The other species are Arctic.

The Michigan fish is reported to grow to nearly two pounds weight ; I never saw one that I thought would weigh much over a pound, and I have taken them in spawning season for the purpose of procuring their eggs. Whether this fish will bear acclimatization to other waters, I cannot say. I raised a few until a year old at my former trout farm in Western New York, and when I left them I opened the pond and let them into the stream below, but none have ever been taken there, as far as I know. It seems a pity to allow this elegant fish to become extinct, as it will in a few years in its limited habitat, and if opportunity offered I would again try to domesticate it.

The trout-fisher needs no special directions nor tackle to fish for grayling; he may cast in the usual manner, only remembering that the fish has a very tender mouth, and must be treated with this fact ever in mind. The Michigan grayling streams are not suited for wading, and, therefore, fishing from a boat is the rule. This may not suit some anglers, to whom I can only say, every one to his fancy, but no wading for me; dry feet are more comfortable than wet ones, and boat-fishing or bank-fishing are more suitable to my taste, than to be immersed up to my hips in cold water for half a day.

I have killed, I believe, every game fish in America east of the Rocky Mountains, except the salmon, for which I have a rod in readiness, that I hope to use soon, and I can say that while I do not think the grayling the superior of all of them for gameness, yet there is something of romance in the remembrance of the grayling, a kind of sentimental retrospect, that endears the fish to me above all others. Whether it was owing to the pine woods and the genial companionship, I do not care to consider; but each year there comes a longing to repeat the pleasant experiences of the Au Sable and its delicate grayling.

" The trout-fly does not resemble any known species of insect. It is a ' conventionalized ' creation, as we say of ornamentation. The theory is, that, fly-fishing being a high art, the fly must not be a tame imitation of nature, but an artistic suggestion of it. It requires an artist to construct one ; and not every bungler can take a bit of red flannel, a peacock's feather, a flash of tinsel thread, a cock's plume, a section of a hen's wing, and fabricate a tiny object that will not look like any fly, but still will suggest the universal conventional fly."—*Charles Dudley Warner.*

" When you fish with a flie, if it be possible, let no part of your line touch the water, but your flie only."—*Izaak Walton.*

1. Coachman.	2. Leadwing Coachman.	3. Royal Coachman.
4. Coachman red tip.	5. Gilt Coachman.	6. Cowdung.
7. Fern.	8. Blue Jay.	9. Abbey.
10. Red Ant.	11. Black Ant.	12. Seth Green.
13. Professor.	14. Blue Professor.	15. Dark Stone.

"A combination of English Jay is one of the most effective flies in the world, as it can be put into as gay a fly as you please, and also into as plain a one as you like."—*Capt. Peel* (" *Dinks* ").

" When I think of the great secrets of Nature locked up from our knowledge (yet under our eyes at every turn of your daily duty), and imagine what a mine of intellectual wealth remains to be opened out by quickness of sight, clearness of intellect, and the pickaxe of hard work, a great panorama opens before me. How ignorant—how terribly ignorant—are we of God's great laws as applied to the creatures that live in the element in which we are forbidden to exist!"—*Frank Buckland*.

" The ancient belief in the stoppage of sport during a thunder storm is not strictly true."—*David Foster*.

" A fish will *hook himself only* in cases where the fly first touches the water at the end of a straight line, or when the line is being withdrawn smartly for a new cast. In all other cases the skill of the angler must be employed."—*Charles Hallock.*

" We had determined on a feast, and trout were to be its daintiest dainty. We waited until the confusing pepper of a shower had passed away and left the water calm. We tossed to the fish humbugs of wool, silk and feathers, gauds such as captivate the greedy or the guileless. The trout, on the lookout for novelty, dashed up and swallowed disappointing juiceless morsels, and with them swallowed hooks. Then, O Walton ! O Davy ! O Scrope! ye fishers hard by taverns! luxury was ours of which ye know nothing. Under the noble yellow birch we cooked our own fish. We used our scanty kitchen-battery with skill. We cooked with the high art of simplicity. Where Nature has done her best, only fools rush in to improve. On the salmonids, fresh and salt, she has lavished her creative refinements. Cookery should only ripen and develop."—*Theodore Winthrop.*

"As a general thing, it is a waste of time to be forever changing your flies. If the trout are not rising, it is entirely useless to fling an assortment of flies at them."—*T. S. Up de Graff, M.D.*

" In taking the fly, I award the palm to the trout, as he usually throws himself out of the water to do so. The salmon does not, he scarcely more than shows himself; but after being hooked the sport commences, and it is all activity to the death, rarely any sulking."—*Charles W. Stevens.*

" ' That old story about the little boy with the pin-hook, who ketched all the fish, while the gentleman with the modern improvements, who stood alongside of him, kep' throwin' out his beautiful flies and never got nothin', is a pure lie.' "—*Frank R. Stockton.*

A TROUTING TRIP TO ST. IGNACE ISLAND.

BY

W. THOMSON

Towards the end of August, 1877, I had become pretty well fagged out with office work and felt that I must have a week or two of out-door recreation or sport of some kind, so I naturally decided upon a trout-fishing expedition ; and I selected, as the scene, the island of St. Ignace, in Lake Superior, of which I had heard most excellent accounts in regard to fish products. I had, it is true, caught a great many brook trout throughout the summer, in small streams close at hand ; but these were mostly fish of inferior size, few indeed reaching one pound in weight ; while I was assured by an ancient fisherman of repute, that at the Island, the real *Salmo fontinalis* often attained to four, five, and even seven pounds.

This was the kind of ground I had been, for many years, anxious to find, and I made up my mind to try it at all events.

The first thing to do was to secure two suitable companions, and a man or boy of all work. The former I quickly enlisted in the persons of a genial M. D. and an overworked limb of the law. The latter opportunely turned up in the shape of "Jim," a colored youth of sixteen, as black as the ten of spades, but no less celebrated for his culinary skill than for his impish tricks and imperturbable good humor and honesty. To banish formality once for all, and put things upon an easy and familiar footing at the start, I christened the M.D. "Squills" and the lawyer "Bluffy," out of compliment to his usual style of treating witnesses in court. In deference to my advanced age and *general good looks,* the boys called me "Governor," I being then about fifty-three and neither of them thirty. Our supplies, consisting of a ten by twelve tent, three camp beds and bedding, two small boats, a stock of provisions for six men for two weeks, one rifle, two fowling pieces, and our fishing tackle, were soon got together, and in twenty-four hours from the first proposal, we were ready to take the cars for Collingwood. At that point we secured an ample supply of ice; and then embarked with our traps on board a steamer bound for Duluth and intermediate ports, and touching at St. Ignace on her way.

This island is situated in Canadian waters, about thirty-five miles from the mouth of Nepigon River, forty-seven miles east of the famous Silver Islet and some seventy from Thunder Bay. I say island, but there are in fact *two* called St. Ignace; the largest being about sixteen miles long by ten wide; with generally bluff shores and high headlands, one of these rising to a height of thirteen hundred and fifty feet above the lake level. The smaller island, at which steamers

touch and upon which we camped, is separated from
the larger by a channel of from fifty to a hundred yards
wide, and is about two miles by a half a mile in size,
having one bold headland five hundred feet high.
Neither island is inhabited except by occasional Indians
and other fishermen ; nor do either of them, so far as I
observed, contain any agricultural land, the formation
being rock.   Both, however, as well as contiguous
groups, are mostly covered with a thick growth of
spruce, balsam, birch and mountain ash.   This last is
so plentiful that in the autumn its brilliant red leaves
may be seen from quite a distance at sea, framed in a
background of dark green spruce, and presenting a
most charming view.   The larger island contains in itself numerous small lakes which abound in pike (*E.
lucius*), and what we Canadians call yellow pickerel
(*Stizostedium vitreum*), really pike-perch.   No one
bothers catching these, however, as the surrounding
waters yield an enormous supply of choicer fish, among
which are said to be ten varieties of the salmon family ;
besides whitefish, some of which attain to seventeen
pounds in weight ! I took some trouble to ascertain
the local names by which the various species of trout
are known, and the greatest attested weight of individuals of each.   I am indebted to Mr. Wm. Boon, of
Barrie, Ontario, a professional fisherman who spends
four months of every year upon the island, for the following list, which I give without vouching in any way
for this queer addition to the salmon family:

 1. Salmon trout, weight up to.................... 70 lbs.
 2. "Siskowitt," weight up to..................... 12 "
 3. Half-breed Siskowitt, weight up to .... 5 "
 4. "Potgut," very inferior fish, weight up to...... 12 "
 5. Rock or black trout, weight up to............. 40 "
 6. Large gray or shovel-nose trout, weight up to.... 70 "
 7. "California trout," yellow spots and flesh, weight
    up to.................................... 10 "
 8. "Half-breed red trout," weight up to .... 15 "
 9. Common brook or speckled trout, weight up to .. 7 "
10. "Red trout," weight up to.................... 42 "

All of these, of course, are local names, but the
fish are all true trout ; crossed and re-crossed, I presume, *ad infinitum.* The brook trout is the only
species found here with a square tail, those of all the
others being more or less forked. The " red trout " is
far superior to any of its confrères, and is called by the
Indians—Pugwashooăneg, that is, Paysplatt—Dis-
trict-fish, as it is taken only in this locality, and only
in the fall of the year as a rule. The Indians come
from Nepigon expressly to fish for it, and care for no
other trout in comparison. It is much more highly
esteemed than the brook trout. This very day on
which I write this article, I had a salted piece of one of
these " red trout " for dinner and found the flesh of a
bright pink, and the flavor exquisite. I shall refer to
it again.

On our passage from Collingwood we touched at the
following ports and " landings," viz. : Meaford, Owen
Sound, Killarney, Little Current, Bruce Mines, Hilton,

or St. Joseph Island, Garden River, and the Sault.
Thence, via Michipicoton Island to St. Ignace. I may
say here, before I forget it, that among the useful pro-
ductions of this last are incredible quantities of huckle-
berries and " sand cranberries." The former were just
in season at the date of our visit, and after the first
day " Jim " always gave us capital puddings and pies
made from them.

We found many pleasant people on board the steamer,
with whom we picked acquaintance in that free and
easy manner peculiar the world over to anglers.

After a delightful trip of four days, we made the
landing on our Island at about five o'clock on a beautiful evening, and, having got our whole outfit ashore,
selected a charming spot in the midst of a spruce grove
as a camping ground. The tent was put up, beds and
bedding arranged, supplies for present use unpacked,
a table improvised and things generally " set out " in
a most orderly manner by the Doctor and "Bluffy,"
while I employed myself in the construction of a fish
corral, the use of which will be seen further on.
Meantime, " Jim " had, with a few loose stones, made
for himself a very passable fire-place, and soon had tea
and coffee prepared, several appetizing dishes cooked,
and called us to supper at 6.30. After a hearty and
enjoyable meal, we proceeded to put the finishing
touches to our work ; sorted out and overhauled our
fishing tackle ; caught a few minnows and placed them
in a perforated bucket in the lake ; and before dark

were all in ship-shape and thoroughly comfortable. "Jim" slung his hammock between and beneath two umbrageous trees, and by eight o'clock, with a full stomach and clear conscience, was roosting in it, happy as a lord ! From this coign of vantage, with the gathering darkness to hide his *blushes,* he favored us with several choice negro melodies rendered in a style and with a pathos which any "professional" might have envied. As the night deepened we drank in with appropriate senses all the delights of our surroundings. The great fire before which we three sat, lighting up with weird and fantastic effects the sombre foliage of the adjacent forest ; the plaintive cry of the distant loon ; the harsher notes of the bittern, and the even, gentle murmur of the softly lapping waves, all united to inspire us with a sense of freedom and happiness unknown to the busy world. Serene and contented, we "turned in" at ten, with blissful anticipations for the morrow. We had not forgotten that prime necessity of a well-ordered camp, light, but had brought with us several pounds of sperm candles, two gallons of oil and a good swinging lamp, which, suspended from the centre-pole, not only rendered the tent cheerful, but gave facilities for performing with ease and comfort the thousand and one little jobs which precious daylight could not be wasted upon. Reader, did you ever "camp out" in the midst of a dense grove of pine or spruce trees ? If not, you have yet to enjoy the luxury of the most balmy and refreshing sleep which can bless mortal

man. There is a something in the delicious aroma of
the resinous woods which induces a perfect repose, ob-
tainable, in my experience, through no other means.
A sound, sweet, wholesome, and yet not heavy sleep ;
quiet and dreamless, and from which you awake, not
drowsy and cross, but with a buoyancy of spirits, a
strength of body and clearness of mind which make
even hard daily toil seem a mere pastime. And so,
with thankful hearts sank we to rest on this our first
night at St. Ignace. There are no black flies on the
Island, and the season was too far advanced for
mosquitoes to be troublesome ; facts which added not a
little to our serenity of mind and took away the last
excuse for ill-humor.

The next morning, after partaking of a breakfast
which fully sustained Jim's reputation as a cook,
" Squills " and " Bluffy " agreed to go out in the larger
of the two boats, leaving the small one for me. They
were provided with various kinds of bait, including frogs,
worms, grubs, grasshoppers, and minnows, as well as a
goodly supply of spoons and other lures. I had decided
upon trying flies for the first day, and if found effective I intended to stick to them. The boys anchored
out at about a hundred yards from shore and went to
work ; and I moved slowly along the coast-line, closely
examining the bottom and the lay of the submerged
rocks, as well as the trend of the contiguous land. When
an angler is in strange waters he will find this preliminary survey to be always a paying operation. By

and by I found a lovely-looking reef which extended from the shore to deep water. This reef or ledge was broad and smooth on one side, but the other dipped down sharply, and presented a rough, jagged, and cavernous face. Here, if anywhere, I judged *fontinalis* would be sure to lurk ; so I anchored within twenty feet of the precipitous edge of the reef, with water apparently about ten feet deep under the boat, but of profound depth a few yards from the ledge. At that time I had no split bamboo rod, a fact which I have ever since regretted, but I had an excellent ash and lancewood, which had killed myriads of fish, and is still to the fore. I never was and never will be a skilful fly-fisherman, or perhaps I should say—as too much modesty savors of affectation—a skilful fly-*caster*.

That is I never could, nor can I yet, make an effective and proper cast of over forty-two feet from reel to fly. I have always found, however, that I *take as many fish* as those artistic anglers who can cast more than double that distance. On this occasion I tried a white miller as tail fly, and a common gray hackle as dropper, and they succeeded so well that I only thereafter changed them as a matter of experiment. I never at any time during this trip used more than two flies at once, as that number gave me quite enough to do.

Well, this morning of which I am now writing, was one to make glad the heart of an angler. A southwest wind blew softly, and the sun was obscured by warm gray clouds. No fish of any decency or self-respect could *help* biting on such a day ! I felt so sure of good luck that I put overboard a wicker-work basket, with a hole in the lid, so arranged, with a falling spring door, that fish could be put in but could not get out. This floated astern and would keep fully a hundred pounds of fish alive, if necessary, for any length of time. Having fixed everything to my liking, I stood up and made my first cast along the edge of the reef. No result ! but I thought I saw a faint suspicion of a shadowy form or two, and a slight movement of the water just behind my flies. Have been too quick, I thought ; and so tried again, letting the flies this time rest until they sank an inch or so below the surface, when I *attempted* to draw them slowly in. I say attempted, because they had not moved six inches when first the dropper and then the tail fly were taken in a rush, by two large trout which didn't draw towards me worth a cent, for some fifteen minutes at least. On the contrary they darted away as if the Old Nick was after them with a red-hot frying-pan ; pulling in unison like a pair of well-broken colts and severely trying my rather too light tackle. Any decided check was out of the question. I could only put on such pressure as the single gut leader would bear, and that was sufficient to make a half-circle of my rod. I had beautiful open water in which to play the fish, but as they rushed along and down the face of the submerged cliff, I did not know what hidden dangers might lurk in the unseen depths, nor at what moment a sharp, jagged rock might cut the line, or some profound recess furnish a retreat from whence it might be impossible to withdraw my prize. So far, however, all went well. The fish in their terror had sought deep water and not touched rock at all. Soon the distraction of the heavy, ceaseless strain caused them to forget the glorious maxim that, " in union is strength," and they began to pull different ways. Now I was sure of them ! and very gradually and gently, inch by inch, I coaxed them away from the dangerous ground, and got them safely above the smooth bottom of the plateau on the farther side of the boat, where I could see their every motion and watch their brave struggles for life. A prettier sight I never witnessed than the curious way in which the movements of one fish neutralized those of the other. If one sought the bottom, his mate went for the surface ; if one rushed away seawards, the other came towards the boat. They literally *played each other*, and I was for awhile a mere spectator ! After looking upon these cross-purposes for some minutes, I noticed that the fish on the tail fly became entangled with the line above his comrade on the dropper, and both then began to whirl furiously round and round after the usual manner of trout in a like predicament. When the wildest of this flurry was over, I drew them cautiously to the boat and dipped up both at once with my landing net. An immediate application of my pocket scale proved their weight to be twenty-nine and thirty-three ounces respectively, the heaviest trout being that on the drop or upper fly. They

Plate VII. Description on page 171.

TROUT FLIES.

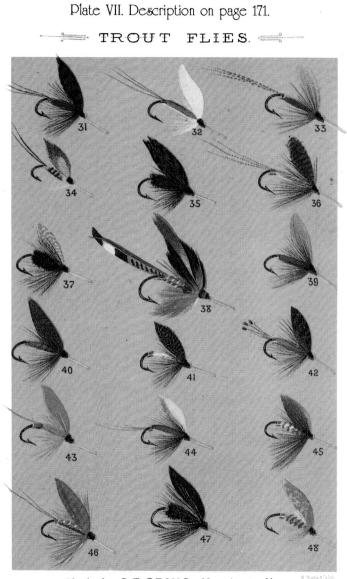

Made by C. F. ORVIS, Manchester, Vt.
COPYRIGHTED.

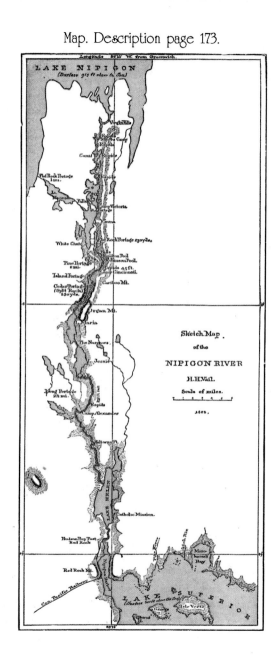

Longitude 88°15' W. from Greenwich.

LAKE NIPIGON
(Surface 913 ft above the Sea)

Virgin Falls
Big Rapids
Miller's Camp
Big Rapids
Canal Rapids
Rapids
Flat Rock Portage
1 mi.
Rapids
Maxwell Falls
Camp Victoria
Portage
Simona
Red Rock Portage 250 yds.
White Chute
Falls
Mission Pool
Robinson Pool
Pine Portage
3 mi.
Rapids 45 ft.
Camp Cincinnati
Island Portage
Cedar Portage
(Split Rock)
250 yds.
Caribou Mt.
Organ Mt.
St. Maria
The Narrows
L. Jessie
Falls
Long Portage
2½ mi.
Rapids
Camp Alexander
Falls
Half-way Pt.
Catholic Mission.
Hudson Bay Post
Red Rock
Red Rock Mt.
Can. Pacific Railway

LAKE HELEN

Sketch Map
of the
NIPIGON RIVER

H. H. Vail.

Scale of miles.

1882.

Pays Plat River
Black Bay River
Mica-katuak
Bay

LAKE SUPERIOR
(Surface 600 ft above the Sea)
St. George
Island
Isle Verte
Orient Island

were evidently a mated pair, and both were broad-shouldered, deep fish, but not very long, the largest being only sixteen and a half inches. Their backs were beautifully clouded and mottled, but the carmine spots on their sides were not quite so vivid as those of dark river-water trout. Fortunately they were merely lip-hooked, and being at once placed in the floating creel, soon revived. Now I began to feel big, and thought myself quite an expert, but in less than five minutes the conceit was taken out of me with a vengeance, for on my very next cast I struck a magnificent fish and lost him, and half my leader, instanter. On feeling the hook old *Salmo* went like a shot over the brow of the declivity and (I suppose) into a hole, and cut the line short off. After that mishap I became more careful, and never dropped my fly more than six inches from the edge of the reef ; and whenever a fish was struck I drew him at once, at all hazards, away from the risky ground and played him on the plateau.

By ten o'clock I had secured fifteen beauties, some running close upon three pounds. Eleven of these were as lively as ever, but four had been hooked in the throat and soon died.

As the day was now becoming bright and hot, I thought it time to look after my boys, who were out of sight around a point. I soon came up with them and found " Squills " asleep in the bottom of the boat while " Bluffy " sat smoking, with his rod lying idly across the gunnel with the line in the water. " What luck,

boys ? " I shouted. " Squills " awoke and replied,
" What luck yourself, Governor ? Not one blessed fish
in this region." I settled on my sculls, ready for a
quick start, and said, " Why, Squills, you don't know
how to fish. Just compound a few of your best pre-
scriptions and throw them overboard. They have generally proved fatal to your patients, and will murder
the fish sure." " Squills " made a wicked dab at my
head with his long-handled net, but a stroke put me in
safety, and I added, " And you, friend ' Bluffy,' just
rehash that famous trespass-case speech of yours, which
gave the judge fits and nearly killed the jury, and if
you don't have lots of dead fish, I'm a Dutchman."
The poor boys, however, were past joking ; and I rowed
back and examined their ground. They had actually
been fishing all the morning in water nine feet deep ;
over a bottom smooth as a billiard table, without a
weed, rock or stone to hide them from the fish ; all
of which, within a hundred yards, could plainly see
them and their boat. So I said, " Come boys, we'll go
to camp and have an early trout dinner, and in the
evening you shall catch fish to your heart's content."
Then up, after this manner, spoke the dolorous
" Squills," " That is all right, Governor, but it strikes
me that in order fully to enjoy a trout-dinner, it is,
above all things, necessary first to have the trout."
" True, most sapient medicus, and here they are," I
rejoined, at the same time lifting the lid of my creel.
" Glory to Galen ! " " Thunder and turf ! " " Ghost of

Walton ! where did you get those, Governor ?" both exclaimed in a breath. "Boys," said I, "you are hungry, tired, and cross ; possess your souls in patience; come to camp ; take some lime-juice and water, with a little of something in it ; eat, drink, and recover your strength, and you shall have the best afternoon's sport you ever saw." These words of wisdom cheered the fellows up wonderfully, and we all put off for camp.

That redolent and shiny youth, Jim, soon cleaned two of the dead fish, together about five pounds, cooked them in a style of his own, and we sat down at the unfashionable hour of eleven to our first camp dinner. I will, for once, give the *menu*, merely to show what awful *hardships* we had to encounter !

Brook trout, fried in red-hot lard, garnished with bread crumbs ; broiled mutton chops ; baked potatoes ; cold tongue ; pickles ; sauces and jellies : aftercourse— pancakes with maple syrup ; wind up—Stilton cheese. Didn't we just suffer for our country ? After the inevitable and welcome pipe (not cigars), and some choice and (I am happy to say) *chaste* anecdotes by " Bluffy," we laid down for a two hours' siesta. Oh, the glory, the happiness of out-door life, away from posts, telegraphs, or newspapers ! Oh, the delight of feeling that every fresh breath of pure ozone-laden air, adds to health and wholesome animal spirits, and is rapidly re-invigorating your system, and fitting you to more effectually take part in renewed and honest work !

At four o'clock the sun was again obscured by kindly

clouds and we all went out to the reef ; the boys, as
before, in one boat, and I in the other. And then occurred sport such as is seldom seen in genuine trout-
fishing. My friends stuck to their minnow and grasshopper bait, while I retained the fly. I induced them
to anchor quite close to the edge of the reef, so that
they might, if necessary, drop their lines perpendicularly down its face. They had not fished five minutes
when " Bluffy " gave a whoop, which might have
awakened a petit-juror or scared a witness out of his
boots. I glanced that way, and found the man of law
standing up in the boat with curved and straining rod
and a glow of intense satisfaction pervading his jolly
countenance. "I've got him, Governor! He's a
whopper; an old he fellow! None of your three
pounders," he yelled in great excitement. Sure enough,
he *had* him, and after ten minutes of skilful play,
landed a trout of over four pounds.

This beat me all hollow ! Indeed the largest *S. fontinalis* I took on this trip weighed three pounds, one
ounce, being two ounces lighter than the heaviest I
have ever yet caught.

" Squills " now got his hand in and brought out a
dashing fish of three and a-half pounds, in a manner so
pretty and artistic as to elicit a warm eulogium from the
" Governor," who, of course, had not meantime been
idle himself. In fact, I had taken a double and single
while the boys got their two ; but these outweighed my
three. All through our excursion the *largest* fish were

invariably taken by bait, but not so many of them as
by the fly. However, the fly was so much less trouble
and so much prettier, and cleaner to handle, I did not
care to change, seeing at once that we should catch
more fish than we wanted anyway.

It was a great treat to me to watch the enjoyment
the boys had in their sport. Neither of them had been
out before for years, and no student at the beginning
of a long vacation could have manifested such un-
bounded delight at his freedom, as did they with their
fishing and its accompanying pleasures. It is a fact
worthy of note that while I, using the fly, took only
speckled trout (*S. fontinalis*), my friends, with bait,
secured several of other and larger kinds.

Well, amid laughter, joke and repartee, the afternoon wore away, and evening shades came all too
quickly.

Our sport had been almost unique in its exhilarating
success and joyousness. When the sun sank below
the waters we had taken in all seventy-six fine trout,
none under one pound. Of this number my fly was
responsible for thirty-two, "Squills" had taken twenty-one, and "Bluffy" twenty-three. A lovelier lot of
fish was never seen ; and with the exception of eight
dead ones, we transferred them all safely to the corral,
built in the edge of the lake near our tent, with large
stones. Here, about eighty per cent. of all the fish
taken on this trip remained alive during the whole time
of our stay. Whenever one showed signs of failing

we dipped him out for present use. This corral, backed up by our supply of ice, gave us full assurances that our good luck would not be followed by reckless waste.

But I had almost forgotten the chief incident of this memorable day. As we approached the camp we saw "Jim" on the shore dancing a double "Virginny break-down" and grinning all over from head to foot; his shining ebony face and gleaming teeth fairly illuminating the coming darkness. On seeing us he yelled out, "I got him, gentlemen; I beats you all; takes this nigger to catch fish!"

The imp had actually made for himself a raft of drift-wood, paddled it out to deep water, and taken with bait a great salmon trout of twenty pounds! and it was now swimming about in the corral like a very leviathan among my morning's catch. This tickled us all so immensely that we then and there bestowed upon "Jim" an extra "quarter" each. This boy was indeed a treasure; a first-class cook and care-taker; willing, faithful, and honest; while his store of songs, exhibits of dancing, and never-failing fun and good-humor, would have sufficed to keep cheerful any camp in the world. Poor fellow! he was drowned two years later in Lake Michigan, while bathing.

If I did not fear to spin out this already dull narrative to an inordinate length, I should like to give a detailed account of each of the twelve days we fished and shot in this vicinity.

Twelve days only, mind you, for not a line was wet on Sunday.

Our one rifle proved a useful adjunct, but we found no use for the shot-guns, the season being too early and the weather too fine for ducks. The delicately sighted Winchester, however, procured us several fine specimens of the loon or great northern diver, and one or two large blue cranes, all of which, I presume, now adorn "Squills'" sanctum in British Columbia.

Almost every day we had choice sport, and we limited our catch only by the facilities we possessed for saving and carrying away the fish.

One particular day we devoted to salmon and red trout, which we fished for away off in very deep water, all of us using either spoons or live herring bait, in trolling. We had plenty of wholesome exercise in rowing, and very fair luck as regards fish; taking in all, seven salmon trout and five red trout.

The honors of this day fell to "Squills," who captured with his spoon a salmon trout of nineteen pounds, while I got a red trout of ten pounds. This last named fish is as pink in the flesh and as fine flavored as *Salmo salar*. It is said by local fishermen to be in fact the same fish, and they suppose that in ages long past sea salmon had some means of reaching this lake, and when the waters subsided some were left, and that from them the red trout is descended. As I have myself no scientific knowledge whatever I cannot offer an opinion upon this point. I can only say that if a

skilled fisherman, or even a scientist, were to receive one
of these fish from, say Quebec, he could hardly distinguish it from the veritable *Salmo salar,* though it bears
even a more exact resemblance to the salmon of Frazer
River, British Columbia.

I am told that this red trout will rise to the fly, but
I cannot vouch for the fact, as all we took were captured
with bait or spoon.

A rather curious, though frequently occurring, thing
happened one evening as we were all fishing, with our
boats not more than fifty feet apart. I had hooked,
and was playing a medium sized speckled trout, when
it was seized and gorged by a sixteen-pound salmon
trout. I realized the situation instantly and gave
line freely, so as to allow the poacher lots of time
to swallow his stolen prey. The rifle was in the
other boat, and I asked the boys to come alongside, as
we should probably have to use cold lead, the fish being
too large for our landing nets. By the time they were
in position, about sixty feet of my line had gone slowly out, and I judged that the large fish had got the
small one fairly in his stomach. I then began to reel
in very gently, and was surprised to find that the big
trout followed my lead with great docility until I had
brought him quite near the surface. Then he became
alarmed and dashed off—a proceeding to which I made
no resistance, as I feared pulling the bait from his
throat. Being apparently satisfied that all was right,
my unknown friend soon became quiescent, and I could

only feel a slight tremor of the line as he settled his
supper satisfactorily in his maw. Again I coaxed him
slowly and cautiously towards the boat in which stood
" Bluffy " with poised rifle. This time I ventured to
make him show himself within twenty feet of the
muzzle of the gun, when " Bluffy " very neatly put a
bullet through his head, and he turned belly up and
was got on board. " Well done, 'Bluffy,' " said
" Squills ; " " your *practice* could not have done greater
execution if you had been making out a bill of costs for
a client." " Well, no," says " Bluffy ; " " but I think
perhaps one of *your curative* pills would have killed the
fish more unutterably dead." " Peace, boys, peace,"
said the " Governor " ; " this is a solemn occasion ; we
have used unlawful and unsportsmanlike means to take
a game fish ; but as it could not be helped we will con-
done the offence by giving the fish away to the first de-
serving object we meet." " And that will be 'Jim,' "
quietly observed " Squills."

But dear me ! what is the use of trying to tell all the
fun and glorious sport we had ? The pen of a " Frank
Forester " or a Hallock might do justice to the subject,
mine cannot. Suffice it to say that, as the days went
on, each one made me feel younger and younger, until
I found it hard to convince myself that I was over
twenty-five. As to my comrades, we had not been out
a week before they were boys of sixteen !

Last days will come, however, and all too quickly, let
us bear up never so bravely. The fifteenth morning

saw us packing up and preparing to return once more
to civilized life and " the busy haunts of men."

I am afraid to say how many trout we had at the
finish, but I know that we packed in ice more than
three hundred pounds weight to take home with us;
and gave away, almost alive from the corral, nearly as
many more to the captain of the steamer, thereby calling down upon our heads the earnest blessings of pas-
sengers and crew.

I find, on looking over this MS. that I have forgotten
to say that we discovered several places along the channel edge of the island where most excellent trout-fishing could be had from the shore ; and that, by the advice of local fishermen, my friends tried the *"hearts"*
of killed trout as bait, and found such very effective.
This " heart " is a piece of flesh which lies inside the
pointed part of the fish's belly which runs between the
gill covers.   It looks much like a genuine heart, and
pulsates for several seconds after being removed from
the fish.   I suppose that it *is* in fact a real heart.
Never once did this bait fail to attract a bite ; but, of
course, not many hearts could be obtained, as we ex-
tracted the delicate morsel only from such fish as were
required for immediate consumption.

We finally bade farewell to our two weeks' elysium,
with sorrowful feelings, but before the lapse of twenty-
four hours, kind and loving thoughts of wives, little
ones, and home re-asserted themselves, and we landed
at Collingwood in jubilant spirits and vigorous health,

fully prepared to resume our several avocations, and fight again the battles of life with renewed courage and hope.

P.S.—We were absent from Barrie twenty-five days in all, and the whole trip cost us only one hundred and thirty-five dollars, or forty-five dollars each. Our ice was kept almost intact by being wrapped in blankets and covered with spruce boughs. Mr. Boon, before referred to, has built and is this winter (1883) filling a large ice-house on the small island for his own use and that of any visitors who may fish in the neighborhood next summer. Mr. Boon took five hundred half barrels of choice fish on these grounds last season ; with nets, of course.

" If there is one day's fishing in the year which the trout-angler looks forward to more keenly than any other, it surely is the first day with his favorite old rod on the bank of some favorite stream."—*R. B. Marston.*

" A salmon will rise again and again at a fly after he has missed it. In this he differs widely from the trout."—*Lorenzo Prouty.*

" Then I gave him a gray hackle and told him that that was to the trout what bread was to civilized man—a staple article of which he seldom grew tired."—" *Bourgeois.*"

" I am inclined to believe that more important than fishing up or down stream, more important than wearing brilliant or sober-tinted clothing, more important than wading rather than fishing from the bank, more important than a dry or a wet fly, more important than being yourself visible or concealed, more important, indeed, than any of the different cautions of the books, is it to have your leader absolutely invisible, or, if that is impossible, then at least that it present to the trout no unusual or unfamiliar appearance."—*Henry P. Wells.*

" The idea that each month has its own killing flies is sheer nonsense ; a fly that is good on a bright day in the spring is good on any other bright day, although it must be admitted that trout are fickle in their tastes."—*Fred Mather.*

" Hackled flies are generally better than those that are winged ; but dress both, and give the fish which they prefer."—*Michael Theakston.*

" After fishing for a time with any one fly, and the salmon refuse to rise at it freely, we change to an opposite color, say from dark to light, or *vice versa*, which we find will bring them up when the former fly has lost its attraction or been regarded with suspicion."—*Allan Gilmour.*

" The rudest appliances of a savage life have been used to aid the angler at his delightful task, and science has not disdained to aid the modern fisherman in his sport."—*Genio C. Scott.*

THE ANGLER'S GREETING.

W. DAVID TOMLIN.

WHITHER away, friend ! Your black slender rod-box
and the creel denote you are on fishing intent, but
where are you bound ?

A momentary glance, a cordial good evening ; the
question then came—To whom am I indebted for this
greeting ? An exchange of cards resulted in a long
and cordial grasp of hands ; glad to meet you ! Is it
possible ? The magic pasteboard revealed two names
not unknown to each other through the columns of
their favorite angling journal, and this visitor had come
to the little country station in quest of some of the fishing often spoken of in the said paper.

The fates had led the correspondent to the railway
station to bid good-bye to a friend when the angler un-
limbered himself therefrom; and was looking around
as strangers do.

"Can you recommend a quiet inn near this point
where I can find decent treatment ? I am not inclined
to be fussy."

A few minutes' walk and I introduced him to mine
host, who was a genuine piscator, and nothing pleased

him better than to have an angler under his roof : he took possession of him and considered nothing too much trouble, so long as he gave his guests good fishing, clean beds, a square meal, and satisfaction.

While supper was being prepared, we pleasantly chatted over the prospect of sport, and the angler's aim and ambition. He wanted a day or two of trouting, and some roach fishing with a fly, as he had read some letters giving an experience in fishing for these dainty fish, and intended trying them. The inspection of a well-filled fly-book showed how carefully he had selected his stock.

The early supper over, we strolled up the hillsides overlooking this lovely vale. On the grassy downs we seated ourselves, and I pointed out to him the various fishing points ; yonder is a splendid reach where the trout are always found ; see that sheeny rivulet coming down through that clump of trees ! that is the best trout stream in this section of country.

Note the different water-courses. The canal runs through the middle of the valley ; see here, clear away to the west, a little brook comes tumbling in ; see just below that point, a silvery-looking stream on the farther side of the canal—that is a fine trout stream ; follow its course until it loses itself in that big clump of willows : a saw-mill is hidden in those willows, and the stream, after supplying the mill with power, drops into a culvert under the bed of the canal ; there it is again in that piece of open moorland ; there it is coming out

from that long clump of willows, and finally joining
the stream mentioned before as the best trout stream
in this region ; thus the two streams, the Gade and the
little Bourne, are swallowed up in the canal ; and have
always been splendid waters for roach fishing.

The hills hide the canal and streams in their winding course, or I would point out to you the best fishing
grounds for miles along this Hertfordshire valley ; but I
presume there lies under your observation enough fishing ground for a day or two.

The sun is tending downward like a huge ball of fire,
the vale is in a dreamy shade ; how glistening the appearance of the water-courses, like a big silvery thread
winding in and out along the vale ! the evening air is
full of music ; the bee is humming around you ; what
a flood of music comes from the throat of that woodland thrush in yonder thorn hedge ! the strain is taken
up, and the very woods echo again with the song of the
black-bird. As he ceases his roundelay, the soft clear
note of another bird strikes on the ear ; for the moment
nature seems hushed ; almost breathless you wait ; the
notes come rich and clear, as silvery as a lute, a flood
of melody ; the sound dies away and instantly the
woods ring again ; all the sweet-throated songsters
seem as if applauding the song of the nightingale ; we
sit and drink in these sounds, until one by one the
songs drop into silence, leaving the nightingale to pour
out its tuneful music until far into the night. At this
moment there comes in the air the quivering boom of a

bell ringing out the hour of nine from the steeple of the church yonder, faintly limned on the evening shadows. Ah ! listen again ! there comes the evening chime. How the quivering notes pulsate up here on these hill-tops ! how silvery the tones ; as the chords of the vesper hymn rings out sweet and clear, our hearts beat in rhythm to the strain ! Lovely vale ! Israel's grandest seer, who with eye undimmed and natural force un-abated, even from Pisgah's lofty heights gazed on no lovelier scene than this we have surveyed. We descend into the shadows ; promising to meet my angling friend some time during the following day, I wend my way homeward and to rest.

The evening shadows were again falling ere I could join our angler, but the flies were on the waters and roach were fairly jumping, the surface of the stream was alive with fish, both roach and dace breaking water around us. My friend was no novice ; I found him whipping the stream from bank to bank, and his creel testified to his success. He was using a tail fly and dropper, a red hackle for the former, and an imitation of the common blue house-fly for the dropper. These fish are fastidious in their tastes; they do not rise at flies like a trout, but come to the surface of the water and just break for the fly and at once turn tail up. He who fishes for them must have a quick eye and steady hand ; then he can kill readily enough. They are a toothsome fish, but a trifle bony. Eye and hand must work together, and when fish are feeding they will readily take the fly. They are tender in the mouth and require care in handling. They afford good sport in streams where they are abundant, and are often killed weighing from one and a-half to two pounds.

My angling friend had come well prepared with letters introducing him to the owners of the fine trout streams, and readily obtained permission to fish these preserved waters. It was rare sport to watch him daintily lay out his line across the stream, his stretcher a June fly, or at times a floating May-fly skittered across the surface until close to the farther bank. Here lay a big *Salmo fario*. We had been watching him lazily coming to the surface to suck in a fly or bug that had tumbled from the trees overhead. A big cock-chafer came spinning and buzzing down stream. All laziness gone in an instant, up came the *Salmo* showing his huge sides. A fierce lunge and a heavy splash and the 'chafer was gone into the cavern of the open mouth. The fly-book was out in an instant. A dark brown fly somewhat resembling the 'chafer replaced the stretcher. A careful cast a little up stream, a lunge and a miss from the trout. Another cast close in to the bank, a slight jerk and the fly assumed the appearance of the buzzing 'chafer; the same sharp dash, the hand was as quick as the trout this time, the hook was driven home and the fun began. Such a dashing, splurging, rushing I had never seen. He was determined to use every art known to trout-lore before he surrendered. The rod bent and sprung, the line fairly swished as he tore up stream ; above him lay the limb of a tree, scraggy and ragged ; toward this he plunged, but the line tightened on him ; he tugged and jerked, but gained not an inch; he came to the surface and thrashed the water with his broad tail. Fatal error! as he did so the line came in as fast as fingers could fly round, the landing net was slipped under him, a quick upward movement and Master *Salmo* was flung high and dry. He was too big for the net and so was ignominiously flung ashore.

What a noble trout! His silver sides and belly gleamed in the light, his blood-red spots seemed to glow with indignation at his cruel death. He had long been a lordling over the other trout and now was strangling ! Kill him ! I cannot bear to see a trout gasping. Killed and scaled he weighs three and a half pounds. A credit to the angler : but at times, during the contest, it was a question to which the honor belonged ; it was: " Splendid rod !" "Ah ! how skilfully he handles his fish." " Who would have dreamt that little thing would have stood such a strain ?"

Gentle angler, let us leave our friend to the contemplation of the beauties of the fairest of all England's garden landscapes, and the preserved trout streams, and plunge with me into an American forest.

By a beautiful lake in the famous State of Michigan a little settlement is springing up. Over in that bay is a trout creek emptying ; it is full of trout—trout *galore*—trout by the hundreds can be seen. Come with

me, I will show them to you. Let me drop a fly
into this hole. Ah! there he is! see him dash for it.
He won't come again, let us push along.

Push along, you say? do you expect I am coming
through that brush? Not much; I am not a crank.
If you are so fond of trying to break your neck for a
string of trout, why go. I go! am quite willing to
be alone on this lovely little creek, for it contains some
of the handsomest trout it has ever been my good luck
to kill. Here and there I drop in a fly; sometimes a
"Yellow May," sometimes a "Professor," sometimes a
"Stone-fly"; once in a while an "Ibis" is fancied by
some fastidious trout. Now and then a "Floating
May-fly" seems a favorite. Where the brush overhangs
and is a darksome, lonely spot, I drop in a "Royal
Coachman," and out comes a big trout lusty and fight-
ing; sometimes fancy flies are spurned and hackles of
all colors kill; then a fly composed of alternate feathers, red and white, of no name, but a favorite with
the writer, will kill when trout will not take any other
fly.

I am enjoying the fun, and the creel is getting
heavy. Half a mile of fishing and twenty-five handsome trout is doing good enough for mid-day fishing.

As the evening falls I take my split bamboo and the
fly-book, pull on the wading boots, and go down to the
mouth of the creek, wading out until I am as far as the
sand runs. I cast out more for practice than to expect
trout. I have on a big bass-fly large enough for a sal-

mon-fly. As it strikes the water twenty-five feet from me there is a commotion. " Ye gods and little fishes ! " What was the fuss ? I cast again, and as true as I am here if a number of trout did not jump clear out for that fly, big as it was ! Hastily reeling in I put on a dun-colored fly, and cast again ; the same jump and dash, but no trout. Changing my flies until at last I put on as a stretcher a " White Miller," I flung out clear beyond any former cast into the midst of what appeared like a boiling spring. The fly dropped softly and out came a host of trout. School kept just then, for I certainly had struck a school of trout. Striking, I fastened into a fine fish ; reeling in, I dried my fly and cast again and hooked again. The fun grew fast and furious ; my little bamboo swished and bent ; hooks were snipped off ; I was excited and jubilant, when along came an itinerant parson. The twenty-five or thirty trout I had, set him longing ; he must fish. Jerking off his boots, pulling up his pants, he waded into the icy cold water equipped with a stick cut from the forest. He had nosed out a line and some hooks from a supply I had left on the bank in my fishing-case, and without so much as "by your leave " began threshing the water as close to the school as he could get his line ; this was baited with a piece of dead fish. To say that I was disgusted faintly expresses my feeling. I would have ceased fishing, but my friend with whom I was staying said, "No, don't stop while sport is so good." I put on a " Royal Coachman " and cast out again, hooking and bringing out trout every second or third cast. I began casting wide, the school followed my flies. I tried the "Professor's," "Dun's," "Hackle's," "Seth Green," "Governor," and "May-flies," with good success. With one pure "Yellow May" I caught a dozen handsome trout, but in this event the evening shadows were fast falling. As they deepened, the "Royal Coachman" and "White Millers" were the killing flies. I cast until I could not see where my flies fell, and even then once in a while hooked and brought in a trout.

I had been thoughtless enough to leave my creel up in the house, never expecting to have this run of good luck. All my trout were taken from the hook and thrown twenty-five feet to shore. I lost many of them in this way. Thirty my friends claimed, yet when I came to count tails, I found forty as handsome trout as ever man wished to see, and all caught from 6 in the evening until dark, about 7.45. I had no net, no creel, therefore had to lead my trout into my hand. The friend at whose house I was staying claims I lost more than I caught by having them flounder off the hook while trying to take them by the gills, and by flinging them ashore.

I have used flies on this creek many times, but never had such luck before nor since. My experience has been that the fine fancy flies of the eastern streams are useless on these Michigan streams ; the nearer the flies approach to a species of small moth found flitting amidst the foliage of the forest, the greater the success. A word, brother angler, and I have done. Learn to cast a fly, and you will never go back to bait fishing from choice. Get good flies, and you won't regret the extra money they cost you ; don't buy cheap imitations or trade made flies—" they are frauds."

Don't buy a pole big enough for the staff of a Philistine Goliath ; to fish for trout, buy a fine rod, take care of it, learn to use it thoroughly. Never buy a cheap rod ; a rod fit for trouting must be as fine as it is possible to make them, and it should not make a shadow on the water. Cheap rods are like cheap guns, schamdahms ! Good trout rods cost a good deal of time and labor ; cheap rods are turned out in a rapid-running lathe. They are a delusion. Get the best materials of everything you need, and buy of a good maker. Never be tempted to buy " cheap flies because they are bargains "—cheap rods because some one is selling out ; " want to get out of the business, no money in it." Remember you are the party who will be sold. Cheap things for trouting are a " fraud, a delusion, and a snare."

Almost every angler has been bitten, but the prevailing opinion is : buy the best tackle your pocket-book can afford and take care of it. And my word for it, as an angler who learned to cast a line for pickerel at ten years old, you will love the sport and think it the best way to spend a summer's vacation of any amusement under the sun.

"In using the fly the object is to imitate the movements of the natural insect as nearly as possible. To drop the line naturally on the water, and then to keep the fly endued with life, is the stratagem. From the moment the fly touches the water the angler should keep his eye on it. Trout often feed a little under the surface ; they do not always break when they rise, but quietly suck in the fly."—*Charles Hallock.*

" 'An angler, sir, uses the finest tackle, and catches his fish scientifically—trout, for instance—with the artificial fly, and he is mostly a quiet, well-behaved gentleman. A fisherman, sir, uses any kind of 'ooks and lines, and catches them any way ; so he gets them it's all one to 'im, and he is generally a noisy fellah, sir, something like a gunner.' "—*Doctor Bethune.*

16. Silver Black.	17. Scarlet Ibis.	18. Stone Fly.
19. White Miller.	20. Fiery Brown.	21. Yellow Drake.
22. Grizzly King.	23. Imbrie.	24. Soldier Palmer.
25. Chantry.	26. Portland.	27. Ethel May.
28. Pale Evening Dun.	29. Great Dun.	30. Whimbrel.

" Be stil' moving your fly upon the water, or casting it into the water ; you yourself, being also alwaies moving down the stream."
—*Izaak Walton.*

" When once alarmed, trout will never bite."—*Seth Green.*

" Fly-fishers are usually brain-workers in society. Along the banks of purling streams, beneath the shadows of umbrageous trees, or in the secluded nooks of charming lakes, they have ever been found, drinking deep of the invigorating forces of nature—giving rest and tone to over-taxed brains and wearied nerves—while gracefully wielding the supple rod, the invisible leader, and the fairy-like fly."—*James A. Henshall, M.D.*

" It is generally true that if a trout is pricked by a fly-hook he will not rise to it again."— *W. C. Prime.*

" CHRISTOPHER NORTH.—Would you believe it, my dear Shepherd, that my piscatory passions are almost dead within me ; and I like now to saunter along the banks and braes, eyeing the younkers angling, or to lay me down on some sunny spot, and with my face up to heaven, watch the slow changing clouds ! "

" SHEPHERD.—I'll no believe that, sir, till I see 't—and scarcely then—for a bluidier-minded fisher nor Christopher North never threw a hackle. Your creel fu'—your shootin'-bag fu'—your jacket-pouches fu', the pouches o' your verra breeks fu'—half-a-dozen wee anes in your waistcoat, no' to forget them in the croon o' your hat,—and, last o' a', when there's nae place to stow awa ony mair o' them, a willow-wand drawn through the gills of some great big anes, like them ither folk would grup wi' the worm or the mennon—but a' gruppit wi' the flee—Phin's delight, as you ca't,—a killen inseck—and on gut that's no easily broken—witness yon four pounder aneath Elibank wood, where your line, sir, got entangled wi' the auld oak-root, and yet at last ye landed him on the bank, wi' a' his crosses and his stars glitterin' like gold and silver amang the gravel ! I confess, sir, you're the King o' Anglers. But dinna tell me that you have lost your passion for the art ; for we never lose our passion for ony pastime at which we continue to excel."

" The fisherman has a harmless, preoccupied look ; he is a kind of vagrant, that nothing fears. He blends himself with the trees and the shadows. All his approaches are gentle and indirect. He times himself to the meandering, soliloquizing stream ; he addresses himself to it as a lover to his mistress ; he wooes it and stays with it till he knows its hidden secrets. Where it deepens his purpose deepens ; where it is shallow he is indifferent. He knows how to interpret its every glance and dimple ; its beauty haunts him for days."—*John Burroughs.*

THE LURE.

BY

"BOURGEOIS."

AMONG the delightful summer resorts of Colorado
Estes Park may be justly considered one of the most
attractive. It is now easy of access. Seven years ago
it began to be frequented, the trail having given way to
the wagon road. Before the days of easy ingress, I had
cast my lures upon the waters of the Thompson and Fall
River, with gratifying success.

In the summer of 1875, the Governor, the Governor's
mother, and myself, determined upon Estes Park for a
six weeks' vacation. With this end in view, in the
latter part of July, I sent off the team loaded with the
camp outfit.

Two days after we took the morning train for Long-
mont, on the Colorado Central, and had an early lunch
at the tail end of the wagon just outside the town. Before noon we were on the fifteen-mile drive into the
cañon of the St. Vrain, for camp.

By sunrise the following morning we had started,
with twenty miles to make over a new road part of the
way, and no road at all in places, and the places were
many. However, we had to hitch on to the end of the

tongue but once, to snake the wagon over an otherwise impassable boulder. The rock stood a foot out of ground, stretched entirely across where the road was to be, and at an angle of 45°. The team could barely get a foothold upon the top, when the traces were let out full, and the double-tree hooked on the end of the tongue. The horses understood their business, and upon a word settled their shoulders into the collars together, the breeching gradually lifted as their knees bent a little ; without a slip their iron-shod hoofs held to the hard granite, and we were up as deftly as a French dancing master would raise his hat to a lady. In travelling in the hills there is nothing so gratifying as a team whose pulling powers you can swear by ; a balky horse is an engine of destruction or death ; if you know his failing, shoot him before you reach the foothills.

As the sun dropped behind the range, lighting up the high peaks with his golden rays, and the pines were beginning to take on tints of darker green, we reached the head of the Park, and within three miles of our camping ground. To the right of us " Olympus," with the dying sunlight dancing on his granite head, to the left Long's Peak, with patches of snow here and there, towering godlike above the surrounding giants. Before us, Prospect Mountain with its rugged front far reaching above its robes of green, while around its base and toward us came leaping the beautiful mountain stream for two miles through the meadow-hued park, with scarce a willow upon its banks. What a place to

cast a fly ! Aye, indeed it is ; and what a place it was
to catch trout. But we must move on around Prospect
Mountain to Ferguson's for camp, which we make on a
little eminence near a great spring and close by the
cabin where we know we shall be welcome.

A late supper disposed of, and the Governor stowed
away in the blankets, Ferguson and I fall talking at
his broad fire-place about Horse Shoe Park and Fall
River ; of course trout are plenty there ; he had been
up the day before and knew whereof he spoke ; yes,
there were quite a number of tourists in the park, but
the streams were not "fished out." He rather thought
that with "a pole" to every rod of the stream the fishing improved ; at least for him.

Our genial friend who obeyed Joshua in the long ago,
was out of bed next day sooner than I. Dick, the pony,
gave me a cheerful good morning as I put in an appearance and changed his picket pin. I received his salu-
tation as a good omen.

Breakfast over and Dick saddled, it was eight o'clock.
We had five miles to go. I strapped my rod and creel
to the pommel, and with a caution to the Governor's
mother not to let him fall into the spring, Ferguson
and I were off. There was no occasion to hurry ; if we
reached the beaver-dams in Horse Shoe Park by ten
o'clock we would be just in time. Experience had
taught me that the two hours before noon, and after
five o'clock were the hours for success.

Our route was a "cut off" without any trail, but

familiar; across the Thompson, up stream, westward for a mile, we turned up a " draw " to the right, for a swale in the ridge dividing the Thompson and its tributary, Fall River.   By nine o'clock we had reached the summit of the divide.   Before and below us lay a beautiful park, three miles in length, by a mile in width toward its upper end, where it rounded at the base of the mountain range, giving it the shape of a horse shoe, which no doubt suggested its name.   To the north it is guarded by an immense mountain of rocks, where towering and impenetrable cliffs stand out against the background of blue sky, as though the Titans had some time builded there, and mother earth had turned their castles into ruins, and left them as monuments of her power.   To the south a long, low-lying, pine-covered hill, while from the range in the west with its snow covered summit and base of soft verdure, comes a limpid stream winding down through the grass-covered park, its course marked by the deeper green of the wild grass and the willows.   A mile away a band of mountain sheep are feeding; they have evidently been down to water and are making their way back to their haunts in the cliffs, and whence we know they will quickly scud when they see or wind us.   Ferguson longed for his rifle; it was just his luck; he had the " old girl " with him the last time, but " nary hoof " had he seen. To me they were precious hints of man's absence, and the wilderness.

Reaching the stream we picketed the ponies in the

grass to their knees ; the nutritious mountain grass, the mother of cream so thick that you have to dip it out of the jug with a spoon. The ponies were happy, and I became nervous ; it seemed half an hour before I could get my tackle rigged. But after I had sent my favorite gray hackle on its mission and had snatched a ten-inch trout from his native element, my nerves were braced. A second and a third followed ; I heard nothing from Ferguson except the " swish " of his old cane pole above the music of the waters. The trout struck and I landed them so fast that the sport began to be monotonous, and I followed up the sound of the cane. Going round a clump of willows I discovered the old gentleman upon the edge of the pool, and that old rod going up and down with the regularity of a trip hammer, the owner combining business and sport. I asked him what he was doing ; he said he was fishing, and I thought he was.

Wandering up stream, taking it leisurely, I had by noon filled my creel, and was enjoying a sandwich under the shelter of some willows, when my companion came along with his sixteen pound lard-can filled, besides a dozen upon a stick. I asked him when he intended to quit. He said he had never seen fish " bite " so ; he hated to stop, and yet had all he could carry, but concluded with me that enough was as good as a feast. Then he began to banter me about my ash and lancewood, and the excess of his catch over mine. I told him to wait till some other day. It came in the course of time, upon the same stream. The trout refused everything I had, grasshoppers included. Finally I fished up an old fly-book from the depths of my coat pocket, and in it were half a dozen nameless blue-bodied flies with a mouse-colored feather upon a number six Kirby. Upon sight, I remembered to have discarded them in disgust, but I thought I would try one for luck, and lo ! the mystery was solved. I had been working industriously for two hours and had two trout. Ferguson had been no more successful, but was in sight when the trout began to rise to my cast-off fly. He came down my way, wanted to know what I was using, and I gave him one ; he lost that and his leader in some half-sunken brush, and I gave him another. But his good genius had deserted him ; I persuaded a trout right away from his lure, and he quit in disgust, while I said never a word. Though a little sensitive upon the score of success, he was and is a genial and companionable angler, and one who can make a good cast withal, an he have proper tools.

Willow Park, an adjunct to Estes Park, through which runs a branch of the Thompson, has afforded me many a day's sport, and is nearer to camp. Upon a memorable occasion I had been fishing down stream, when, with a well-filled creel, I encountered a gigantic boulder on the bank. Just beyond it was a pool that was suggestive ; to reach the base of the boulder it was necessary to get over a little bayou of about five feet in width and three in depth. To jump it were easy but for the willows, yet I must get to that pool. Selecting a place where I think the willows will give way to my weight, I essay the leap. My feet reach the opposite bank, my body presses back the brush, but I feel a rebound that assures me of my fate. I clutch frantically at the swaying bush ; it breaks in my hand, and I sit down quite helplessly, muttering a prayer till the cold water bids me shut my mouth. Emerging I hear a well defined laugh, but not being in the mind to fear the spirits that haunt these wilds, I make for the base of that boulder and the coveted pool. A moment after I discover a face bedecked with glasses upon the opposite side of the brook, and recognize the smiling countenance of a genial member of the guild looking at me through the willows.

" Oh, is that you ? "

To this lucid inquiry I reply in the affirmative.

" Where's Ferguson ? "

" At home, I suppose."

" I thought I heard him fall in the creek."

I told him I did not think Ferguson had a monopoly of the bathing privileges of the Thompson and its tributaries.

" Well, I thought it was funny."

" Thought what was funny ? "

" Why, I heard the splash, and supposed it was Ferguson ; then I remembered Ferguson was a church member in good standing."

I took my revenge by competing with my brother for

the contents of that pool, and beat him by one. But to this day he greets me with a smile. When I got back to camp I learned that the Governor had been trying to follow in the footsteps of his father, and had tumbled into the spring. He had been fished out by the combined efforts of his mother and Mrs. Ferguson, and I discovered him swathed in a blanket by the kitchen stove, mad as a hornet; I shook hands with him.

Our camp is pitched in a pleasant spot, with two tall pines, a hundred feet away, for sentinels. *Coup de soleil* is unknown in Colorado, so I prefer the sun's rays to lightning, especially while trees seared from top to bottom are plentiful in the Park as monitors. To the right is Prospect Mountain, with its west end a beetling cliff, perhaps two thousand feet high, where I once had the buck-ague during an interview with a " big-horn." To the left and in front, the range, where the storm-king holds high carnival, while lower down and nearer is a mountain of towers and pinnacles of brown and red and gray, carved out by that whimsical sculptor, Old Time. With the sun for my artist, the range for both his easel and background, I have lounged away many an hour under one of the old pines. My gaze wandering down the green slope to the river half a mile away, and with the weird music of the tumbling waters coming and receding on the summer breeze to help my dreams, we have together wrought out fantastic ruins and ghostly shapes to people them. A drifting cloud, perhaps, will change a barbacan to a spire, and a Doric

capital to a Corinthian, or the knight panoplied to a
brownie with a lily for a throne, and

> " —— jolly satyrs, full of fresh delight,
> Come dancing forth, and with them nimbly ledd
> Faire Helenore, with girlonds all bespredd,
> Whom their May-lady they had newly made; "

to give place again, as the golden meshes weave, to
cowled monks or ladies fair, as suits the whim of the
artist's patron. Again, the goblins of the range begin
their game of nine-pins, and the fleecy clouds that have
been slowly drifting, drifting all the day, settle down
upon the mountain top and change from white to gray
and from gray to black as the sport grows furious.
Something these elves must have to light up their
frolic, and presently it comes in great flashes of wicked
steel-blue and red, zigzaging down the mountain side,
or in straight blinding bolts that rive paths in the hard
granite, scattering the loose rock and shivering the
pines, while the noise of the jolly nine-pins rattles and
re-echoes among the crags, and dies away to come again
more quickly, until the mountain-top is a sheet of lurid
flame and the din unceasing, so closely follows peal
upon peal. The game is too violent to last, but the
gnomes love to hug the range in their pastime, and
I, understanding the signs, and having no fear of their
electric lights, watch the fast growing rift of azure that
crowds hard upon the driving blackness. At last the
mellow rays touch up my mountain ruins, and they

are arrayed in new splendors and peopled with other
phantoms.

So I have dreamed, and might go on dreaming, but this
time I am brought back to the green slope and a little
figure. The Governor is toiling up the trail with a quart
bucket, his special chattel, from the spring, whence he
volunteered to bring a drink for his mother. I can see
no impediment in his path, yet he stumbles and falls.
Would I had been there to warn him ; but the water is
spilled. He does not cry, but gathers himself and his
property up, and goes back to begin his task over again.
Just then there came to me pat, an aphorism, I think,
of " Poor Goldsmith " : " True greatness consists not
in never falling, but in rising every time we fall ; " and
I took it as an omen of good for the boy.

The time is approaching when we must break camp
and go back to the brick and mortar and the realities
of civilization. Duties to be performed will be under-
taken with better zest when I get to them, but I cast
lingering looks toward my mountain ruins as the day
of departure draws nigh. I even have a thought that
it would be pleasant to relapse into barbarism, if out of
such as mine our civilization has grown—we might
build up a better. As this may not be, I am encour-
aged by the thought that another season will come, and
with hope in my heart I am better prepared for the
work awaiting me. I know that I shall go back with
a fresher feeling for my kind, and more charity. So
when one September morning, after a day of gray mist

hanging over the range, the wind comes down chill from the heights, and the morning sun lights up my castles and pinnacles in diadems of new-fallen snow, I say we must be off. We gather together our lares of nomadic life, and with a regretful farewell to those I cannot bring away, we make the journey home, a better man and woman, with a nut-brown, healthy boy, for much of which I give credit to the artificial fly, and the beautiful denizens of the mountain streams.

" Fishing for lake trout is about as much sport as dredging for oysters, and boat-fishing for brook trout is merely a refinement of sitting on the corner of the dock and bobbing for eels. In wading a stream all the muscles are called into play and the mind is strung so tightly with anticipation of a rise, new views and surprises, care where the feet are planted, and watchfulness that the bushes do not capture the flies, that there is a sense of generalship in steering clear of all dangers and in capturing your game."— *Fred Mather.*

" The true angler touches no net, but that with which he lands the heavy struggler hung on his tiny hair."— *G. W. Bethune, D.D.*

" The Western trout takes the fly well, but not so greedily as the Eastern fish. The reason is, that they are from early spring gorged with food in the myriads of young grasshoppers that fall into the streams before getting their wings. The best months for trout fishing in the Rocky Mountains are August and September, although good sport may be had in July and October."— *Lieut.- Col. R. I. Dodge, U. S. A.*

" If you eat your kind, I will eat you."—*Benjamin Franklin.*

" What may appear the right color when looking down upon the fly, may be found quite wrong when viewing it between the eye and the light—the way in which fish must, from their position *beneath* the object, always see it."—*Hewett Wheatley.*

"Although I am a great advocate for the system of matching your artificial flies with the natural ones upon the water at the time of fishing, still I am of the opinion that an unnecessary number of patterns only confuses the tyro."—*Francis M. Walbran.*

" Light is light. And by its aid all animated beings see, and in its absence all alike are blind. The laws of nature operate equally and invariably both above and below the surface of the water, and, until it is demonstrated to be otherwise, I cannot think trout see in any different manner, or by any different means, than do we. There may be a difference in degree, but I cannot believe in kind."—*Henry P. Wells.*

FLY FISHING IN THE YOSEMITE.

BY

A. LOUIS MINER, JR.

A MERRY party had come for a holiday to the Yosemite, and their camp was established between the north and south domes near the forks of the Merced. Toward the east the Tenajo Cañon opened, revealing through its vista of granite crags the highest peak of "Clouds' Rest," crowned with eternal snows. Westward, the Sentinel Rock, like a minaret among the domes, pierced the sky.

There were seven in the party, including a heathen from the flowery kingdom, almond-eyed—Ah Yang. His nominal function was to do as he was bid, and serve as man of all work, but in reality he ruled ; and ruled with a rod of iron. Yang had been induced to come by motives purely sordid ; but the others, aside from seeing the wondrous valley, had various reasons for making the journey.

The Judge came for relaxation. He needed it. For the last dozen years he had devoted himself to reading the morning papers, lunching at his club, and entertaining his friends sumptuously at dinner.

His wife, who, in the levelling atmosphere of camp,

came to be styled the *Judgess,* imagined herself on the verge of a decline, and sought recuperation in the forest.   If the Judgess were described as fat and forty, omitting the fair, the description would fall far short of truth.   In spite of her ailments, the Judgess would have enjoyed herself in a way, had it not been for the young woman she was chaperoning.   This was Madge. Certain young men in San Francisco called her a *rattler,* and certainly there was nothing slow about her.   The chief end of her existence, at home and everywhere, seemed to be the pursuit of fun ; to this end she flirted with anything that came in her way, from stray herds- men on the plains to an English baronet at a Yosemite hotel.   When nothing else was at hand, and to the Judgess' indignation, she flirted with the Judge.   With charming zest she played continued games of poker with him till his honor's purse was far thinner than its owner.   The Judge's admiration for Madge was pro- found, but after an hour at cards, he would usually re- mark, "that girl has the devil in her, *as it were,* bigger than a wolf."

It is said that all men have a ruling passion.   Be that as it may, a passion certainly ruled a worthy clergyman of the company.   The men of our generation affected with beetle mania are many, but his Reverence was absolutely devoted to bugs.   The Judgess, a zealot to such a degree that Mary of England was but lukewarm in comparison, said that his Reverence valued a butter- fly more than a human soul ; and Madge insisted that, while he pretended to read his office, he was engaged in dissecting a coleoptera or something.

The Doctor, who was Madge's unworthy brother, had come with the avowed intention of sketching. All the long way from San Francisco he had been at work with brushes and blotting paper. Often the "prairie schooner," in which the party travelled, had "lain to" while the Doctor washed in patches of blue and white to represent cloud-effects, or a jagged gray band against streaks of orange, portraying sunrise in the Sierras.

The last member of the party without professional distinction, and familiarly called "Jack," had also a *penchant*, though many years had passed since it had been gratified. When they had left the San Joaquin plain and its sluggish rivers oozing their way through mud and reeds, and had climbed into the mountain, a halt was made in a deep cañon. Here was a stream indeed. How blithely it danced along, eager to find the Golden Gate and the Pacific! How it sang to Jack of fellow streams near the other ocean! How it whispered of trout streams ahead! Presently a long-cherished fly book was produced and Jack was poring over it. His Reverence, attracted by the little volume, looked over Jack's shoulder. He was entranced. A volume of ecclesiastical Latin would not have interested him half so much. He began to criticise and expound. Some were perfect. Some were caricatures of diptera. The other members of the party drew around. "Pooh!" said the Doctor, "I hope you don't expect to catch any

trout with those things in Yosemite ! Everybody knows
that the Merced trout don't take the fly." The Doctor
went on to say, "that with a common string, such as
any grocer would use to tie up a package of tea, a good
strong hook, and a worm," he would catch in the same
time, more fish than could all the sportsmen of California, fishing with fancy flies.

The Doctor, like most cynics, was somewhat given to
hyperbole.

During the remainder of the journey into the valley,
Jack felt himself regarded as the victim of a mild halu-
cination.

The Doctor could sketch ; beetles were awaiting his
Reverence's microscope ; flirtation and frolic were dawn-
ing on Madge's horizon ; even the Judge and Judgess
could get rid of a stone or two avoirdupois if they tried ;
but poor Jack had come, it appeared, to fish, and there
were no fish to catch, or at least to catch with a fly.
Such was the tradition, and so the Doctor had asserted,
and no one ever disputed the Doctor excepting Yang,
the Chinaman.

Our friends had been revelling in the enchantments
of the valley a week ; had climbed the trails that crept
zig-zag up the dizzy heights ; had spent hours among
the soft mist and rainbows at the first landing of that
wonder of the world, the Yosemite Falls ; and still Jack
had not accomplished the cherished desire of his heart.
He had not the moral courage to take from its swad-
dling clothes his beloved rod (which the Doctor would

persist in calling "your fish-pole"). Never had he so longed to cast a fly ; but he thought of the teasing Madge and waited. At best, he was but a poor male creature. Madge, in his place, would have been whipping the stream, with defiance and determination, an hour after her arrival.

His Reverence and the Doctor had arranged to ascend Clouds' Rest on a Thursday and return next day. Early Thursday morning, before Yang or the birds were stirring, Jack sauntered forth to his morning bath in the icy waters of the river. This Rio de la Merced, would it prove to him indeed a *river of mercy,* or a river of humiliation? But what a glorious stream it was ! Here it glided through wooded banks, the opposite side black in the shadow of overhanging manzanita, while nearer the rippling waters were checkered with the shadows of the cotton-wood leaves, trembling in the growing light. Further on, the river whirled and eddied around great boulders, resting among the mossy rocks in deep, dark pools, bordered with fern and flecked with patches of lace-like foam. Further still, it wound silently through the sedges, reflecting on its glassy surface the stormed-carved Cathedral Rocks, or the huge mass of El Capitan. Here was an ideal trout stream, but were there trout in it ! No doubt, for the Doctor had taken his grocers' string and a worm and a veritable pole, and after a day's tramp had returned to camp wet, hungry, in a sulphurous mood, but with four unmistakable trout. These, served up the next

morning, were appropriated by the Judgess, and made
an excellent appetizer to more abundant bacon and
flap-jacks.

Jack had reached that pearl of waters, the Mirror
Lake, and was watching the marvellous beauties pict
ured on its bosom, when suddenly there was a soft
plash, the sleeping depths were troubled, a circling
ripple crept toward him, and Jack's pulses bounded.
A trout had risen !

Through the dewy chaparral and the fragrant whispering pines, our friend hurried back to camp in a
fever of impatience. He tried to help Yang with
breakfast, but was told by that dignitary to " giv' us a
rest," and so humbly retired. He then waked his
Reverence. He wakened the Doctor and was greeted by
language far from complimentary. He aroused the
Judgess, and was pierced with daggers from her eyes
while she hurriedly adjusted her teeth.

After breakfast more torturing delays, the Judgess
declined to join the mountain party. The others must
not think that she feared to ride the mules, for she
adored mountain climbing, and the exercise and all
that. (This was a dreadful fib, which was probably
made use of at her next confession.) Both the Judge
and herself were pining for a few refinements of life
at the hotel. Without napkins and finger-bowls, life
became a burden. The poor Judge had to acquiesce
and said : " She wants a little civilization *as it were.*"
Then Jack rebelled. There was a general confusion,

in the midst of which Yang began to fire his pistol. This pistol was the idol of his pagan soul, and his frequent salutes the terror of the party. No one dared to interfere. At this time the volley was continued and promiscuous. The Judgess screamed, and having no immediate revenge in the shape of ill-cooked dinners to fear, sharply expostulated. Thereupon Yang, with utmost *sang froid,* told her to "shut your head" and journey to regions he had probably heard the Doctor name. This was too much. The Judgess climbed into the wagon and stated her opinion of people who permitted such "goings on" and of a priest who allowed a Christian woman to be sworn at. Madge was convulsed with laughter, even his Reverence smiled, while the Judge, poor man, looking as if every brewery on the continent had been burned, snapped his whip, and the wagon was lost to sight beneath the arching sequoias.

It was high noon when the sure-footed mules had arrived and the party fairly started off. Jack waved an adieu with one hand, and with the other reached down his rod from the branches of a live oak. Yang proceeded to dissect a sucker he had caught for bait, saying : "If you fishee, me fishee too, but you no sabee nothing."

Later in the afternoon Jack stood on the grassy point where the lake narrows into the river. He had adjusted his flies, and everything was in readiness. He paused to watch Yang, who was stationed below on the

river, fasten a cubic inch of sucker to his hook, ex-
pectorate upon it, turn around three times, and fling
it with a tremendous splash into the water. Whether
these performances were the result of Oriental supersti-
tion, or whether the Chinaman imitated some American example, he did not stop to consider. His long
unpractised hand, trembling a little now, had sent the
flies far out beneath the shadows of some willows.
Another cast was made, and then another. At the
fourth there was a rise, and the fish was hooked. The
struggle was short but spirited. Yang, abandoning his
primitive tackle, was ready with the landing-net, and
the fish was killed. As the sport continued, Jack
grew calmer, while Yang's excitement increased. He
trembled as if the ague were upon him. His stoicism
was laid aside. He laughed, jabbered, and Jack was
obliged to address him as the Chinaman had addressed
the Judgess. Yang begged to try the rod, and by reason of his imitative faculties might have made good
use of it, but he had to content himself with the net.

At last the lengthening shadows deepened into twilight, and the gathering darkness put an end to the
sport. The great dome of Mt. Watkins, inverted in the
motionless water, had changed from gold to crimson,
and from crimson to violet; they paid no heed until
the reflection faded, then, looking up, the real mountain, circled by rising mists, seemed to float in the
darkening sky, and Jack, with that feeling of perfect
content and peace which kings can never know unless

they are anglers, stowed away his flies, unjointed his rod, while Yang shouldered the catch.

It was a happy couple that went down the Tenajo cañon that evening. The moon smiled upon them ; an owl hooted enviously ; Jack softly whistled a strain from Schubert, while Yang made the towering rocks echo and re-echo to the joyous banging of the pistol.

The fish were dressed, supper eaten, Yang's tin dishes washed, and everything was snug for the night. Jack, stretched beneath a giant pine and smoking his evening pipe, was watching the weird play of the fire-light in the canopy of foliage above. The Celestial appeared.

" Me heap lonesome, got no more cartridges ; you no care ; go down hotel stay Chinaboy to-night."

Unselfish, devoted, and charitable as Yang claimed to be, he could hardly pretend to heroism. The China-man was permitted to go, and Jack, appropriating the Judgess' hammock, turned in. This hammock owed Jack a lodging. All the way across the plains, and up the mountains, and in the valley, that hammock had almost nightly collapsed. Perhaps the Judge did not know how to tie a knot ; perhaps the ample physique of the Judgess was too much for any knot, but the thing kept occurring, to the great discomfiture of the Judgess and all the rest of the party. As Jack, with his feet at the fire, and his head on a sack of barley, lay studying the midnight heavens, there would come a shock as of an earthquake. The Judge was a little deaf

and after a night or two of experience, would lie just
beyond reach of whatever member his better half could
disentangle with which to punch him.   First, his Reverence would be summoned ; but he slept the sleep of
the just.   Then cries for Ah Yang and the others would
follow.   Yang was too wise a Chinaman to awaken.
Jack sometimes rolled over and kicked the Doctor till
he roused, and the good lady hearing his exclamations,
claimed his assistance ; but sometimes Jack also shed
his blankets and relieved the massive limbs from a state
of suspension.

With content Jack rolled himself in the hammock.
Never had he slept in such profound solitude.   The
nearest camp was far away down the valley ; and towards the east, beyond the mountain-barrier, nothing
but the wild desert, and solitary, sage-clad hills of
Nevada.

The river murmured over the pebbles, the pines
faintly whispered, and that was all.   For once he was
alone, and oh ! the peace of it !   Was it such a night as
this that tempted men to leave their fellows for a her-
mitage ?   Such visions came to him as seldom visit men
beneath a roof.   At last he slept, and dreamed of the
first trout he had killed in a little New England
meadow-brook.   He was filling a creel with bass from a
fair Wisconsin lake.   He was in a plunger off Montauk
Point, striking the blue-fish.   He was trolling for pike
through Champlain, and casting a fly from a canoe on
Adirondack waters.

The South Dome was glowing in the ruddy morning light ; a flock of blackbirds were piping cheerily ; an odor of fried trout and coffee was in the air, and Yang was tugging at the blankets, and saying :

" Come, you heap laze, bleakfast all leddy. Git up! "

* * * * * * * * *

What a dinner Yang and Jack had in readiness for the party that night ! The Judge and spouse, after much pressing, had come. The lady could not withstand the trout, especially on a Friday. The judicial pair arrived just as Madge and his Reverence raced into camp on the sturdy mules. The Doctor and guide fol_ lowed. Madge's cheeks were glowing, her eyes sparkling, and her tongue rattling, as she leaped from her saddle. " Such a time as they had had ! His Reverence had been a duck, and the Doctor for once had behaved himself and kept civil." She gave her hand to the Judgess, but kissed the Judge.

At Yang's summons, a jovial company sat down to such a table as campers in the Sierras seldom see. Madge was in ecstacies, and even the Judgess expressed approval. There was real damask upon it, with napkins and silver forks and wine from the hotel, with all sorts of garnitures of Yang's contrivance.

The dinner began, continued, and ended with fish ; but fish cooked in every way which Oriental imagination could devise, and camp facilities permit. Even "Simpson's Fish Dinner," of seven courses, in Billingsgate, could not surpass it. The Judgess, having disposed of about a dozen fish, remarked that, after all, these were *only* California trout, and entirely lacked the flavor, as they lacked the beauty, of their Eastern cousins. She thought, however, that Yang's salad—of cresses from the Merced—was not bad ; but wine—even if it was champagne—when sipped from a tin cup, left much to be desired. Alas ! Jack had forgotten to borrow the glasses.

All that evening, around the camp-fire, the party listened to an account of the catch. The Doctor did not hesitate to express his entire disbelief in the story. It was his opinion that Jack had hired the Indians to fish for him, and bribed Yang to hold his tongue. Then Yang spoke :

" You think you heap smart. Jack heap sabee how fish, and you *no* sabee, but me sabee *you.* Last Fliday you go fish, and when me water horse, see Injun sellee you fish. I sabee *you.*"

In the peals of laughter which followed, the Doctor went away to his blankets muttering. So the trout the Judgess had enjoyed a week before were not the Doctor's catching, after all.

A week longer the party lingered in the valley. Madge and his Reverence became quite expert with the fly. The lake seemed to have yielded all its finny treasures to Jack, but the Merced afforded ample sport. Many strings of trout were sent to fellow-campers, and to friends at the hotel ; and one little hamper made the long journey by stage and rail to San Francisco.

Plate VIII. Description on page 197.

TROUT FLIES.

Made by C.F. ORVIS, Manchester, Vt.
COPYRIGHTED

Plate IX. Description on page 225.

TROUT FLIES.

Made by C.F. ORVIS, Manchester, Vt.
COPYRIGHTED

The "trout-camp" became famous in the valley, and paragraphs noticing the catch appeared in the *Stockton Independent*, and even in the *Sacramento Bee*. Jack had accomplished his purpose, and had not come to the Yosemite in vain.

Then the prairie schooner sailed away through the mountains, Madge and his Reverence driving by turns, while the Judge held his ponderous foot on the brake. Yang was mounted on a mustang, while the doctor and Jack trudged through the dust. Frequent halts were made, the Judgess taking her noon-day siesta, the "three fishers," as she called Madge, his Reverence and Jack, striking out for some neighboring stream. Near the Tuolumne big trees his Reverence took the largest trout of the trip—a four-pounder. On the Tuolumne River the three met with fair success ; but on the upper waters of the Stanislaus the sport was better. They tarried by the stream winding through that dead little mining town, Big Oak Flat. The banks of the little river were honey-combed by the old placer mining. The population of the Flat wondered to see Madge cast a fly. Even the Chinamen who were still washing for gold, would throw aside their cradles and pans to gaze.

An ancient beau of the town stranded there fifteen years ago (such a man as Bret Harte would have gloried in), became so enamored with the fair angler that he would have followed in her wake ; but the fickle object of his admiration eluded her admirer, and the miner sadly headed his mustang toward his mountain home, promising to call "next time he went to 'Frisco."

The schooner dropped anchor in Oakland. The Judge asked all to dine with him that day week—"a sort of a re-union, *as it were,* you know." His Reverence hastened to don something more in keeping with his cloth than a blue shirt; Madge threw a kiss to Jack as the Doctor handed her into a carriage; and Jack was left to cross the ferry alone. Yang, however, had not abandoned him. He produced a piece of red paper and asked Jack to write his address upon it.

"I hab one fliend who come get your washee Monday."

Jack, inured to submission, could not refuse, and Yang's "fliend" still does his "washee."

Since the Yosemite excursion Jack has trailed salmon flies on the noble Columbia River, and whipped the California trout streams from the cactus-covered plains of the Mexican border to the glaciers of Mount Shasta, but he has never had such keen enjoyment with the fly as on that afternoon at Mirror Lake.

When he arranges his tackle for a little holiday sport on the Russian River, or the streams among the red woods of Santa Cruz, he sees again the reflected fir-trees and granite dome trembling in the water as the trout leap to his fly; he again hears Yang's ejaculations and commands. "Fifty-sleven, Jack. Hi! that big fish; fifty-eight. You *heap* sabee. Hold him tight. 'Rusalem, him sabee how swim! Pull like hella, fifty-nine!"

"Trout take some flies because they resemble the real fly on which they feed. They take other flies for no such reason."— *W. C. Prime.*

"The oft-repeated quotation, 'Spare the rod and spoil the child,' has been misconstrued for many a long day, and if I had known early in life its real significance it would hardly have made so doleful an impression. There is no doubt to-day in my mind that this 'rod' meant a *fishing-rod*, and the timely cherishing of it in youth tends to develop that portion of one's nature to which the former use was entirely innocent."—*Thomas Sedgwick Steele.*

"My favorite fly of all is a snipe feather and mouse body."— *"Frank Forester."*

31. Cinnamon.	32. Deerfly.	33. Red Fox.
34. Camlet Dun.	35. Governor.	36. Green Drake.
37. Alder.	38. Cheney.	39. Soldier.
40. Hod.	41. Kingdom.	42. Oak Fly.
43. Gray Coflin.	44. Fin Fly.	45. Beaverkill.
46. Yellow May.	47. Black June.	48. Quaker.

"Often the whereabouts of a trout is betrayed by a break or a leap from the surface, and the wide-awake angler will make it his business to toss his fly over the spot sooner or later. Sometimes the trout rush at the lure like a flash, leaping clear over it in their eagerness. They are difficult to hook then."—*Charles Hallock.*

"No description of the brook trout, that has ever been given, does him justice. It stands unrivalled as a game fish."—*Theodatus Garlick, M.D.*

"The best flies to use are imitations of those which are born on the water; for, though trout will often take land flies, and indeed almost any insect you can throw on the water, yet it is on the water-flies which he chiefly depends for his sustenance."—*Francis Francis.*

" A trout does not always get the fly when he attempts to; it may be lying against the leader, making it impossible for him to get it in his mouth; you may strike too quickly, taking it out of reach; the strike may be too hard, tearing his mouth. More trout by far are pricked than hooked. Practice only can teach you when to strike; you see a faint gleam under the surface, when you instinctively twitch, to find you have hooked a beauty. Few fishermen can separate force from quickness of motion. Never use your arm in making the strike, only your wrist; then will the difficulty be overcome."—*T. S. Up de Graff, M.D.*

" Innocent stranger! Thou who readest these lines! perhaps you never caught a trout. If so, thou knowest not for what life was originally intended. Thou art a vain, insignificant mortal ! pursuing shadows ! Ambition lures thee, fame dazzles, wealth leads thee on, panting! Thou art chasing spectres, goblins that satisfy not. If thou hast not caught a trout, this world is to thee, as yet, a blank, existence is a dream. Go and weep."—*Thaddeus Norris.*

"On one occasion the writer was awakened at a very early hour, when, lo! Mr. Webster, who happened to be in a par- ticularly playful mood, was seen going through the graceful mo- tions of an angler throwing a fly and striking a trout, and then, without a word, disappeared. As a matter of course, that day was given to fishing."—*Lanman's Life of Webster.*

" There is some difference of opinion as to the working of the flies after they have fallen. Mr. Francis objects to any movement beyond that of the stream. Others like to impart a gentle trem- ulous motion—as being more consistent with the notion that the fly is drowning. Of course, it is not here advised that the fly be drawn along with a series of jerks, but that just such motion shall be imparted, and no more, as shall render the fly a simulated drowning fly."—*G. Little.*

FLY-FISHING ON THE NIPIGON.

CINCINNATI, June 2, 1884.

MR. CHARLES F. ORVIS, MANCHESTER, VT. :

MY DEAR SIR—The box of flies made to my order, and according to samples furnished by me, came just one day too late to reach me at the Sault Ste. Marie as I went north to the Nipigon River last July.

To a fly-fisherman whose usual resort is some New England brook or river, such flies as these are simply enormous ; but I believe that the trout in the Nipigon River would rise freely to a moderate-sized canary bird if it could be properly cast. Although I missed this fresh supply of flies, perfectly adapted to the stream, our party of two were tolerably well supplied. We had an abundance of small trout flies, tied in London, which were not even noticed by the uneducated Nipigon trout. We also had flies such as we had thrown for trout and land-locked salmon on the Maine Lakes, and a few samples of your large "Lake flies" and two or three immense gray hackles like those ordered. The large lake flies and the large hackles were the correct thing where the large trout were to be found.

At the risk of telling you what you already know, I will remark that the Nipigon River constitutes the real upper course of the St. Lawrence. It is the largest stream flowing into Lake Superior. Its source, Lake Nipigon, is about two-thirds as large as Lake Erie ; it is irregular in shape, deep, with rocky shores and innumerable islands. This lake is fed by twelve small rivers, each one with an unpronounceable name nearly the length of its course. Lake Nipigon is 313 feet higher than Lake Superior, and as the course of the river is less than forty miles and one-third of that distance is occupied by four small lakes through which it passes, the remainder has an exceedingly rapid current. The water of the Nipigon is cold and clear. It enters Lake Superior at the northern point of Nipigon Bay between two huge precipices of red sandstone which gave the name of Red Rock to the Hudson Bay Company's post which lies on the right bank just at the foot of the first rapids.

I advise no one to try to ascertain the meaning of the word *Nipigon*. *Nipi* means *water* in several Indian dialects. When J. E. Cabot coasted along the southern part of Nipigon Bay with Prof. Agassiz, in 1848, the water had been stirred near the islands by a recent storm, and he understood that *Nipigon* meant *dirty water* and he so recorded it. Prof. Bell in his report says that his Indians interpreted it as meaning *deep, clear water lake.* Our Indians declared that Nipigon was a "white man's name ; " but that the original name meant *water with many channels.* On the earliest map of this region which I have seen, the lake is called *Alemipigon.* When the guide-

book writers get up there, they will probably discover a
new meaning, now unknown even to the natives.

We commenced fishing July 11th, on the first rapids
of the river, from our canoes, with two ordinary flies such
as we have often used in Maine. The first day I caught
two pairs. After the second full catch I removed one fly.
The trout were feeding in the rapids where the water was
so active that it was almost impossible for a fly-rod to drag
up two two-pound trout within reach of the landing-net.
We found it necessary to shorten the leaders from nine
to six feet, so as to spare the rods in getting the trout to
the net. Our total catch this afternoon in three hours
for two rods was twenty pounds. The fish averaged a
pound each. While we were camped at the Hudson
Bay Post we had no difficulty in disposing of any
amount of fish. Farther up the river we returned
more than half of the uninjured fish to the water, except
on such days as transient Indians camped near us. We
took sixty-four pounds of trout one afternoon, and
thirteen Indians consumed all of them before they slept.

The Nipigon is a large and strong stream of water exactly suited to trout. The fish are well fed, and average
larger than I have found them in any waters that I have
fished in Maine.

Our second camp was at Alexandra Falls, fifteen miles
up the river. Here there is a mile of rapid water and
most excellent fishing. The trout were larger than were
taken below, averaging nearly two pounds. We soon
found that small flies could not be seen in very quick

water, and that small hooks would not hold two-pound trout in a roaring, raging torrent. We fished from our canoes. If we found a place where trout were plentiful we anchored below some big rock, or in an eddy, and cast on either side. The trout, when struck, had usually to be pulled up through the rapids in a manner that seriously threatened to break our bamboo rods.

From Alexandra Falls we crossed a portage of two and a half miles, and afterward some lesser portages, to a point known as Camp Cincinnati. Here we had excellent fishing in about a mile of rapids, with falls above and below. There are two fine large pools above, which we visited. In one of them I took three two-pound fish within ten minutes. The three all dashed at my hook the first time it was cast near them. One was happy enough to get it, and the others chased him around even when we were netting the first one, and made efforts to snatch the fly from his mouth. My guide tried to net one of the free fish, but missed him. One rod this day took fifty-six pounds of trout.

At Camp Victoria, some miles farther up the river, we stayed several days, making excursions across to Lake Nipigon, about six miles away, and to the Virgin Falls, seven miles up the river, near where the river leaves the lake. The Hudson Bay employees do not follow the river to the lake ; they cut across through Lake Hannah, and carry over a low divide a mile wide to the south shore of Lake Nipigon.

At Camp Victoria the fishing-grounds were on the

rapids, in sight from our tent. I should think that the water fell twenty feet in about a hundred yards. A canoe could be anchored in almost any part of it, and the trout were found in every part.

We took one morning all the fish we could possibly use in the day; but the afternoon was perfect weather for fishing, and we could not lie quiet in the tent within sight of the leaping fish. Thus far we had neither of us taken a trout at any place weighing more than three pounds, and we agreed that we would not kill a fish unless it weighed more than five pounds. I was called upon, in accordance with this agreement, to toss overboard one four-pounder and a dozen of smaller size. I find in my note-book for this day the following memoranda of one perfect catch. I saw a trout rise at my right some fifty feet below us. I threw over the place, and he sprang clear from the water in the most graceful curve imaginable, and fastened himself firmly on the hook as he came down. He took a rapid run to my left for some fifty feet, and at the end threw himself boldly out of the water, showing his broad red-spotted sides, and dashing the sparkling drops of water high in the air. Then he sought the bottom, and worked his way back to my right, and at last, when well wearied, he took a clever run up stream, and as I brought him to the surface he floated gently down beside the canoe and dropped into the landing-net. He was quickly weighed, and dropped from the scales into the river, and he darted away unharmed by the perilous adventure.

I recollect also the particulars of the last double catch I made on the stream. The pair were of nearly the same size and were struck well down the stream. The dropper or hand-fly was taken last, and it was some minutes before my light rod could hold him up to the surface long enough to take the fight out of him. The trout on the tail-fly was still as active as ever. The reel line was all in, and I could not pull the two up near enough for my guide to net the rear fish first. I would not consent to a possible loss of either of them. I directed him to net the upper fish quickly and cut the snell with my knife. This he did, and the fish that had temporary possession of the tail-fly darted off and had his own fun before he would consent to be led into the landing-net. The two weighed five and a half pounds.

Our day at the Virgin Falls, July 19th, was the successful termination of our northward journey. We paddled up the stream with both birch-bark canoes and reached the falls at about 10 A.M. We carried our canoe around a sharp rapid at Miner's Camp and came in sight of the falls as we cleared the pine forest which covered our path. The falls, thirty feet high, were right in front of us, half a mile away, and a great eddy, white with foam, filled the space between us and the foot of the fall where the river turns at a right angle. Gulls, eagles, and fish-hawks were soaring over the white water of the rapids and diving occasionally for their prey. We soon landed at the rocky point below the falls. The trout could be seen throwing themselves clear from the

water in the eddy. I did not strike one until we had
been there half an hour. I was greatly puzzled to place
my fly far out on the deep water where the trout were
to be seen feeding. It was too deep to anchor, too
swift to hold the canoe with paddles, and too far to
cast. I had with me a multiplying bass-reel with click
and drag, both removable, allowing free play of the reel.
I cast from the point into the swift current at my right
hand, and as soon as my reel-line was straightened I
released the click and the line spun out in five seconds
fully two hundred feet. I then reeled in slowly, and
rarely did I have to repeat my cast without capturing a
fish. My first was a five-pound brook trout. The eddy
helped to bring the fish in even to my feet, and it was
soon in the meshes of the landing-net. At this place
the largest flies were needed, and a bit of pork-rind the
size of a small steel pen, or a small shiner was sure to
take a trout. There was no striking *short* or delay.
The trout were there; they were feeding, and we were
constantly occupied, except when we stopped to take a
generous lunch and a short rest, until four o'clock, when
we ceased fishing and attempted to photograph the falls
and our string of fish.

We then had in our pool among the rocks, dug out
by some clever predecessor, the largest trout that the
writer ever took. We weighed thirteen trout that aggregated fifty-five and a half pounds, and four Mackinaw
trout averaging eight pounds each. We killed four of
the speckled trout weighing as follows: Five and a

half pounds, five and a half pounds, five and a quarter pounds, five pounds, and returned all the others in good condition to the water. These trout were from twenty-two to twenty-four inches long, and from thirteen to thirteen and a half inches in shoulder girth. They were all fine breeding trout, with the sexual differences strongly marked even in the middle of July. We took trout with eggs fully developed in the middle of July.

It may be well to remark here that the biting on the Nipigon River is not all done by the fish. There are three varieties of "fly" that bite. The mosquitoes are thick and hungry. They are sometimes too hungry to be driven away by endurable smoke or by the usual "fly iles." Tar and olive-oil well daubed on will keep them off for a few minutes. The mosquitoes do not bite when the sun is hot on the water or when the wind is high. The black fly is to some persons more annoying than the mosquitoes. He is indifferent to the sacrifice of his individual life. The angler wipes off a hundred or two from under the protecting brim of his hat and from behind his ears, and the eager swarms are instantly replaced. More than one man has been confined to his camp for a day or two because the black flies closed his eyes by their bites.

When these two torments are quiet or absent, the sportsman may be assailed by sand flies. These are almost invisible, but they bite as energetically as a New Jersey mosquito. When all three kinds assail the sportsman at once, he might well flee for his life.

Now one word as to requisites for a trip to the Nipigon River. The sportsman from the States must have a permit from the Government authorities. He needs a good large birch-bark canoe and two experienced men. He will provide a tent (mosquito tight), provisions and clothing suited to a cool and bracing climate. He wants good tackle, two or more steely, stiff fly-rods, because one may break. Good, long, heavy reel lines ; short and strong gut leaders and plenty of *large* flies. Hackles of all kinds, white moths, royal coachmen, silver doctor, Montreal, Canada, captain, and most of the salmon flies are all good flies for the Nipigon. A large and deep landing-net with long staff is also wanted, but there is no need to take a creel.

It is fortunately against the law to use a spoon, or to kill fish that cannot be used. It is not a safe place for pot-fishermen to go.

At times bait is of no use at all. At Virgin Falls on a bright warm day, we found that the fish took eagerly any bait that resembled a shiner, and only took the fly when it was under water and resembled a small fish. One night at Camp Alexander the stone flies were on the water in the greatest abundance ; the trout were rising to them all over the rapids ; but the fish took some other artificial fly more eagerly than they did the close imitations of the natural fly. At times the trout seemed to strike at any small object moving in the water which excited their curiosity. At several points on the river, particularly in the wild water at the foot of falls, the

Mackinaw trout, *salvelinus namaycush*, was abundant and took the fly with as much vigor as any *salvelinus fontinalis* (I believe that these are the correct names unless some new professor has changed them to-day). We could not tell which we had struck except from a flirt of the caudal fin. The " well-forked " caudal fin of the Mackinaw trout was frequently distinguished by our guides at a great distance. They do not play toward the surface so much as the brook trout. They were fat and lazy, two or three long runs generally wearied them so that they led peacefully into the net.

In the small lakes connected with this river there are plenty of pike. We took several with the spoon on our trip through Lake Hannah. They were very numerous in the small bays of shallow water within a mile of wild rapids where trout were equally abundant. This is the first water I have fished that contained both pike and trout. Small fish of several kinds were so abundant that, when we wished to try bait, we had no difficulty in taking " shiners " with a quick swoop of a fine-meshed landing-net near the shore.

I took one small black bass at the mouth of the brook just below Camp Alexander. It was the first one that any of our party had ever heard of in the Nipigon waters.

With such abundant ever-flowing water so stocked with game fish and their prey, there is not the slightest danger that the fishing in this river will be spoiled so long as the bites of mosquitoes, sand flies, and black flies are painful to men.

There are no houses on or near the Nipigon above the first lake, and there is no good reason why there should be any built for many years to come. The Canadian Pacific Railroad is graded from the west to the Nipigon River, but the trains were not running nearer than Port Arthur, close by Fort William. The Nipigon is easily reached by the steamers which follow the north shore. The trip is well worth the time spent.

Last year we were the first sportsmen on the upper part of the river. Others came while we were there, and we have learned that several parties had good success.

I had almost forgotten to say that the scenery of the Nipigon is "alone worth the price of admission" in the language of the show-bills. The rapids are the only fishing-grounds for trout, but there are beautiful lakes, quiet reaches of still-flowing water, lofty cliffs of brightly colored rock, magnificent combinations of water, rock, and woods that charm the eye and give quiet and rest to nerves that have been overstrained by work and care.

Very respectfully,

HENRY H. VAIL.

"We do not expect to get practical instructions from the old writers on angling, but we do learn from them that it was an honorable pastime and so held by those high in the various walks of life. You know that in this country not many years ago a fish-rod and line were considered the belongings of a sort of vagabond. I have tried to show, by quoting from various writers, that angling was held in esteem by men whose opinions were entitled to respect. Thank heaven, we no longer have this Puritanical horror of a fish-rod in America, the only place where it ever had growth."—*A. N. Cheney.*

"I have a few rules for the care of my rods which I always bear in mind, and wish I could urge upon every man who values a fishing-rod. You may not need cautioning, but you will undoubtedly meet some one who does, therefore I give them to you, as follows:

"Put tips and second-joints large end DOWN in sack.

"Straighten each joint of wood rods after use.

"NEVER twist your rod in putting it together or taking it apart, especially a bamboo rod.

"Don't tie your rod up too tight in sack, it crooks the joints.

"Don't put a rod away in a wet sack.

"Keep rod in dry, cool place when not in use.

"If you would not snap your flies off, treat them with the *utmost* gentleness until the leader and snells become softened by the water."—*C. F. Orvis.*

"Long woollen stockings reaching midway between the knee and hip, and supported by elastic side garters with breeches buttoning or buckling just below the knee, is the perfection of wading costume."—*Fitz James Fitch.*

"When I come to rapids I cast far down the foaming yeast of waters and draw my dancing, leaping flies swiftly up stream. The water throws the flies hither and thither in the most natural way, and often from a single cast in such a place I have three trout on."—"*Ned Buntline.*"

Plate X. Description on page 241.

HACKLES & GNATS.

Plate XI. Description on page 257.

BASS FLIES.

Made by C.F.ORVIS, Manchester,Vt.
COPYRIGHTED.

HOW TO CAST A FLY.

BY

SETH GREEN.

I AM asked a great many times what is the secret of fly-casting ? There are three principles. First, quick out of the water ; second, give the line time to straighten behind you ; third, throw. I will explain these principles more definitely.

Raise your rod straight up, or nearly so, the inclination being backward ; then make a quick stroke forward. When you take the line from the water it should be done with a quick jerk ; then give your line time to straighten behind ; then give it the same stroke forward that you did to get it out of the water.

Why so many fail in fly-casting is, they throw the rod backward too near the ground behind them, and when they make the forward stroke, and the line gets straightened out, it is some distance above the water and kinks back, so that when it falls upon the water it lies crooked, and is some distance short of what it would have been if it had struck the water as soon as it was straightened out.

If a fish should strike at your flies at this time you are pretty sure to miss him. By never throwing your rod back more than to a slight angle from the perpendicular, and making the stroke forward your line goes straight out and the flies go to the point you desire.

Great care should be taken when you have thrown the line behind you, that the line is given time to straighten before making the stroke forward. I have thrown seventy feet of line against a strong wind, first, by giving my rod a quick, strong back stroke, carrying my rod but slightly back of the perpendicular, and giving my line time to straighten behind me, then making the same stroke forward that I did to get it back of me.

I nearly forgot to mention that it is more important to have your line fit your rod than it is to have your coat fit your back.

You may think it strange that I should tell you three or four times over in the same article, that in order to do good fly-casting you must throw your rod back only just so far, and then wait for your line to straighten behind you ; and when your line is straight, to make a quick stroke forward, without carrying your rod forward, even a little, before delivering your line, but these movements are the essential principles in fly-casting. By observing them one may hope to become a skilful fly-caster.

TROUT :

MEETING THEM ON THE " JUNE RISE."

BY

" NESSMUK."

There is a spot where plumy pines
  O'erhang the sylvan banks of Otter ;
Where wood-ducks build among the vines
  That bend above the crystal water.

And there the blue-jay makes her nest,
  In thickest shade of water beeches;
The fish-hawk, statuesque in rest,
  Keeps guard o'er glassy pools and reaches.

'Tis there the deer come down to drink,
  From laurel brakes and wooded ridges ;
The trout, beneath the sedgy brink,
  Are sharp on ship-wrecked flies and midges.

AND of the scores of mountain trout-streams that I have fished, the Otter is associated with the most pleasing memories.

It is, or was, a model trout-stream ; a thing to dream of. Having its rise within three miles of the village, it meandered southward for ten miles through a mountain valley to its confluence with the second fork of Pine Creek, six miles of the distance being through a forest without settler or clearing.

The stream was swift, stony, and exceptionally free of brush, fallen timber and the usual *débris* that is so trying to the angler on most wooded streams. Then, it was just the right distance from town. It was so handy to start from the village in the middle of an afternoon in early summer, walk an hour and a half at a leisurely pace, and find one's self on a brawling brook where speckled trout were plenty as a reasonable man could wish.

Fishing only the most promising places for a couple of miles always gave trout enough for supper and breakfast, and brought the angler to the "Trout-House," as a modest cottage of squared logs was called, it being the last house in the clearings and owned by good-natured Charley Davis, who never refused to entertain fishermen with the best his little house afforded. His accommodations were of the narrowest, but also of the neatest, and few women could fry trout so nicely as Mrs. Davis. True, there was only one spare bed, and, if more than two anglers desired lodgings, they were relegated to the barn, with a supply of buffalo skins and blankets. On a soft bed of sweet hay this was all that could be desired by way of lodgings, with the advantage of being free from mosquitoes and punkies. The best of rich, yellow butter with good bread were always to be had at Charley's, and his charges were 12½ cents for meals, and the same for lodging.

The two miles of fishing above the "Trout-House" led through clearings, and the banks were much overgrown with willows, making it expedient to use bait, or a single fly. I chose the latter ; my favorite bug for such fishing being the red hackle, though I am obliged to confess that the fellow who used a white grub generally beat me.

But the evening episode was only preliminary ; it meant a pleasant walk, thirty or forty brook-trout for supper and breakfast, and a quiet night's rest. The real angling commenced the next morning at the bridge, with a six-mile stretch of clear, cold, rushing water to fish. My old-fashioned creel held an honest twelve pounds of dressed trout, and I do not recollect that I ever missed filling it, with time to spare, on that stretch of water. Nor, though I could sometimes fill it in a forenoon, did I ever continue to fish after it *was* full. Twelve pounds of trout is enough for any but a trout-hog.

But the peculiar phase of trout lore that most interested me, was the "run" of trout that were sure to find their way up stream whenever we had a flood late in May or the first half of June. They were distinct and different from the trout that came up with the early spring freshets. Lighter in color, deeper in body, with smaller heads, and better conditioned altogether.

They could be distinguished at a glance; the individuals of any school were as like as peas in color and size, and we never saw them except on a summer flood. The natives called them river trout. They came in schools of one hundred to five times as many, just as the flood was subsiding, and they had a way of halting to rest at the deep pools and spring-holes along their route. Lucky was the angler who could find them at rest in a deep pool, under a scooped out bank, or at the foot of a rushing cascade. At such times they seemed to lose their usual shyness, and would take the fly or worm indifferently, until their numbers were reduced more than one-half. To "meet them on the June rise" was the ardent desire of every angler who fished the streams which they were accustomed to ascend. These streams were not numerous. The First, Second, and Third Forks of Pine Creek, with the Otter, comprised the list so far as I know. And no man could be certain of striking a school at any time; it depended somewhat on judgment, but more on luck. Two or three times I tried it on the Otter and missed; while a friend who had the pluck and muscle to make a ten-mile tramp over the mountain to Second Fork took forty pounds of fine trout from a single school. It was a hoggish thing to do; but he was a native and knew no reason for letting up.

At length my white day came around. There was a fierce rain for three days, and the raging waters took mills, fences and lumber down stream in a way to be

remembered. Luckily it also took the lumbermen the
same way, and left few native anglers at home. When
the waters had subsided to a fair volume, and the streams
had still a suspicion of milkiness, I started at 3 P. M.
of a lovely June afternoon for the Trout-House. An
easy two hours walk, an hour of delightful angling,
and I reached the little hostelry with three dozen brook
trout, averaging about seven inches in length only, but
fresh and sweet, all caught on a single red hackle,
which will probably remain my favorite bug until I go
over the last carry (though I notice it has gone well
out of fashion with modern anglers).

A supper of trout ; an evening such as must be seen
and felt to be appreciated ; trout again for breakfast,
with a dozen packed for lunch, and I struck in at the
bridge before sunrise for an all day bout, "to meet 'em
on the June rise." I didn't do it. I took the entire
day to whip that six miles of bright, dashing water. I
filled a twelve-pound creel with trout, putting back
everything under eight inches. I put back more than
I kept. I had one of the most enjoyable days of my
life ; I came out at the lower bridge after sundown—
and I had not seen or caught one fresh-run river trout.
They were all the slender, large-mouthed, dark-mottled
fish of the gloomy forest, with crimson spots like fresh
drops of blood. But I was not discouraged. Had the
trout been there I should have met them. I walked
half a mile to the little inn at Babb's, selected a dozen
of my best fish for supper and breakfast, gave away the

rest, and, tired as a hound, slept the sleep of the just man.

At 4 o'clock the next morning I was on the stream again, feeling my way carefully down, catching a trout at every cast, and putting them mostly back with care, that they might live ; but for an hour no sign of a fresh-run river trout.

Below the bridge there is a meadow, the oldest clearing on the creek ; there are trees scattered about this meadow that are models of arborial beauty, black walnut, elm, ash, birch, hickory, maple, etc. Most of them grand, spreading trees. One of them, a large, umbrageous yellow-birch, stood on the left bank of the stream, and was already in danger of a fall by

> "The swifter current that mined its roots."

It was here I met them on the June rise.

I dropped my cast of two flies just above the roots of the birch, and on the instant, two fresh-run, silver-sided, red-spotted trout immolated themselves, with a generous self-abnegation that I shall never forget.

Standing there on that glorious June morning, I made cast after cast, taking, usually, two at each cast. I made no boyish show of "playing" them. They were lifted out as soon as struck. To have fooled with them would have tangled me, and very likely have scattered the school.

It was old-time angling ; I shall not see it again.

My cast was a red hackle for tail-fly, with something

like the brown hen for hand-fly. I only used two, with four-foot leader; and I was about the only angler who used a fly at all in those days, on these waters.

I fished about one hour. I caught sixty-four trout, weighing thirteen and three quarter pounds. I caught too many. I was obliged to *string* some of them, as the creel would not hold them all. But my head was moderately level. When I had caught as many as I thought right I held up; and I said, if any of these natives get on to this school, they will take the last trout, if it be a hundred pounds. And they will *salt them down.* So when I was done, and the fishing was good as at the start, I cut a long "staddle," with a bush at the top, and I just went for that school of trout. I chevied, harried and scattered them, up stream and down, until I could not see a fish. Then I packed my duffle and went to the little inn for breakfast. Of course every male biped was anxious to know " where I met 'em." I told them truly; and they started, man and boy, for the " Big Birch," with beech rods, stiff linen lines, and a full stock of white grubs.

I was credibly informed afterward, that these back-woods cherubs did not succeed in " Meeting 'em on the June rise." I have a word to add, which is not important though it may be novel.

There is a roaring, impetuous brook emptying into Second Fork, called " Rock Run." It heads in a level swamp, near the summit of the mountain. The swamp contains about forty acres, and is simply a level bed of loose stones, completely overgrown with bright green moss.

"Rock Run" heads in a strong, ice-cold spring, but is soon sunken and lost among the loose stones of the swamp. Just where the immense hemlocks, that make the swamp a sunless gloom, get their foothold, is one of the things I shall never find out. But, all the same, they are *there.* And "Rock Run" finds its way underground for 80 rods with never a ray of sunlight to illumine its course. Not once in its swamp course does it break out to daylight. You may follow it by its heavy gurgling, going by ear ; but you cannot see the water. Now remove the heavy coating of moss here and there, and you may see glimpses of dark, cold water, three or four feet beneath the surface. Drop a hook, baited with angle-worm down these dark watery holes, and it will be instantly taken by a dark, crimson-spotted specimen of simon pure *Salmo fontinalis.* They are small, four to six inches in length, hard, sweet ; the *beau ideal* of mountain trout. Follow this subterranean brook for eighty rods, and you find it gushing over the mountain's brink in a cascade that no fish could or would attempt to ascend. Follow the roaring brook down to its confluence with Second Fork, and you will not find one trout in the course of a mile. The stream is simply a succession of falls, cascades, and rapids, up which no fish can beat its way for one hundred yards. And yet at the head of this stream is a subterranean brook stocked with the finest specimens of *Salmo fontinalis.* They did not breed on the mountain top. They *cannot* ascend the stream. Where did they originate ? When, and how did they manage to get there ? I leave the questions to *savans* and *naturalists.* As for myself, I state the fact—still demonstrable—for the trout are yet there. But I take it to be one of the conundrums "no fellah can ever find out."

P. S.—A word as to bugs, lures, flies, etc. Now I have no criticism to offer as regards flies or lures. I saw a Gotham banker in 1880, making a cast on Third lake, with a leader that carried *twelve flies.* Why not? He enjoyed it ; and he caught some trout. Even the guides laughed at him. I did not : he rode his hobby, and he rode it well. Fishing beside him, with a five-dollar rod, I caught two trout to his one. What did he care ? He came out to enjoy himself after his own fashion, and he did it. Like myself, he only cared for the sport—the recreation and enough trout for supper. (I cannot cast twelve flies.)

Now my favorite lures—with forty years' experience —stand about thus. Tail fly, red hackle ; second, brown hen ; third, Romeyn. Or, tail fly, red ibis ; second, brown hackle ; third, queen of the waters. Or, red hackle, queen, royal coachman. Sometimes trout will *not* rise to the fly. I respect their tastes. I use then —tail fly, an angle worm, with a bit of clear pork for the head, and a white miller for second. If this fails I go to camp and sleep. I am not above worms and grubs, but prefer the fly. *And I take but what I need for present use.* Can all brother anglers say the same ?

"It has so happened that all the public services that I have rendered in the world, in my day and generation, have been connected with the general government. I think I ought to make an exception. I was ten days a member of the Massachusetts Legislature, and I turned my thoughts to the search of some good object in which I could be useful in that position; and after much reflection I introduced a bill which, with the consent of both houses of the Legislature, passed into a law, and is now a law of the State, which enacts that no man in the State shall catch trout in any manner than in the old way, with an ordinary hook and line."—*Daniel Webster.*

"If you do not know a river it is always most desirable to have someone with you who does."—*Francis Francis.*

49. The Teal.	50. Reuben Wood.	51. Red Spinner.
52. No. 68.	53. Hawthorne.	54. Dorset.
55. Widow.	56. Grasshopper.	57. Stebbins.
58. March Brown.	59. Shoemaker.	60. Orange Black.
61. King of the Water.	62. Gen. Hooker.	63. Gray Drake.

"The angler atte the leest, hath his holsom walke, and mery at his ease, a swete ayre of the swete savoure of the mede floures, that makyth him hungry ; he hereth the melodyous armony of fowles; he seeth the yonge swannes, heerons, duckes, cotes, and many other fowles, wyth theyr brodes; whyche me semyth better than alle the noyse of houndys, the blastes of hornys, and the scrye of foulis, that hunters, fawkeners, and fowlers can make. And if the angler take fysshe ; surely, thenne, is there noo man merier than he is in his spyryte."—*Dame Juliana Berners.*

"Skill, and trained skill at that, does the good work, and the angler's score is just in proportion to his knowledge of 'how to do it.'"—*Wm. C. Harris.*

"A gray-haired bait-fisher is very rare, while the passion for fly-casting, whether for trout or salmon, grows by what it feeds upon, and continues a source of the highest pleasure even after the grasshopper becomes a burden."—*George Dawson*.

"It is not the number of fish he captures that makes the angler contented, for the true angler can enjoy the mere casting of the fly if he has only an occasional fish to reward his efforts."—"*Random Casts*."

"The great charm of fly-fishing for trout is derived from the fact that you then see the movements of your fish, and if you are not an expert hand, the chances are that you will capture but one out of the hundred that may rise to your hook. You can seldom save a trout unless you strike the very instant that he leaps. The swiftness with which a trout can dart from his hiding-place after a fly is truly astonishing ; and we never see one perform this operation without feeling an indescribable thrill quivering through our frame."—*Charles Lanman*.

"There is nothing grovelling in fly-fishing—nothing gross or demoralizing."—*Charles Hallock*.

"Angling is a maist innocent, poetical, moral and religious amusement. Gin I saw a fisher gruppin creelfu' after creelfu' o' trouts, and then flingin' them a' awa among the heather and the brackens on his way hame, I micht begin to suspec that the idiot was by nature rather a savage. But as for me, I send presents to my freens, and devour dizzens on dizzens every week in the family—maistly dune in the pan, wi' plenty o' fresh butter and roun' meal—sae that prevents the possibility o' cruelty in my fishin', and in the fishin' o' a' reasonable creatures."—*James Hogg*.

"People that have not been inoculated with the true spirit may wonder at the infatuation of anglers—but true anglers leave them very contentedly to their wondering, and follow their diversions with keen delight."—*William Howitt*.

"WHY PETER WENT A-FISHING."

W. C. PRIME.

NEVER was night more pure, never was sea more
winning ; never were the hearts of men moved by
deeper emotions than on that night and by that sea
when Peter and John, and other of the disciples, were
waiting for the Master.

Peter said, "I go a-fishing." John and Thomas,
and James and Nathanael, and the others, said, "We
will go with you," and they went.

Some commentators have supposed and taught that,
when Peter said, "I go a-fishing," he announced the
intention of returning to the ways in which he had
earned his daily bread from childhood ; that his Master
was gone, and he thought that nothing remained for
him but the old, hard life of toil, and the sad labor of
living.

But this seems scarcely credible, or consistent with
the circumstances. The sorrow which had weighed
down the disciples when gathered in Jerusalem on that
darkest Sabbath day of all the Hebrew story, had given
way to joy and exultation in the morning when the
empty tomb revealed the hitherto hidden glory of the

resurrection, joy which was ten-fold increased by an interview with the risen Lord, and confirmed by his direction, sending them into Galilee to await Him there. And thus it seems incredible that Peter and John— John, the beloved—could have been in any such gloom and despondency as to think of resuming their old employment at this time, when they were actually waiting for His coming, who had promised to meet them.

Probably they were on this particular evening weary with earnest expectancy, yet not satisfied ; tired of waiting and longing, and looking up the hillside on the Jerusalem road for His appearance ; and I have no doubt that, when this weariness became exhausting, Peter sought on the water something of the old excitement that he had known from boyhood, and that to all the group it seemed a fitting way in which to pass the long night before them, otherwise to be weary as well as sleepless.

If one could have the story of that night of fishing, of the surrounding scenes, the conversation in the boat, the unspoken thoughts of the fishermen, it would make the grandest story of fishing that the world has ever known. Its end was grand when in the morning the voice of the Master came over the sea, asking them the familiar question, in substance the same which they, like all fishermen, had heard a thousand times, "Have you any fish ?"

*   *   *   *   *   *

The memory of this scene is not unfitting to the

modern angler. Was it possible to forget it when I
first wet a line in the water of the Sea of Galilee ? Is
it any less likely to come back to me on any lake among
the hills when the twilight hides the mountains, and
overhead the same stars look on our waters that looked
on Gennesaret, so that the soft night air feels on one's
forehead like the dews of Hermon ?

I do not think that this was the last, though it be
the last recorded fishing done by Peter or by John. I
don't believe these Galilee fishermen ever lost the love
for their old employment. It was a memorable fact for
them that the Master had gone a-fishing with them on
the day that He called them to be His disciples ; and
this latest meeting with Him in Galilee, the commis-
sion to Peter, "Feed my sheep," and the words so
startling to John, "If I will that he tarry till I
come,"—words which He must have recalled when He
uttered that last longing cry, "Even so come, Lord"
—all these were associated with that last recorded fishing scene on the waters of Gennesaret.

Fishermen never lose their love for the employment,
and it is notably true that the men who fish for a living love their work quite as much as those who fish for
pleasure love their sport. Find an old fisherman, if
you can, in any sea-shore town, who does not enjoy his
fishing. There are days, without doubt, when he does
not care to go out, when he would rather that need did
not drive him to the sea ; but keep him at home a few
days, or set him at other labor, and you shall see that he

longs for the toss of the swell on the reef, and the sudden joy of a strong pull on his line. Drift up along side of him in your boat when he is quietly at his work, without his knowing that you are near. You can do it easily. He is pondering solemnly a question of deep importance to him, and he has not stirred eye, or hand, or head for ten minutes. But see that start and sharp jerk of his elbow, and now hear him talk, not to you— to the fish. He exults as he brings him in, yet mingles his exultation with something of pity as he baits his hook for another. Could you gather the words that he has in many years flung on the sea winds, you would have a history of his life and adventures, mingled with very much of his inmost thinking, for he tells much to the sea and the fish that he would never whisper in human ears. Thus the habit of going a-fishing always modifies the character. The angler, I think, dreams of his favorite sport oftener than other men of theirs.

There is a peculiar excitement in it, which perhaps arises from somewhat of the same causes which make the interest in searching for ancient treasures, opening Egyptian tombs and digging into old ruins. One does not know what is under the surface. There may be something or there may be nothing. He tries, and the rush of something startles every nerve. Let no man laugh at a comparison of trout-fishing with antiquarian researches. I know a man who has done a great deal of both, and who scarcely knows which is the most absorbing or most remunerating ; for each enriches mind and body, each gratifies the most refined taste, each becomes a passion unless the pursuer guard his enthusiasm and moderate his desire.

*   *   *   *   *   *

To you, my friend, who know nothing of the gentle and purifying association of the angler's life, these may seem strange notions—to some, indeed, they may even sound profane. But the angler for whom I write will not so think them, nor may I, who, thinking these same thoughts, have cast my line on the sea of Galilee, and taken the descendants of old fish in the swift waters of the Jordan.

Trout fishing is employment for all men, of all minds. It tends to dreamy life, and it leads to much thought and reflection. I do not know in any book or story of modern times a more touching and exquisite scene than that which Mrs. Gordon gives in her admirable biography of her father, the leonine Christopher North, when the feeble old man waved his rod for the last time over the Dochart, where he had taken trout from his boyhood. Shall we ever look upon his like again ? He was a giant among men of intellectual greatness. Of all anglers since apostolic days, he was the greatest ; and there is no angler who does not look to him with veneration and love, while the English language will forever possess higher value that he has lived and written. It would be thought very strange were one to say that Wilson would never have been half the man he was were he not an angler. But he would have said so himself, and I am not sure but he did say so, and, whether he did or not, I have no doubt of the truth of the saying.

It has happened to me to fish the Dochart, from the old inn at Luib down to the bridge, and the form of the great Christopher was forever before me along the bank, and in the rapids, making his last casts as Mrs. Gordon here so tenderly describes him :

" Had my father been able to endure the fatigue, we too would have had something to boast of, but he was unable to do more than loiter by the river-side, close in the neighborhood of the inn—never without his rod.   *   *   *

" How now do his feet touch the heather ? Not, as of old, with a bound, but with slow and unsteady step, supported on the one hand by his stick, while the other carries his rod.   The breeze gently moves his locks, no longer glittering with the light of life, but dimmed by its decay.   Yet are his shoulders broad and unbent.   The lion-like presence is somewhat softened down, but not gone.   He surely will not venture into the deeps of the water, for only one hand is free for a ' cast,' and those large stones, now slippery with moss, are dangerous stumbling-blocks in the way.   Besides, he promised his daughters he would not wade, but, on the contrary, walk quietly with them by the river's edge, there gliding ' at its own sweet will.' Silvery band of pebbled shore leading to loamy colored pools, dark as the glow of a southern eye, how could he resist the temptation of near approach ? In he goes, up to the ankles, then to the knees, tottering every other step, but never falling.   Trout after trout he catches, small ones certainly, but plenty of them.   Into his pocket with them all this time, manœuvering in the most skilful manner both stick and rod ; until weary, he is obliged to rest on the bank, sitting with his feet in the water, laughing at his daughters' horror, and obstinately continuing the sport in spite of all remonstrance. At last he gives in and retires. Wonderful to say, he did not seem to suffer from these imprudent liberties."

And Mrs. Gordon gives us another exquisite picture in the very last day of the grand old Christopher :

* * * " And then he gathered around him, when the spring mornings brought gay jets of sunshine into the little room where he lay, the relics of a youthful passion, one that with him never grew old. It was an affecting sight to see him busy, nay, quite absorbed with the fishing tackle scattered about his bed, propped up with pillows—his noble head, yet glorious with its flowing locks, carefully combed by attentive hands, and falling on each side of his unfaded face. How neatly he picked out each elegantly dressed fly from its little bunch, drawing it out with trembling hand along the white coverlet, and then replacing it in his pocket-book, he would tell ever and anon of the streams he used to fish in of old, and of the deeds he had performed in his childhood and youth."

There is no angler who will not appreciate the beauty of these pictures, and I do not believe any one of us, retaining his mental faculties, will fail, in extremest age, to recall with the keenest enjoyment, of which memory is capable, the scenes of our happiest sport.

Was Peter less or more than man ? Was John not of like passions with ourselves ? Believe me, the old dweller on Patmos, the old Bishop of Ephesus, lingering between the memories of his Lord in Galilee and the longing for Him to come quickly yet again, saw often before his dim eyes the ripple on Gennesaret and the flashing scales of the silver fish that had gladdened him many a time before he knew the Master.

It is one of the most pleasant and absorbing thoughts which possess the traveller in those regions, that the child Christ was a child among the hills of Galilee, and loved them with all the gentle fervor of his human soul. Doubtless many times before He had challenged the fisher on the sea with that same question which we anglers so frequently hear, " Have you taken any fish ? " He may have often seen Peter and the others at their work. Perhaps sometimes He had talked with them, and, it may well be, gone with them on the sea, and helped them. For they were kindly men, as fishermen are always in all countries, and they loved to talk of their work, and of a thousand other things, of which, in their contemplative lives, they had thought without talking.

In an age when few men were learned, and, in fact, few in any grade or walk of life could even read or write, I am inclined to think there was no class from whom better trained intellects could be selected than from among these thoughtful fishermen. They had doubtless the Oriental characteristics of calmness and reserve, and these had been somewhat modified by their employment. Given to sober reflection, patient to investigate, quick to trust when their faith was demanded by one whom they respected, slow to act when haste was not necessary, prompt and swift on any emergency, filled full of love for nature, all harsh elements of character softened into a deep benevolence and pity and love—such are the fishermen of our day, and such, I doubt not, were the fishermen of old. They were men with whom a mother would willingly trust her young boy, to whom he would become attached, with whom he would enjoy talking, and, above all, who would pour out their very souls in talking with him, when among their fellow-men they would be reserved, diffident, and silent. They were men, too, who would recognize in the boy the greatness of his lineage, the divine shining out from his eyes. Who shall prevail to imagine the pleasantness of those days on the sea when Peter and John talked with the holy boy, as they waited for the fish, and their boat rocked to the winds that came down from Lebanon. Who can say that there were not some memories of those days, as well as of the others when we know Christ was with him, which, when he was tired of the waiting, led Peter to say, "I go a-fishing!"

I believe that he went a-fishing because he felt exactly as I have felt, exactly as scores of men have felt who knew the charm of the gentle art, as we now call it. No other has such attraction. Men love hunting, love boating, love games of varied sorts, love many amusements of many kinds, but I do not know of any like fishing to which men go for relief in weariness, for rest after labor, for solace in sorrow. I can well understand how those sad men, not yet fully appreciating the grand truth that their Master had risen from the dead, believing; yet doubting, how even Thomas, who had so lately seen the wounds and heard the voice; how even John, loving and loved, who had rejoiced a week ago in Jerusalem at the presence of the triumphant Lord; how Peter, always fearful; how Nathanael, full of impulsive faith, how each and all of them, wearied with their long waiting for Him on the shore of the sea, sought comfort and solace, opportunity and incitement to thought in going a-fishing.

I can understand it, for, though far be it from me to compare any weariness or sorrow of mine with theirs, I have known that there was no better way in which I could find rest.

I have written for lovers of the gentle art, and if this which I have written fall into other hands, let him who reads understand that it is not for him. We who go a-fishing are a peculiar people. Like other men and women in many respects, we are like one another, and like no others, in other respects. We understand each other's thoughts by an intuition of which you know nothing. So closely are we alike in some regards, so different from the rest of the world in these respects, and so important are these characteristics of mind and of thought, that I sometimes think no man but one of us can properly understand the mind of Peter, or appreciate the glorious visions of the son of Zebedee.

FROM " GAME FISH OF THE NORTH."

BY

R. B. ROOSEVELT.

THERE are innumerable rules applicable to trout-
fishing, and innumerable exceptions to each ; neither
man nor fish is infallible. A change of weather is
always desirable ; if it has been clear, a rainy day is
favorable ; if cold, a warm one ; if the wind has been
north, a southerly one is advantageous ; a zephyr if
it has been blowing a tornado.   Generally, in early
spring, amid the fading snows and blasts of winter, a
warm day is very desirable ; later, in the heats of summer, a cold, windy day will insure success.   Dead calm
is dangerous, although many trout are taken in water
as still, clear and transparent as the heavens above.
The first rule is never to give up ; there is hardly a
day but at some hour, if there be trout, they will rise,
and steady, patient industry disciplines the mind and
invigorates the muscles.   A southerly, especially a
south-easterly wind, has a singular tendency to darken
the surface, and in clear, fine waters is particularly
advantageous ; a south-wester comes next in order ; a
north-easter, in which, by-the-by, occasionally there is
great success, is the next ; and a north-wester is the

worst and dearest of all.   Give me wind on any terms,
a southerly wind, if I can have it; but give me wind.
It is not known what quality of wind darkens the
water; it may be a haziness produced in the atmosphere, although with a cloudy sky the water is often
too transparent; it may be the peculiar character of
the waves, short and broken, as contra-distinguished
from long and rolling; but the fact is entitled to re
liance.

Slight changes will often affect the fish.   On one
day in June, in the writer's experience, after having no
luck until eleven o'clock, the trout suddenly commenced rising, and kept on without cessation, scarcely
giving time to cast, till two, when they as suddenly
stopped.   There was no observable change in the
weather, except the advent of a slight haze, the wind
remaining precisely the same.   I was much disappointed, not having half fished the ground, and being
prevented, by the numbers that were taken, from casting over some of the largest fish that broke.   As it
was I caught seventy trout in what are ordinarily considered the worst hours of the day.   But in this particular, also, the same rules apply as to the warmth of
the weather.   In early spring it is useless to be up
with the lark, even supposing such a bird exists; no
fish will break water till the sun has warmed the air;
but in summer, the dawn should blush to find the
sportsman napping.   In fact, trout will not rise well
unless the air is warmer than the water.   They do not

like to risk taking cold by exposing themselves to a sudden draught.

There is a very absurd impression that trout will not take the fly early in the season ; this is entirely unfounded. As soon as the ice disappears they will be found gambolling in the salt-water streams, and leaping readily at the fly. At such times, on lucky days, immense numbers are taken. In March they have run up the sluice-ways and are in the lower ponds, lying sullenly in the deepest water ; then is the Cowdung, politely called the Dark Cinnamon, the most attractive fly. In April, May and June they are scattered, and entrapped by the Hackles, Professor, Ibis, and all the medium-sized flies. In July and August they have sought the head-waters of navigation, the cool spring brooks, and hide around the weeds and water-cresses, whence the midges alone can tempt them.

Any flies will catch fish, cast in any manner, if the fish are plenty and in humor to be caught. A few feathers torn from the nearest and least suspicious chicken, and tied on an ordinary hook with a piece of thread, will constitute a fly in the imagination of a trout, provided he follows, as he sometimes appears to do, the advice of young folks—shuts his eyes and opens his mouth. I cannot recommend such tackle, being convinced the most skilfully made is the best ; but I do advise simplicity of color.

* * * * * *

Good luck, that synonym for all the virtues, does

not depend so much upon the kind of flies as the skill in casting, and a poor fly lightly cast into the right spot will do better execution than the best fly roughly cast into the wrong place. The lure must be put where the fish habit, often before their very noses, or they will not take it; and when they lie, as they generally do in running streams, in the deep holes under the banks, where the bushes are closest and cause the densest shade, it requires some skill to cast properly into the exact spot. Sacrifice everything to lightness in casting; let the line go straight without a kink if you can, drop the fly into the right ripple if possible, but it must drop gently on the surface of the water. An ugly splash of a clear day in pure water, and the prey will dart in every direction, and the angler's hopes scatter with them.

A beginner may practice a certain formula, such as lifting the line with a wave and smart spring, swinging it backward in a half circle, and when it is directly behind him, casting straight forward; but as soon as he has overcome the rudimentary principles, he should cast in every manner, making the tip of his rod cut full circles, figure eights, and all other figures, behind him, according to the wind; bearing in mind, however, ever to make his fly drop as lightly as a feather. He should use his wrist mainly, and practice with each hand, and should never be otherwise than ashamed of a bungling cast, though he be alone, and none but the fish there to despise him. If the line falls the first time with a heart-rending splash, all in a tangle, it is useless to make the next cast properly. The fish have found out the trick, and know too much to risk their necks in any such noose.

A skilful fisherman can cast almost any length of line, but practically, fifty feet, counting from the reel, is all that can be used to advantage. Some English books say only the leader [gut links] should alight in the water ; but this is nonsense, for at least one-half the line must fall into the water, unless the fisherman stand on a high bank. With a long line, the difficulties of striking and landing the fish are greatly increased. In striking, there is much slack line to be taken up. In landing, it requires some time to get the fish under control, and he is apt to reach the weeds or a stump.

That most excellent fisherman and learned scholar, Dr. Bethune, in his edition of Walton, Part II., page 73, says that candid anglers must confess that nine out of ten trout hook themselves. This may be so in streams teeming with fish, where a dozen start at once, frantically striving to be the first ; but in clear, well-fished streams, not one fish in a thousand will hook himself ; and on Long Island, an angler would grow gray ere he filled his basket if he did not strike, and that quickly. Striking, to my mind, is by far the most important point, and hundreds of fish have I seen escape for want of quickness. It must be done quickly but steadily, and not with a jerk, as the latter is apt, by the double action of the rod, to bend the tip forward, and loosen instead of tightening the line.　There are days when fish cannot be struck, although they are rising freely.　Whether they are playing or over-cautious, I never could determine; whether they are not hungry, or the water is too clear, they put a man's capacities at defiance.　Their appearance must be signalled to the eye, by that reported to the brain, which then directs the nerves to command the muscles to move the wrist; and ere this complicated performance is completed, the fish has blown from his mouth the feathery deception, and has darted back to his haunts of safety.　A fish will occasionally leap up, seize the fly, discover the cheat, and shaking his head, jump several feet along the surface of the water to rid his mouth of it, and do this so quickly as not to give a quick angler time to strike.　How often fish are caught when they rise the second time, as then the angler is more on the alert; whereas, on the first rise, he was off his guard!　How often fish rise when the angler's head is turned away from his line, or when he is busy at something else, and how rarely are they caught!　In my experience, it is so great a rarity, that it might almost be said they never hook themselves.　In the language of youth, the only hooking they do, is to hook off.

Dr. Bethune, page 97, says the rod should not exceed one pound in weight.　Indeed, it should not; and if it does, it exemplifies the old maxim, so far as to have a fool at one end.　If we could fish by steam, a rod exceeding a pound and measuring over fourteen feet might answer well; but in these benighted days, while wrists are of bone, muscles, cartilages, and the like, the lighter the better. A rod—and if perfection is absolutely indispensable, a cedar rod—of eleven or twelve feet, weighing nine or ten ounces, will catch trout. Cedar rods can only be obtained in America, and then only on compulsion; but this wood makes the most elastic rods in the world. They spring instantly to every motion of the hand, and never warp. They are delicate. The wood is like woman—cross-grained, but invaluable, if carefully treated. The reel should be a simple click, never a multiplier, but large-barrelled, and fastened to the butt with a leather strap. The line silk, covered with a preparation of oil, tapered, if possible, at each end, and thirty to forty yards long. The basket—positive—a fish basket; the angler—comparative—a fisherman.

Thus equipped, go forth mildly, approving where the writer's opinions coincide with yours, simply incredulous where they do not.

*　　　*　　　*　　　*　　　*　　　*

There are several ways of landing a trout, but not all equally sportsmanlike. Large trout may be gaffed; small ones landed in a net; and where neither of these means is at hand, they must be dragged out of the water, or floated up among the bushes, according to the taste of the angler and the strength of his tackle.

A tyro was once fishing in the same boat with me, using bait, when he struck his first trout. One can imagine how entirely misspent had been his previous existence, when it is said he had never taken a trout,

no, nor any other fish, before.   It was not a large fish ;
such luck rarely falls to the share of the beginner; and
in spite of what elderly gentlemen may say to the contrary, an ignorant countryman, with his sapling rod
and coarse tackle, never takes the largest fish nor the
greatest in quantity.   Were it otherwise, sportsmen had
better turn louts, and tackle-makers take to cutting
straight saplings in the woods.   My companion, nevertheless, was not a little surprised at the vigorous rushes
the trout made to escape, but his line being strong and
rod stiff, he steadily reeled him in.   Great was the
excitement ; his whole mind was devoted to shortening
the line, regardless of what was to be done next.   We
had a darkey named Joe with us, to row the boat and
land the fish, and our luck having been bad during the
morning he was delighted with this turn of affairs, and
ready, net in hand, to do his duty.   The fish was being
reeled up till but a few feet of the line remained below
the top, when with a shout of " land, Joe, land him !"
my companion suddenly lifted up his rod, carrying the
trout far above our heads.   There it dangled, swaying
to and fro, bouncing and jumping, while the agonized
fisherman besought the darky to land him, and the
latter, reaching up as far as he could with the net, his
eyes starting out of his head with wonder at this novel
mode of proceeding, came far short of his object.   Never
was seen such a sight ; the hopeless despair of my friend,
the eagerness of the darky, who fairly strove to climb
the rod as the fish danced about far out of reach.   What

was to be done ?   The line would not render, the rod
was so long we could not reach the tip in the boat; and
the only horrible alternative appeared to be my friend's
losing his first fish. The latter, however, by this remarkable course of treatment, had grown peaceable,
and when he was dropped back into the water, made
but feeble efforts, while my companion, as quietly as he
could, worked out his line till he could land him like a
Christian. Great were the rejoicings when the prize
earned with so much anxiety was secured. That is the
way not to land a trout.

One afternoon of a very boisterous day, I struck a large
fish at the deep hole in the centre of Phillipse's Pond, on
Long Island. He came out fiercely, and taking my fly as
he went down, darted at once for the bottom, which
is absolutely covered with long, thick weeds. The
moment he found he was struck he took refuge among
them, and tangled himself so effectually that I could not
feel him, and supposed he had escaped. By carefully
exerting sufficient force, however, the weeds were loos-
ened from the bottom, and the electric thrill of his
renewed motion was again perceptible. He was allowed
to draw the line through the weeds and play below
them, as by so doing they would give a little, while if
confined in them he would have a leverage against them,
and could, with one vigorous twist, tear out the hook.
When he was somewhat exhausted, the question as to
the better mode of landing him arose. The wind was
blowing so hard as to raise quite a sea, which washed

the weeds before it in spite of any strain that could be
exerted by the rod, and drifted the boat as well, render-
ing the latter almost unmanageable, while the fish was
still so vigorous as to threaten every moment to escape.
I besought the boatman, who was an old hand, and
thoroughly up to his business, to drop the boat down
to the weeds and let me try and land my fish with one
hand while holding the rod with the other. He knew
the dangers of such a course, and insisted upon rowing
slowly and carefully for shore at a shallow place sheltered from the wind, although I greatly feared the
hook would tear out or the rod snap under the strain
of towing both weeds and fish; once near shore, he
deliberately forced an oar into the mud and made the
boat fast to it, and then taking up the net watched
for a favorable chance. He waited for some time,
carefully putting the weeds aside until a gleaming
line of silver glanced for a moment beneath the water,
when darting the net down he as suddenly brought it
up, revealing within its folds the glorious colors of a
splendid trout. That was the way to land a trout
under difficulties, although I still think I could have
done it successfully by myself.

Generally the utmost delicacy should be shown in
killing a fish, but there are times when force must be
exerted. If the fish is making for a stump, or even
weeds, he must be stopped at any reasonable risk of
the rod's breaking or the fly's tearing out. A stump is
the most dangerous; one turn around that and he is

off, leaving your flies probably in a most inconvenient place and many feet below the surface of the water. But remember the oft-repeated maxim of a friend of the writer, who had been with him many a joyous fishing day, " That one trout hooked is worth a dozen not hooked." Small trout are more apt to escape than large ones, because the skin around the mouth of the latter is tougher. With either, however, there is risk enough. The hook is small, and often takes but a slight hold ; the gut is delicate, and frequently half worn through by continual casting. Fish are, in a majority of instances, hooked in the corner of the upper jaw, where there is but a thin skin to hold them ; by long continued struggling the hole wears larger, and finally, to the agony of the fisherman, the hook slips out.

There are occasions when force must be exerted, and then good tackle and a well-made rod will repay the cost. At dusk, one night, I cautiously approached the edge of a newly made pond, that was as full of stumps as of fish, both being about the extreme limit, and casting into the clear water struck a fine fish of three-quarters of a pound. Not a minute's grace did he receive, but I lugged and he fought, and after a general turmoil I succeeded in bringing him to land, in spite of weeds and stumps and twigs, which he did his best to reach. The same was done with seven fish after a loss of only three flies and with a rod that weighed only eight ounces.

In landing a fish wait till he is pretty well exhausted, bring his mouth above water, and keep it there till he is drawn into the net, and warn your assistant to remove the net at once if he gets his head down. By diving after him with the net the assistant would certainly not catch the fish and might tangle one of your other flies. The fish should be led into the net, and the latter kept as still as possible ; he knows as well as you do what it is for, and if his attention is drawn to it will dart off as madly as ever.

*   *   *   *   *   *

The trout is admitted to be the most beautiful of all our fish ; not so large or powerful as the salmon, he is much more numerous, abounding in all the brooks and rivulets of our Northern States. He lives at our very doors ; in the stream that meanders across yon meadow, where the haymakers are now busy with their scythes, we have taken him in our early days ; down yonder in that wood is a brook filled with bright, lively little fellows ; and away over there we know of pools where there are splendid ones. Who has not said or thought such words as he stood in the bright summer's day under the grateful shade of the piazza running round the old country house where he played—a boy ?

He does not make the nerves thrill and tingle like the salmon, he does not leap so madly into the air nor make such fierce, resolute rushes ; he has not the silver sides, nor the great strength ; but he is beautiful as the sunset sky, brave as bravery itself, and is our own home darling. How he flashes upon the sight as he grasps the spurious insect, and turns down with a quick little slap of the tail ! How he darts hither and thither when he finds he is hooked ! How persistently he struggles till enveloped in the net ! And then with what heart-rending sighs he .breathes away his life ! Who does not love the lovely trout ? With eye as deep and melting, skin as rich and soft, and ways as wildly wilful as angelic woman—who loves not one loves not the other. Who would not win the one cares not to win the other. Strange that man should " kill the thing he loves ;" but if to possess them kills them, he must kill. If women, like the *Ephemeræ*, died, as they often do, in their love, we should still love them. Such is man ; do not think I praise him. No one kills fish for the pleasure of killing ; but they cannot live out of water, nor we in it, therefore one of us must die.

The man who kills to kill, who is not satisfied with reasonable sport, who slays unfairly or out of season, who adds one wanton pang, that man receives the contempt of all good sportsmen and deserves the felon's doom. Of such there are but few.

We seek this, our favorite fish, in early spring, when the ice has just melted, and the cold winds remind one forcibly of bleak December, and when we find him in the salt streams, especially of Long Island and Cape Cod ; but we love most to follow him in the early summer, along the merry streams of old Orange, or the mountain brooks of Sullivan county ; where the air is full of gladness, and the trees are heavy with foliage—where the birds are singing on every bough, and the grass redolent of violets and early flowers. There we wade the cold brooks, leafy branches bowing us a welcome as we pass, the water rippling over the hidden rocks, and telling us, in its wayward way, of the fine fish it carries in its bosom. With creel upon our shoulder and rod in hand, we reck not of the hours, and only when the sinking sun warns of the approaching darkness do we seek, with sharpened appetite, the hospitable country inn, and the comfortable supper that our prey will furnish forth.

*   *   *   *   *   *

There is no fish more difficult to catch, nor that gives the true angler more genuine sport, than the trout. His capture requires the nicest tackle, the greatest skill, the most complete self-command, the highest qualities of mind and body. The arm must be strong that wields the rod, the eye true that sees the rise ; the wrist quick that strikes at the instant ; the judgment good that selects the best spot, the most suitable fly, and knows just how to kill the fish. A fine temper is required to bear up against the loss of a noble fish, and patient perseverance to conquer ill luck.

Hence it is that the fisherman is so proud of his basket of a dozen half-pound trout. He feels that any one more awkward or less resolute could not have done so well. He feels conscious that he does not owe his success to mere luck, but has deserved the glory. He feels that he has elevated himself by the very effort. Do not suppose I mean that there is no skill in other fishing ; there is in all, even in catching minnows for bait, but most of all in trout-fishing.

"It is well to have in your fly-books a little of everything, but of gray and brown hackles, coachmen and professors, an abundance."—" *Bourgeois.*"

"When a plump, two-pound trout refuses to eat a tinselled, feathered fraud, I am not the man to refuse him something more edible."—" *Nessmuk.*"

"Many of what are considered fancy flies, because not in standard lists, succeed when the known insect is uncared for."— *Hewett Wheatley.*

"The best imitations can scarcely be pronounced good until tested by the fish."—*Michael Theakston.*

"The traveller fancies he has seen the country. So he has, the outside of it at least; but the angler only sees the inside. The angler only is brought close, face to face with the flower and bird and insect life of the rich river banks, the only part of the landscape where the hand of man has never interfered."—*Charles Kingsley.*

"The editor of the *Angler's Souvenir*, from a praiseworthy pride in his nominal ancestors, says the Saxon race were called *Anglo*, because of their skill with the *angle*."—*G. W. Bethune, D.D.*

"Vast varieties of the spinners, beetles, gnats, midges, etc., are perpetually progressing, and pouring their winged progeny on the waters daily throughout the season, making ample store and choice for the fish, and a task for the fly-fisher to discover and imitate the fly they prefer."—*Francis M. Walbran.*

"The single hook salmon flies have been abandoned by nearly all experienced Canadian salmon fishers. The double hook keeps its hold much better and saves many fish that would be lost with the single one. Besides we consider that the double-hook fly floats, or rather, holds its position better *in* the water than the single hook, for no salmon, with us, will take the fly skipping *out* of the water, but often take it a foot or more below the surface. The double-hook fly is our recognition of the evolution theory, or doctrine, in the "survival of the fittest."—*Allan Gilmour.*

" That *we are* wise men, I shall not stoop to maintain, but that we do love angling we are assured of, and therein we know that we are in unison with very many greatly wise and wisely good men."—*Thaddeus Norris.*

" The true angler is not confined to fly-fishing, as many imagine. When the fly can be used it always should be used, but where the fly is impracticable, or where fish will not rise to it, he is a very foolish angler who declines to use bait."— *W. C. Prime.*

" The creative power of genius can make a feather-fly live, and move, and have being ; and a wisely stricken fish gives up the ghost in transports."—" *J. Cypress, Jr.*"

64. Jungle Cock.	65. Lake Green.	66. Jenny Lind.
67. Poor Man's Fly.	68. Pheasant.	69. Romeyn.
70. Morrison.	71. Katy-did.	72. Claret.
73. Hoskins.	74. Caldwell.	75. Iron Dun.
76. Queen of the Water.	77. Olive Gnat.	78. Brown Coflin.

" The deftly-tossed fly, taking wing on the nerve of a masterly cast, will drop gracefully far out in the stream where the heavier gear of the bait rod would never aspire to reach."—*Charles Hallock.*

" Fly-fishing may well be considered the most beautiful of all rural sports."—" *Frank Forester.*"

" To be a perfect trout fisher, to my mind, a man should follow no other branch of fishing. It spoils his hand if he does. I myself, from the practice of striking so hard in both salmon, pike and other fishing, lose numbers of fish and flies in the course of the season ; and what makes it the more vexing is that they are nearly always the best and heaviest fish."—*Francis Francis.*

" If a pricked trout is chased into another pool, he will, I believe, soon again take the artificial fly."—*Sir Humphry Davy.*

" It is only the inexperienced and thoughtless who find pleasure in killing fish for the mere sake of killing them. No sportsman does this."—*W. C. Prime.*

" We persevered, notwithstanding the storm, and got our hundred trout, all alive and active, into Lake Salubria. They did not, however, multiply as we hoped they would. For years one would hear occasionally of a great trout being caught in the lake, till at last they were all gone. They lacked the ripples and the running water. They lived to be old, and then died without progeny, ' making no sign.' "—*S. H. Hammond.*

" The trout is such a light food, that eight of them, some ten inches long, will not make a supper for a hearty man, leading this wilderness life."—*"Porte Crayon."*

" I believe I am sincere in saying that I enjoy seeing another man throw a fly, if he is a good and graceful sportsman, quite as much as doing it myself."—*W. C. Prime.*

" I was content with my one glimpse, by twilight, at the forest's great and solemn heart ; and having once, alone, and in such an hour, touched it with my own hand and listened to its throb, I have felt the awe of that experience evermore." — *A. Judd Northrup.*

" When the May-fly is full on the water, every fish in the river is feeding."— *T. C. Hofland.*

" I never let considerations of the wind or weather interfere with angling arrangements, for the simple reason that I have so often experienced the best sport on the most unlikely days."—*R. B. Marston.*

THE POETRY OF FLY FISHING.

BY

F. E. POND.

It has been said that the angler, like the poet, is
born, not made. This is a self-evident fact. Few men
have risen to the dignity of anglers who did not in
early youth feel the unconquerable impulse to go a-
fishing. There are, of course, noteworthy exceptions,
but the rule holds good. It might be added, too, that
the genuine angler is almost invariably a poet, although
he may not be a jingler of rhymes—a ballad-monger.
Though, perhaps, lacking the art of vesification, his
whole life is in itself a well-rounded poem, and he
never misses the opportunity to "cast his lines in
pleasant places."

This is particularly true of the artistic fly-fisher, for
with him each line is cast with the poetry of motion.
Ned Locus, the inimitable character of J. Cypress'
"Fire Island Ana," is made to aver that he "once
threw his fly so far, so delicately, and suspendedly, that
it took life and wings, and would have flown away, but
that a four-pound trout, seeing it start, jumped a foot
from the water and seized it, thus changing the course
of the insect's travel from the upper atmosphere to the

bottom of his throat." Being quoted from memory, these may not be the words exactly, as Toodles would say, but the sentiment is the same. There is the true poetical spirit pervading the very air, whispering from the leaves, murmuring in the brook, and thus the sur· roundings of the angler complete that which nature began, and make him a poet. In common with other sports of the field, though in greater degree :

> " It is a mingled rapture, and we find
>   The bodily spirit mounting to the mind."

Bards have sung its praises, traditions have hallowed it, and philosophers have revelled in the gentle pastime, from the days of Oppian and Homer down to Walton, Christopher North and Tennyson.

Although the art of fly-fishing was not known to the ancients, the poetry of angling has been enriched by the bards of ye-olden-time to a remarkable degree. In Pope's translation of the *Iliad,* the following passage occurs :

> " As from some rock that overhangs the flood,
>   The silent fisher casts the insidious food ;
>   With fraudful care he waits the finny prize,
>   Then sudden lifts it quivering to the skies."

One of the most familiar of Æsop's fables, in rhyme, is that of the Fisherman and the Little Fish, while Theocritus, who flourished about the year 270 B. C., gives us a spirited idyl representing the life of a Greek fisherman. Oppian and Aristotle each prepared a classical volume on fish and fishing. Pliny in his "Historia Naturalis" treats at length of the finny tribes, and Ansonius in his poem, "Mostella," describes the tench, salmon and other varieties of fish.

Among the early contributions to English literature on angling, the "Poeticæ," generally attributed to a Scottish balladist known as Blind Harry, is conspicuous. Then the "Boke of St. Albans," by Dame Juliana Berners, and quaint old Izaak Walton's "Compleat Angler"—a brace of classic volumes dear to the heart of all who love the rod and reel.

In modern times the literature of angling has had scores of staunch and able supporters among the writers of Britain and our own land. Sir Humphry Davy's "Salmonia"; Christopher North's essays on angling, in "Noctes Ambrosianæ"; Stoddart's Angling Songs; all these and a score of others are familiar to rodsters on both sides of the Atlantic. The clever poet and satirist, Tom Hood, discourses thus in praise of the gentle art :

" Of all sports ever sported, commend me to angling. It is the wisest, virtuousest, discreetest, best; the safest, cheapest, and in all likelihood the oldest of pastimes. It is a one-handed game that would have suited Adam himself; and it was the only one by which Noah could have amused himself in the ark. Hunting and shooting come in second and third. The common phrase, 'fish, flesh and fowl,' clearly hints at this order of precedence. * * * To refer to my own experience, I

certainly became acquainted with the angling rod soon
after the birchen one, and long before I had any practical knowledge of 'Nimrod' or 'Ramrod.' The truth
is, angling comes by nature. It is *in the system,* as the
doctors say."

It is no exaggeration to state that the real poetry of
fly-fishing, as given in the grand old book of Nature,
is appreciated to the fullest by American anglers. The
breezy air of the forest leaves is found in the charming
works of Bethune, of Herbert, Hawes, Norris, Dawson,
Hallock and many other worthies, past and present.
The modern Horace—he of the traditional white hat—
never wrote a better essay than that descriptive of his
early fishing days. The same is true of Rev. Henry
Ward Beecher, and Charles Dudley Warner's most
graphic pen picture is his inimitable sketch, "A Fight
with a Trout." The number of really good books on
American field sports is principally made up of angling
works, a fact which goes far to establish the truth of
Wm. T. Porter's assertion, namely : "No man ever
truly polished a book unless he were something of an
angler, or at least loved the occupation. He who steals
from the haunts of men into the green solitudes of
Nature, by the banks of gliding, silvery streams, under
the checkering lights of sun, leaf and cloud, may
always hope to cast his lines, whether of the rod or the
' record book,' in pleasant places."

This may be appropriately supplemented by the
opinion, poetically expressed by the same author, with

reference to the art of fishing with the artificial fly, thus : "Fly-fishing has been designated the royal and aristocratic branch of the angler's craft, and unquestionably it is the most difficult, the most elegant, and to men of taste, by myriads of degrees the most pleasant and exciting mode of angling. To land a trout of three, four or five pounds weight, and sometimes heavier, with a hook almost invisible, with a gut line almost as delicate and beautiful as a single hair from the raven tresses of a mountain sylph, and with a rod not heavier than a tandem whip, is an achievement requiring no little presence of mind, united to consummate skill. If it be not so, and if it do not give you some very pretty palpitations of the heart in the performance, may we never wet a line in Lake George, or raise a trout in the Susquehanna."

Thomson, the much admired author of "The Seasons," was in his youth a zealous angler, frequently casting his fly in the rippling waters of the Tweed, a trout-stream justly famous along the Scottish border. The poet has eulogized his favorite pastime of fly-fishing in the following elegant lines :

> "Now, when the first foul torrent of the brooks,
>   Swell'd with the vernal rains, is ebb'd away ;
>   And, whitening, down their mossy tinctur'd stream
>   Descends the billowy foam, now is the time,
>   While yet the dark brown water aids the guile
>   To tempt the trout. The well-dissembled fly—
>   The rod, fine tapering with elastic spring,

Snatch'd from the hoary stud the floating line.
And all thy slender wat'ry stores prepare ;
But let not on thy hook the tortur'd worm
Convulsive twist in agonizing folds,
Which, by rapacious hunger swallow'd deep,
Gives, as you tear it from the bleeding breast
Of the weak, helpless, uncomplaining wretch,
Harsh pain and horror to the tender hand."

*   *   *   *   *   *

" When, with his lively ray, the potent sun
Has pierc'd the streams, and rous'd the finny race,
Then, issuing cheerful to thy sport repair ;
Chief should the western breezes curling play,
And light o'er ether bear the shadowy clouds,
High to their fount, this day, amid the hills
And woodlands warbling round, trace up the brooks ;
The next pursue their rocky-channel'd maze
Down to the river, in whose ample wave
Their little Naiads love to sport at large.
Just in the dubious point, where with the pool
Is mix'd the trembling stream, or where it boils
Around the stone, or from the hollow'd bank
Reverted plays in undulating flow,
There throw, nice judging, the delusive fly ;
And, as you lead it round the artful curve,
With eye attentive mark the springing game.
Straight as above the surface of the flood
They wanton rise, or, urged by hunger, leap,
Then fix, with gentle twitch, the barbed hook ;
Some lightly tossing to the grassy bank,
And to the shelving shore slow dragging some
With various hand proportion'd to their force.
If yet too young, and easily deceiv'd,
A worthless prey scarce bends your pliant rod.

Plate XII. Description on page 273.

BASS FLIES.

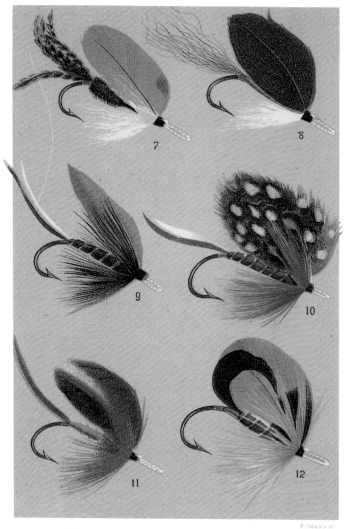

Plate XIII. Description on page 289.

BASS FLIES.

Him, piteous of his youth, and the short space
He has enjoy'd the vital light of heaven,
Soft disengage, and back into the stream
The speckl'd captive throw ; but, should you lure
From his dark haunt, beneath the tangled roots
Of pendent trees, the monarch of the brook,
Behooves you then to ply your finest art.
Long time he, following cautious, scans the fly,
And oft attempts to seize it, but as oft
The dimpled water speaks his jealous fear.
At last, while haply o'er the shaded sun
Passes a cloud, he desperate takes the death
With sullen plunge : at once he darts along,
Deep struck, and runs out all the lengthen'd line,
Then seeks the farthest ooze, the sheltering weed,
The cavern'd bank, his old secure above,
And flies aloft, and flounces round the pool,
Indignant of the guile.   With yielding hand,
That feels him still, yet to his furious course
Gives way, you, now retiring, following now,
Across the stream, exhaust his idle rage,
'Till floating broad upon his breathless side,
And to his fate abandon'd, to the shore
You gayly drag your unresisting prize."

Angling, like every other manly pastime, has had
numerous assailants—some of them "men of mark,"
as in the case of Lord Byron, whose "fine phrensy" in
denouncing Walton and the gentle art failed not to
draw down upon himself the laughter of a world. The
plaint of Lord Byron runs thus :

"Then there were billiards ; cards, too ; but no dice,
Save in the clubs no man of honor plays—

Boats when 'twas water, skating when 'twas ice,
  And the hard frost destroy'd the scenting days;
And angling, too, that solitary vice,
  Whatever Izaac Walton sings or says ;
The quaint old cruel coxcomb in his gullet,
Should have a hook, and a small trout to pull it."

Another famous satirist of the old school defines angling as "a stick and a string, with a fish at one end and a fool at the other," while a third, the well-known Peter Pindar, in closing a " Ballad to a Fish in the Brook," takes occasion to say :

" Enjoy thy stream, oh, harmless fish,
  And when an angler for his dish,
    Through gluttony's vile sin,
  Attempts—a wretch—to pull thee *out*,
  God give thee strength, oh, gentle trout,
    To pull the rascal *in.*"

All who love to go a-fishing can well afford to smile at the malicious flings of morbid critics, and while recreating both mind and body in casting the mimic fly along the dashing mountain stream, think of the deluded satirists in pity rather than condemnation.

Let us, then, in unison with the quaint and charming poet, Gay :

"Mark well the various seasons of the year,
  How the succeeding insect race appear,
  In their revolving moon one color reigns,
  Which in the next the fickle trout disdains;
  Oft have I seen a skilful angler try

The various colors of the treach'rous fly ;
When he with fruitless pain hath skim'd the brook,
And the coy fish rejects the skipping hook.
He shakes the boughs that on the margin grow,
Which o'er the stream a weaving forest throw ;
When if an insect fall (his certain guide)
He gently takes him from the whirling tide ;
Examines well his form with curious eyes,
His gaudy vest, his wings, his horns, his size.
Then round his hook the chosen fur he winds,
And on the back a speckled feather binds ;
So just the colors shine through every part,
That nature seems to live again in art."

" In this rude sorte began this simple Art,
    And so remained in that first age of old,
When *Saturne* did *Amalthea's* horne impart
    Vnto the world, that then was all of gold;
The fish as yet had felt but little smart,
    And were to bite more eager, apt, and bold;
        And plenty still supplide the place againe
        Of woefull want whereof we now complaine.

" But when in time the feare and dread of man
    Fell more and more on every liuing thing,
And all the creatures of the world began
    To stand in awe of this vsurping king,
Whose tyranny so farre extended than
        That Earth and Seas it did in thraldome bring;
        It was a work of greater paine and skill,
        The wary Fish in Lake or Brooke to kill.

" So, worse and worse, two ages more did passe,
    Yet still this Art more perfect daily grew,
For then the slender Rod invented was,
    Of finer sort than former ages knew,
And Hookes were made of siluer and of brasse,
        And Lines of Hemp and Flaxe were framed new,
        And Sundry baites experience found out more,
        Than elder times did know or try before.

" But at the last the Iron age drew neere,
    Of all the rest the hardest and most scant,
Then lines were made of Silke and subtile hayre,
    And Rods of lightest Cane and hazell plant,
And Hookes of hardest steele inuented were,
        That neither skill nor workmanship did want.
        And so this Art did in the end attaine
        Vnto that state where now it doth remaine."
                            —*John Dennys* (1613)

A PERFECT DAY.

GEO. W. VAN SICLEN.

————

I TAKE my rod this fair June morning, and go forth
to be alone with nature. No business cares, no roar of
the city, no recitals of others' troubles and woes which
make the lawyer a human hygrometer, no doubts nor
fears to disturb me as, drinking in the clear, sweet air
with blissful anticipation, I saunter through the wood-
path toward the mountain lake. As I brush the dew
from the bushes around me, I spy in a glade golden
flowers glowing on a carpet of pure green, mingled
with the snowy stars of white blossoms; with their fragrance comes the liquid, bell-like voice of the swamp-
robin, hidden from curious eyes. Soon seated in my
boat, I paddle to the shade of a tall, dark hemlock and
rest there, lulled by the intense quiet. Ever and anon
as I dreamily cast my ethereal fly, a thrill of pleasure
electrifies me, as it is seized by a vigorous trout.

I have long classed trout with flowers and birds, and
bright sunsets, and charming scenery, and beautiful
women, as given for the rational enjoyment and delight
of thoughtful men of æsthetic tastes. And if

" By deeds our lives shall measured be,
    And not by length of days,"

then a perfect life has been lived by many a noble trout
whose years have been few, but who, caught by the fisher's lure (to which he was predestined, as aforesaid),
has leaped into the air and shaken the sparkling drops
from his purple, golden, crimson, graceful form and
struggled to be free, to the intense delight of the artist
who brought him to the basket, where he belonged.

Thus resting, and floating apparently between the
translucent crystal and the blue ether, silent, I have
felt the presence of a spirit who inspires one with pure
thoughts of matters far above the affairs of daily life
and toil, of the universe and what lies beyond the blue
sky, and of the mind and soul of man, and his future
after death.

I *love* the mountains, and the meadows, and the
woods.

Later satisfied, but not satiated, with fair provision
of corn, and wine, and oil, and my creel well filled, the
shadows lengthen and the day begins to die.

Some day I shall hear no more forever the birds sing
in the sylvan shade.   My eyes will no more behold the
woods I love so well.   For the last time my feet will
slowly tread this woodland road, and I shall watch for
the last time the changing shadows made by the clouds
upon the hillsides.

There will come a time when the setting sun will
paint the west as the bridegroom colors the cheek of

the bride ; but I shall not know it, and I shall never again share such hours of peace with the leafy trees. Then, with folded hands upon my quiet breast, my friends will briefly gaze upon my face and I shall be gone. In that last day, so full of deepest interest to me, may my soul be pure.

Filled with such thoughts, I regret that I cannot express them like the poet, whose name I know not, but whose words I will recall :

" Good-bye, sweet day, good-bye !
I have *so* loved thee, but I cannot hold thee ;
Departing like a dream the shadows fold thee.
Slowly thy perfect beauty fades away ;
　　Good-bye, sweet day.

" Good-bye, sweet day, good-bye!
Dear were the golden hours of tranquil splendor.
Sadly thou yieldest to the evening tender,
Who wert so fair from thy first morning ray.
　　Good-bye, sweet day.

" Good-bye, sweet day, good-bye !
Thy glow and charm, thy smiles and tones and glances
Vanish at last and solemn night advances.
Ah! couldst thou yet a little longer stay.
　　Good-bye, sweet day.

" Good-bye, sweet day, good-bye!
All thy rich gifts my grateful heart remembers,
The while I watched thy sunset's smouldering embers
Die in the west beneath the twilight gray.
　　Good-bye, sweet day."

As the balsam-breathing night wind begins to blow, I turn my back upon the silver glancing of the moonlight on the rippling waves of the fairy lake, and step bravely into the darkness of the woods, where I cannot see the places where my foot shall fall, but I know that others have safely passed it before, and that I shall find comfort and home at the end.

NOTE.—" Description of a day on Balsam Lake (headwaters of the Beaverkill) where no house was ever built. From the lake it is two miles through the woods (about *ten miles in the dark*) to the nearest house,"—*Extract from letter accompanging article.*

"I handle this 'brown hackle' as gently as a relic, not alone because it is the memento of an unusual achievement, but because the sight of it brings up vividly before me the beautiful lake where the trout lay ; its crystal waters; the glinting of its ruffled surface as the bright sun fell upon it; the densely wooded hills which encircled it; the soughing of the tall pines as the summer's breeze swept through their branches; and the thrill which coursed through every nerve as trout after trout leaped to the cast, and, after such manipulation and 'play' as only those who have had personal experience can comprehend, were duly captured."— *George Dawson.*

" Don't be in too great a hurry to change your flies."—*Francis Francis.*

1. Brown Hackle.	2. Scarlet Hackle.	3. White Hackle.
4. Yellow Hackle.	5. Ginger Hackle.	6. Gray Hackle.
7. Black Hackle.	8. Coch-y-Bonddu.	9. Gray Hackle.
1. Emerald Gnat.	2. Black Gnat.	3. Soldier Gnat.
	Pennell Hackles.	
1. Brown Pennell.	2. Yellow Pennell.	3. Green Pennell.

" And now we have got through the poetry of the art. Hitherto things have gone happy as a marriage bell. I unhesitatingly declare, and I confidently appeal to my brother Angler, whether he, a fly fisherman, does not feel similarly. To me fly-fishing is a labor of love; the other is labor – alone. But notwithstanding such are my feelings, it by no means follows that every one else so fancies it. Every one to his taste."—*Capt. Peel* (" *Dinks* ")

" When Spring comes round, look to your tackle with careful inspection, and see that all are in perfect order. Above all, look well to your flies; reject all specimens that have been injured by use, and all frayed gut lengths. It is better to throw away a handful now, than to lose flies and heavy fish together the first time you fasten to a rise."—*Charles Hallock.*

" That hook is for a very little fly, and you must make your wings accordingly; for as the case stands it must be a little fly, and a very little one too, that must do your business."—*Charles Cotton.*

" For some reason which I have not succeeded in fathoming, the yellow fly always seems to kill best in the position of dropper, or bob-fly, and the green when employed as the stretcher, or tail-fly. The brown can be used in either position."—*H. Cholmon-deley-Pennell.*

" Note that usually, the smallest flies are best; and note also, that the light flie does usually make most sport in a dark day; and the darkest and least flie in a bright or clear day."—*Izaak Walton.*

" No description with pen or tongue can teach you how to cast a fly. Accompany an expert and watch him."—*T. S. Up de Graff, M.D.*

"There is no more graceful and healthful accomplishment for a lady than fly-fishing, and there is no reason why a lady should not in every respect rival a gentleman in the gentle art."— *W. C. Prime.*

" Everything which makes deception more alluring should be resorted to by an Angler; for, let his experience be ever so great, he will always find opportunities to regret his deficiencies."— *Parker Gilmore.*

"The Bisby Lake trout are not partial to the artificial fly, though occasionally one is taken. The lure of this kind that is most successful is a slate-olive colored fly remotely resembling the caddis fly, and this they are more likely to take when trolled a few feet under water, than when cast and drawn on the sur face."—*Richard U. Sherman.*

" The water is full, I'll try a red hackle, its tail tipped with gold tinsel ; for my dropper I'll put on a good-sized coachman with lead-colored wings."— *Thaddeus Norris.*

SUGGESTIONS

CHARLES F. ORVIS.

DURING my long intercourse with the angling fraternity, I have always found its members very ready to receive and impart suggestions, in the most friendly manner. It appears to me that those who are devoted to "the gentle art," are especially good-natured; and while very many have their own peculiar ideas as to this or that, yet they are always willing and anxious to hear the opinions of others. Believing this, I am prompted to make a few suggestions, in regard to fly-fishing for trout, and the tackle used for that purpose ; and if I differ from any, which will be very likely, I trust that what appears erroneous will be regarded charitably ; and if I shall be so fortunate as to make any suggestions that will add to the enjoyment of any "brother of the Angle," I shall be content.

The rod, of course, is of the first importance in an outfit, as very much depends on its perfection.

For ordinary fly-fishing for trout, a rod from ten to twelve feet in length will be found most convenient.

I use a ten-foot rod, and find it meets all my requirements.

It is well to let your rod have weight enough to have some "back-bone" in it; *very* light and *very* limber rods are objectionable, because with them one cannot cast well against, or across the wind; and it is impossible to hook your fish with any certainty—especially with a long line out—or to handle one properly when hooked.

A *very* limber rod will not re-act quickly enough, nor strongly enough to lift the line and fix the hook firmly; because, when the upward motion is made, in the act of striking, the point of the rod first goes down; and, unless it is as stiff as it will do to have it and cast well, it will not re-act until the fish has found out his mistake and rejected the fraud.

Rods ten to twelve feet long should weigh from seven and one-half to ten and one-half ounces, depending on the material and weight of mountings, size of hand-piece, etc. Many, perhaps, would say, that eight to ten ounces, for a single-handed fly-rod, is too heavy; that such rods would prove tiresome to handle. Much depends on how the rod hangs. If a ten-ounce rod is properly balanced, it will be no harder work to use it than a poorly balanced seven-ounce rod—in fact, not as fatiguing. Some men can handle an eleven-foot rod with the same ease that another could one that was a foot shorter. Hence, the rod should be adapted to the person who is to use it.

The stiffness of a split bamboo rod is one of its great

merits. When I say stiffness, I mean the steel-like elasticity which causes it to re-act with such quickness.

For material for fly-rods, bamboo ranks first, lance-wood next; after mentioning these, there is not much to say. Green-heart is too uncertain. Paddlewood is very fine, but as yet, extremely difficult to obtain in any quantity.

The balance, or " hang," of a rod is of the greatest importance. Let it be never so well made otherwise, if not properly balanced it will be worthless.

The elasticity should be uniform, from tip to near the hand; a true taper will not give this, because the ferules interfere with the uniform spring of the rod. For this reason a little enlargement between the ferules should be made, to compensate for the non-elasticity of the metal. These enlargements cannot be located by measurements, as much depends on the material and the length of the joint.

Spliced rods can be made nearer a true taper, for obvious reasons; although there is no doubt that a spliced rod is stronger and much more perfect in casting qualities, yet they require such care to preserve the delicate ends of the splice, and are so troublesome in many ways, that few will use them.

The details of rod-making having been so often told, I do not purpose making any suggestions on that subject, but will say that, in order to make a good fly-rod, the maker ought to know how to handle it, when finished.

I believe in a very narrow reel, and use one that is only one-half inch between outside plates. As both outside and spool plates are perforated, my line never mildews or gets tender. Hence, it is unnecessary to take the line off to dry it, as should be done when solid reel plates are used.

With such a reel my line never tangles. If your reel be narrow between plates, and large in circumference, it will take up line rapidly, and obviate the use of a multiplier, which is objectionable for fly-fishing. A light click is desirable, just strong enough to hold the handle and keep the line from over-running. More friction is of no use, and may cause you the loss of many fish.

Experience satisfies me that you should use your reel on the under side of your rod, with handle towards the right—because the weight of the reel so placed holds the rod in proper position without your giving it a thought, and your right hand finds the reel handle without trouble ; because your reel is thus entirely out of the way of your arm ; because with the rod always in proper position, your left hand finds the line every time, to draw it from the reel when wanted for a longer cast ; because with the reel on the under side the rod is always exactly balanced, and you will not have to grasp it with anywhere near the force required with the reel on the upper side. And you can make your casts with ease and lay out your flies gently and more accurately than you could with the firmer grip needful to be kept on the rod with the reel in the latter position, and because, without constant attention, your reel is never on the upper side of the rod to any certainty, but anywhere and everywhere. Keep your reels well oiled.

Enamelled, or water-proof, braided silk, tapered, American fly-lines, are the best made for fly-fishing. It is important that the size of the line should be adapted to the rod. A heavy line on a very light rod would be bad. A very light line on a heavy rod would be worse. No. 3 or E, and No. 4 or F, are the two best sizes. I find many are inclined to use too light lines, supposing the lighter the line the less trouble there will be in casting it. This, I think, is an error.

It is impossible to cast well against or across the wind, with a very light line ; and very light lines do not "lay out" as easily or accurately as heavier ones.

Leaders, or casting lines, I like rather heavy, proportionate to the line. To use a very light leader on a No. 4 line is not well ; for what is the leader but a continuation of the line ? Therefore it should approximate the size of the line, that there may be no sudden change in size where the leader begins, in order that the flies shall keep ahead, where they belong.

Leaders should be made with loops at proper intervals, to which the flies are to be attached. Leaders with such loops will last at least twice as long as those without them.

Three flies are generally used ; perhaps two are just as good. But I use three and often find the increased number to work well, as presenting a greater variety to the fickle notions of the many trout, and it is best to take all the chances.

The first dropper loop should be about thirty inches from the stretcher, or tail-fly. Second dropper, twenty-four inches above first dropper—depending somewhat on the length of the leader. Let the flies be as far apart as I have indicated. A greater distance is not objectionable—a *lesser* is.

Leaders should be tapered and made of the best quality of round gut. " Mist colored " or stained leaders are, by many, thought to be better than the clear white gut ; but I must say I never have been able to see that they are, or that there is any difference, practically. There is no great objection to the colored leaders, and I use them myself usually. I will not undertake to settle the much-discussed question. Either plain or colored are good enough, if properly made and from good gut.

Always let your leader lie in the water awhile before commencing to cast, that the gut may soften—or you may lose your leader, fish and temper, and blame some one because you think you have been cheated, when no one was in fault but yourself in your haste. When you have finished fishing, wind your leader around your hat, and the next time you use it it will not look like a cork-screw, and bother you half an hour in casting.

To one who has not acquired the art of fishing with the fly, let me suggest that a day or two with an expert will save much time and trouble. There are many

Plate XIV. Description on page 307.

BASS FLIES.

Plate XV. Description on page 327.

BASS FLIES.

little things that cannot well be described, and would take a long time to find out by experience, that can be learned very quickly when seen. It is not easy to tell one exactly how to fish with the fly.

I remember well my first trout; I remember as well, the first fine rod and tackle I ever saw, and the genial old gentleman who handled them. I had thought I knew how to fish with the fly; but when I saw my old friend step into the stream and make a cast, I just wound that line of mine around the "pole" I had supposed was about right, and I followed an artist. (I never used that "pole" again.) I devoted my time that afternoon to what to me was a revelation, and the quiet, cordial way in which the old gentleman accepted my admiration, and the pleasure he evidently took in lending to me a rod until I could get one, is one of the pleasant things I shall always retain in memory.

To really enjoy fly-fishing one must be able to cast at least fairly well; to cast a very long line is not at all important—to cast easily and gently is. Fifty to sixty feet is all that is necessary for practical purposes, the great majority of trout are taken within forty feet.

It is not easy to tell one how to cast. The art must be acquired by practice. As I have said, much can be learned by observing an expert. There is one great mistake made by most beginners; *i. e.,* far too much strength is used. Let me suggest to the novice to begin with the line about the length of the rod; learn to lay that out gently, and as you take your flies off the

water, do it with a quick movement, decreasing the
motion until your rod is at an angle of not quite forty-
five degrees behind you, this angle to be varied according to circumstances which cannot be foreseen. Then
the rod must come to a short pause, just long enough
to allow the line and leader time to straighten out
fairly, no more. Then the forward motion must be
made with a degree of force and quickness in proportion to the length of line you have *out*, decreasing the
force until the rod is about horizontal ; do not bring
your rod to a sudden stop, or your line and your flies
will come down with a splash and all in a heap ; but
lay your line out gently, my friend, and your flies will
fall like snowflakes. It is not muscle but " gentle art "
that is required. " Take it easy " and keep trying.

In an open space, from a boat for instance, take
your flies very nearly straight off the water ; never
dropping the point of your rod much to the right,
as this leaves your line on the water and makes it hard
to lift. Take your flies up with a quick movement,
nearly vertical, and wait for them to straighten and
cast again directly towards the point to which you wish
them to go.

After you have acquired the skill to cast straight
before you will be time enough for you to practise side
casts, under casts, etc., that you will have to use where
there are obstacles before and behind you. The same
movements to cast and retrieve your lines, will apply
under all circumstances, whether in open water or on

streams overhung with trees, or fringed with bushes. Much vexatious catching of flies may be avoided by not being too eager, and by not using too long a line. Let me add—just before your flies touch the water, draw back your rod slightly and gently; this will straighten the line, and your flies will fall exactly where you want them.

Cast your flies so that they fall as lightly as possible, with your leader extended to its full length; then draw your flies in the direction you wish, being careful not to draw them too far, or you will have trouble in retrieving your line for another cast. With your rod too perpendicular you cannot lift your line quickly enough to carry it back with sufficient force to straighten it out, and your next cast will be a failure. There is also much danger of breaking your rod. Usually you will get your rise just an instant after your flies touch the water, or before you have drawn them more than a little distance. It is better to cast often and draw your flies back just far enough so that you can easily lift your line for another cast. Moreover, with your rod too perpendicular it is not easy to hook your fish ; so cast often and cover all parts of the pool.

I think most skilful fly-fishers draw their flies with a slightly tremulous motion, to make the flies imitate the struggles of an insect, and I believe it to be a good method. It certainly is not objectionable, and you will find it can be done without thought ; the habit once formed and it will be difficult for you to draw your flies otherwise.

The instant you see a rise at one of your flies, strike quickly, but not too strongly, nor with a long pull, but with a short, sharp motion, not too strong or long enough to raise even a small fish from the water, but just enough to drive the hook firmly in. This may be done by an upward and inward motion, or a side motion, as circumstances may dictate. A slight turn of the wrist is often all that is required ; but if you have a long line out, you will have to use your arm and more force. Your fish hooked, keep him well in hand ; don't give him any more line than is necessary. When he is determined to run, let him do so ; but keep your fingers on the line and put all the strain on him you safely can, increasing the strain the further he goes. Turn him as soon as possible, and the instant you have done so, begin to reel him in. When he runs again, repeat the dose and get his head out of the water a little as soon as you dare. This exhausts him quickly. Don't raise him too far out of the water, or in his struggles he will break loose.

Should a fish try to run under the boat, reel up until your line is no longer than your rod, or nearly so, then firmly guide him around the end—remembering always " it is skill against brute force."

In stream-fishing, always wade if you can. When fishing from a boat never stand up if you can help it, but learn to cast sitting down. It is just as easy if you once learn how. On streams it is better to wade, because your feet produce no jar for you cannot well raise them out of the water, and dare not often. And for various reasons a person alarms the fish less in wading than in fishing from the bank.

Fish down stream always if possible. You can, in so doing, look over the pools and approach them to the best advantage. It is easier to wade with the current, and as you cast your flies you can let them float naturally for just an instant, without their being drawn under the surface. This instant is the time that, in a great majority of cases, you get your rise. Every one who has fished much with a fly knows how often he has whipped every inch of a pool and failed to get a rise where he was sure his flies could be seen from any part of it, and at last, when he placed his flies in one particular spot, his hopes were realized in an instant.

Why did not the trout rise before? Because he waited until his food came to him.

In streams, especially, trout usually rise an instant after the flies touch the water, and I believe that trout in streams commonly wait for their food to come to them, and do not often dart out from where they are lying to any great distance, but wait until the fly comes nearly or quite over them, and then rise to the surface and take the fly with a snap and instantly turn head down to regain the position they had left. In doing this they often turn a somersault and throw themselves out of the water; as they go over, their tails come down on the water with a splash, which some persons think is intentionally done to strike the fly or insect in order to kill or injure it and then afterwards capture it. Such persons fail to see the trout's head at all, for very often it barely comes to the surface, but the quick motion to go down throws the tail up and over—hence the error, as I consider it. Any one who will take the trouble to throw house flies to trout in an aquarium, will never again think trout strike their prey with their tails.

The kinds of flies to be used vary with the locality, stream, state and stage of the water, weather, etc. The fly that pleased the fancy of the trout to-day—to-morrow perhaps in the same stream and under the same conditions, as far as any one could see, would fail. The only way is to keep trying until the one is found that *does* please. Don't change too often, but give each "cast" a fair trial.

I do not believe in certain flies for certain months in the year. I have stood up to my knees in snow and taken trout, in mid-winter, with the same flies I had used in mid-summer.

In low, clear water, especially in streams, small flies should be used. In higher water, larger flies are better, as a rule. When the water is high—as early in the season—larger and brighter-colored flies may be used to more advantage. Later, when the water is low and clear, smaller flies and more sober colors are best. I believe, however, that rules for the choice of flies have a great many exceptions, and the best rule I know of, is to keep trying different kinds and sizes until successful.

It is often said, "there is no need of so great a variety of flies." I do not think this is true. Doubtless there are many styles that might well be dispensed with, but one never knows which to discard, and no man can tell him, for the very flies one man would say were worthless, another would consider the best—and prove it, plainly, by the success he had had with that very fly. So it is well to be provided with many kinds and sizes. I have learned of the merits of so many different kinds of flies that I sometimes think nearly all are good—at some time or under some circumstances. There is much doubt in my mind as to the necessity of having the artificial flies like the insects that are near or on the water. One of the best flies that has ever been known—the Coachman—does not in the least resemble any known insect, I believe—and but few of the many patterns made imitate anything in nature. The Cowdung fly, another one of the most "taking" flies—*does* very much resemble the natural fly of that name—but I never saw or heard of their being on or near the water.

Early in the season, while the weather is yet cold, the middle of the day is usually quite as good, and I think the best time for fly-fishing. Later, in warm weather, the evening is the best, and often the last two hours of a pleasant day are worth all the rest of it.

Generally speaking, a gentle southerly breeze is the most favorable wind ; yet I have had splendid sport during a strong north-easterly wind, but not often.

In conclusion, be patient and persevering, move quietly, step lightly, keep as much out of sight of the fish as possible, and remember, trout are not feeding all the time. Perhaps during the last hour before dark you may fill your basket, that has been nearly empty since noon. Don't give up, as long as you can see —or even after—and you may when about to despair take some fine large fish.

Unless one can enjoy himself fishing with the fly, even when his efforts are unrewarded, he loses much real pleasure. More than half the intense enjoyment of fly-fishing is derived from the beautiful surroundings, the satisfaction felt from being in the open air, the new lease of life secured thereby, and the many, many pleasant recollections of all one has seen, heard and done.

" Doubt not, therefore, sir, but that angling is an art, and an art worth your learning ; the question is, rather, whether you be capable of learning it, for angling is somewhat like poetry, men are to be born so : I mean with inclinations to it, though both may be heightened by discourse and practice ; but he that hopes to be a good angler must not only bring an inquiring, searching, observing wit, but he must bring a large measure of hope and patience, and a love and propensity to the art itself ; but having once got and practised it, then doubt not but angling will prove to be so pleasant that it will prove to be like virtue, a reward to itself."—*Izaak Walton.*

" The black bass are unquestionably as fine a fish for angling purposes as any we possess, and as an article of food are equal to our best."—*Parker Gilmore.*

1. Cheney.   2. White Miller.
3. La Belle.   4. Scarlet Ibis.
5. Shad-Fly.   6. Green and Gold.

"Never use too much power in casting ; it is not only not necessary, but it is injurious. You cast the line with the top and half the second joint, and very little force suffices to bring this into play. If you use more, all the effect is to bring the lower part of the rod into action, which has very little spring compared with the top of it."—*Francis Francis.*

" Although trout are taken with numerous grub and angle worms, still frequently all these will fail, and a brilliant colored imitation of a fly will lure them, and herein largely consists the science of the fisherman, in judging what style of fly is appropriate to a peculiar state of the atmosphere or locality."—*T. Robinson Warren.*

" Black bass when struck and played will always head down stream."—*W. C. Harris.*

" Fish always lose by being 'got in and dressed.' It is best to weigh them while they are in the water. The only really large one I ever caught got away with my leader when I first struck him. He weighed ten pounds."—*Charles Dudley Warner.*

" The aim of the angler ought to be, to have his artificial fly calculated, by its form and colors, to attract the notice of the fish ; in which case he has a much greater chance of success, than by making the greatest efforts to imitate any particular species of fly." —*Professor Rennie.*

" I fear it will be almost deemed heresy to place the black bass on a par with the trout ; at least, some such idea I had when I first heard the two compared ; but I am bold, and will go further. I consider he is the superior of the two, for he is equally good as an article of food, and much stronger and untiring in his efforts to escape when hooked."—*Parker Gilmore.*

" The one great ingredient in successful fly-fishing is patience. The man whose fly is always on the water has the best chance. There is always a chance of a fish or two, no matter how hopeless it looks. You never know what may happen in fly-fishing."— *Francis Francis.*

" In bass fishing we have thought the moon to be an advantage. If it does not guide the prey to the lure, it at least lends beauty to the scene and bathes in its pale light the surroundings of the fisherman, which are often so exceedingly beautiful. In addition, it assists him in his work and enables him to handle his tackle more easily and play his fish more comfortably."—*Seth Green.*

" Recreation and amusement are the objects we seek ; and therefore is it not reasonable to conclude that whatever methods and whatever appliances best conduce to these results are the best in themselves, even though the total catch were a little diminished thereby ?"—*Henry P. Wells.*

THE RESOURCES OF FLY-FISHING.

BY

DR. JAMES A. HENSHALL.

THE charms of fly-fishing have been sung in song and story from time immemorial by the poetically gifted devotees of the gentle art, who have embalmed the memory of its æsthetic features in the living green of graceful ferns, in the sweet-scented flowers of dell and dingle, and in the liquid music of purling streams.

The fly-fisher is a lover of Nature, pure and simple, and has a true and just appreciation of her poetic side, though he may lack the artist's skill to limn her beauties, or the poet's genius to describe them.

> " To him who in the love of Nature holds
> Communion with her visible forms, she speaks
> A various language."

And what delightful converse she holds with the fly-fisher, as with rod and creel he follows the banks of the meandering stream, or wades its pellucid waters, casting, ever and anon, the gossamer leader and feathery lure into shadowy nooks, below sunny rapids, over foam-flecked eddies, and on silent pools. She speaks to him through the rustling leaves, murmurs to him from the flowing stream, and sighs to him in the summer breeze. She is vocal in a myriad of voices, and manifest in innumerable ways.

The still fisher, reclining on the mossy bank, is disposed to dreamy reveries, to pleasant fancies; but the fly-fisher, with quickened senses, has an ear for every sound, an eye for every object, and is alive to every motion. He hears the hum of the bee, the chirp of the cricket, the twitter of the sparrow, the dip of the swallow; he sees the gay butterfly in its uncertain flight, the shadow of the drifting cloud, the mossy rock, the modest violet, the open-eyed daisy; he is conscious of the passing breeze, of the mellow sunlight, of the odors of the flowers, of the fragrance of the fields. Nothing escapes his keen notice as he casts his flies, hither and yon, in the eager expectation of a rise.

Fly-fishing is, indeed, the poetry of angling. The capture of the salmon is an epic poem, the taking of the trout an idyl. But it is not my presumptuous purpose to ring the changes on the delights of salmon or trout fishing, for they have been immortalized by the pens of gifted anglers for ages. My feeble effort would be but a sorry imitation of those glorious spirits who have made their last cast, who have crossed to the other side of the river, and

> " Gone before
> To that unknown and silent shore."

So, leaving the salmon, the trout, and the grayling to their well-earned laurels, I wish to say a word for several less pretentious, because less known, game-fishes, whose merits are perhaps as great for the fly-fisher as those familiar game-beauties of the waters.

It is among the possibilities, in this world of transitory things, that fly-fishing for the salmonids in the United States will, in the near future, be known only by tradition. It should, therefore, be a source of great consolation to the fly-fisher to know that there are now, and perhaps will ever be, in the streams and lakes of this broad land, percoid game-fishes equally worthy of his skill, which require only to be known to be properly appreciated.

First among these is the black bass, which already ranks the brook trout in the estimation of those anglers who know him best ; and when I say black bass, I include both species. The black bass is, at least, the peer of the trout in game qualities, and in rising to the artificial fly, under proper conditions. An allusion to a few of these conditions may not seem out of place.

As a rule, the best time of day for fly-fishing for the black bass is from an hour before sunset until dark, though there are times when he will rise to the fly at almost any hour of the day.

It is important that the angler keep out of sight, and that the shadow of his rod be not disclosed to the wary and suspicious bass ; for if he sees either, he will not notice the flies, however skillfully and coaxingly they may be cast. Thus it is that the earlier and later hours of the day are best ; the angler, facing the sun, the

shadows are cast far behind him ; or, before sunrise or
after sunset, or on cloudy days, the shadows are not so
apparent, and the bass are more apt to rise. If the fly-
fisher for black bass will faithfully follow these precau-
tions, he will not be disappointed at the result.

There is another condition, equally important, that
must ever be borne in mind : The black bass will rise
to the fly only in comparatively shallow water, say from
one to six feet in depth. This is a feature often overlooked by many fly-fishers in their first experiences in
black bass fishing. They seem to think that he should
rise to the fly in any situation where he can be taken
with bait ; but a moment's consideration will show this
to be fallacious. A brook trout will take a bait twenty
feet below the surface, but will not rise to a fly from
the same depth. Trout streams are generally shallow,
while the salmon swims very near the surface ; thus it
is that the angler is seldom disappointed in their rising
to the fly. On the other hand, the black bass, while
inhabiting larger and deeper streams, is, unlike the
trout, a great rover, or forager, frequenting both deep
and shallow waters. As a rule, he is in shallow water
early in the season, retiring to the depths in the hottest
weather; again appearing on the shallows in the fall,
and in winter seeking the deepest water to be found.
Trout inhabiting deep ponds and lakes rise to the fly
only when in comparatively shallow water, or when near
the surface. The fly-fisher, therefore, must expect to
be successful only when the proper conditions exist. I

would like to pursue this subject further, but in so brief an article as this, only the most general and important features can be noticed.

Any good trout fly-rod, from ten to eleven feet long, and from eight to nine ounces in weight, will answer for black bass fishing; the heavier rod to be used only where the bass run quite large, averaging three pounds or more. The best line is one of braided silk, tapered, waterproof, and polished. The leader should be six feet of strong single gut, and but two flies should be used in the cast. As to flies, the angler must take his choice. My experience has led me to confine myself to a dozen varieties for black bass fishing, and they are usually, though not always, best in the order named: Polka, King of the Waters, Professor, Oriole, Grizzly King, Coachman, Henshall, Oconomowoc, Red Ibis, Lord Baltimore, White and Ibis, and the various hackles (palmers), the best being the brown. The Abbey, or Soldier, may often be substituted for the King of the Waters, being similar in appearance, and others may be substituted in like manner for several in the above list.

The Polka, Oriole, Oconomowoc and Henshall, are flies of my own designing, and are usually very killing, especially the Polka. Their construction is as follows:

POLKA.—Body, scarlet, gold twist; hackle, red; wings black with white spots (guinea fowl); tail, brown and white, mixed.

ORIOLE.—Body, black, gold tinsel; hackle, black;

wings, yellow or orange ; tail, black and yellow, mixed.

OCONOMOWOC.—Body, creamy yellow ; hackle, white and dun (deer's tail) ; tail, ginger ; wings, cinnamon (woodcock).

HENSHALL.—Body, peacock herl ; hackle, white hairs from deer's tail ; wings, light drab (dove); tail, two or three fibres of peacock's tail-feather.

The Lord Baltimore fly originated with Prof. Alfred M. Mayer, of the Stevens Institute of Technology, Hoboken, New Jersey, its formula being as follows :

LORD BALTIMORE.—Body, orange ; hackle, tail, and wings black, with small upper wings of jungle-cock.

Professor Mayer and myself, being natives of Baltimore, designed, unknown to each other, a fly to embody the heraldic colors of Lord Baltimore and the coat of arms of Maryland—black and orange. He named his fly, "Lord Baltimore," while mine I designated the "Oriole," from the Baltimore oriole, or hanging bird, which beautiful songster was named in honor of Lord Baltimore, its colors being black and orange.

Black bass flies should not be too large, nor yet too small, the largest brook trout flies being about the right size. They should be tied on Sproat or O'Shaughnessy hooks, the first-named being the best, from Nos. 2 to 5. In the above list of flies, most of them are "general" flies, one of which, at least, can be used in the cast under almost any circumstances. The darkest ones are best for bright days and clear water, the brighter ones for dark days or high water, and the lightest ones, *e. g.*, Coachman and White and Ibis, after sundown.

There are several other inland fishes belonging to the same family (*Centrarchidæ*) as the black bass, which, though generally lightly esteemed, are good pan-fishes, are quite gamy, will rise eagerly to the fly, and in the absence of more desirable fishes, afford good sport to the fly-fisher with light and suitable tackle.

The ROCK BASS (*Ambloplites rupestris*), sometimes called " Red-eye," is well-known west of the Alleghanies. Its color is olive-green, with dark mottled markings and brassy and coppery reflections. The iris of the eye is scarlet. The dorsal fin has eleven spines and eleven soft rays ; anal fin, six spines and ten soft rays. It has a large mouth, rises well to the fly, and when it attains its maximum weight of a pound or two, fights vigorously on a six-ounce fly-rod and light tackle. Any of the " general " trout flies, tied on Sproat hooks, Nos. 5 to 7, will answer for rock bass.

The CALICO BASS (*Pomoxys sparoides*), variously known as " Northern Croppie," " Strawberry Bass," " Grass Bass," " Silver Bass," " Chincapin Perch," etc., is a very handsome fish, bright green and silvery, with purplish reflections, and numerous dark spots or blotches. The fins are also much mottled, especially the anal fin. It has a smaller mouth, and is not quite so gamy as the rock bass, but is, withal, a great favorite with many anglers. The radial formula of its fins are : Dorsal, seven spines, fifteen soft rays ; anal, six spines, eighteen soft rays.

The SOUTHERN CROPPIE (*Pomoxys annularis*) is also called " Bachelor," " Tin-mouth," " Speckled-perch," " New-light," "Campbellite," etc. It is closely allied to the last-named species, but is not quite so deep in body, and has a larger, thinner, and more delicate mouth. It is also much lighter in color, olivaceous, and silvery, sometimes quite pale, with much smaller spots, and the anal fin is pale and scarcely marked. Its dorsal fin has but six spines, and fifteen soft rays ; anal fin, six spines, eighteen rays. Both the "Croppies" have large anal fins, fully as large as the dorsals. They grow to two or three pounds in weight, usually swim in schools, and lurk about logs, brush, or fallen trees, under dams, etc. They give fair sport on a five-ounce rod. Trout flies of subdued tints should be used for croppies, as the gray, brown and red hackles, gray drake, brown drake, stone fly, black gnat, blue dun, etc.

The BLACK SUNFISH (*Chænobryttus gulosus*), known in the South as the " War-mouth Perch," is more nearly related to the black bass than any other member of the family in its large mouth, the radial formula of its fins, and to some extent in its coloration ; it also partakes of the gamy nature of the black bass to no inconsiderable degree. Its color is dark olive-green on the back, the sides lighter, with blotches of blue and coppery red, the belly brassy or yellowish ; iris red ; ear-flap black, bordered with pale red. It has teeth on the tongue. Dorsal

fin, ten spines, nine soft rays ; anal, three spines, eight
rays. With a six-ounce fly-rod, and any of the flies
named for black bass, the fly-fisher will find this fish
worthy of his steel, as it grows to two pounds in
weight.

The BLUE SUNFISH (*Lepomis pallidus*) is a very
common and widely-diffused species. In the South, it
is known as .the " Blue Bream," and " Copper-nosed
Bream." Its mouth is quite small. In color it is olivaceous or bluish-green, with a distinct dusky spot on the
last rays of dorsal and anal fins. The dorsal has ten
spines, eleven rays ; anal, three spines and ten soft rays.
It is closely allied to the following species.

The LONG–EARED SUNFISH (*Lepomis megalotis*), or
" Red-bellied Bream," or " Red-bellied Perch," of the
Southwest, is one of the handsomest sunfishes. Its
color is bluish on the back, with the belly red or orange ;
cheeks with blue and red stripes ; colors very brilliant ;
iris bright red ; ear-flap very large, black, with pale
border. Dorsal fin with ten spines, ten soft rays ; anal,
three spines, ten rays. Both this and the last-named
species are quite wary, very gamy, and are greatly esteemed by Southern anglers, and not without reason.
When they reach a pound or two in weight they furnish
excellent sport on a five-ounce rod. Any of the trout-
flies of gay patterns, as Red Ibis, White and Ibis,
Professor, Grizzly King, etc. on Sproat hooks, Nos. 8 to
10, will answer, if the day be not too bright, in which
event less showy flies should be used. As a rule, any of

the hackles (palmers), are good flies for these or any fishes of this family.

The striped-bass group, or sub-family (*Labracinæ*), is composed of some of our best game-fishes. They will all rise to the fly, but more especially the fresh water species. Those of the coast, the striped-bass or rock-fish (*Roccus lineatus*), and the white perch (*Roccus americanus*), when they enter brackish and fresh-water streams, are frequently taken with a gaudy fly.

The WHITE BASS (*Roccus chrysops*), also called "Striped Lake Bass," and "Fresh-water Striped Bass," is a well-known game-fish of the great lakes and Upper Mississippi Valley, and is rightly held in much favor by western anglers. Its color is silvery, darker above, with a number of dark stripes along the sides, four or five being above the lateral line. The mouth is large. There are two distinct dorsal fins, being entirely separated. The first dorsal has nine spines; the second dorsal, one spine and fourteen soft rays; anal fin has three spines and twelve soft rays. A patch of teeth on base of tongue. Its usual weight is one to three pounds, though it is occasionally taken up to four or five pounds. It is good game, rises well to the fly, and on a six or seven-ounce rod is capable of giving fine sport.

The YELLOW BASS (*Roccus interruptus*), or "Brassy Bass," or "Short Striped Bass" takes the place of the white bass in the Lower Mississippi Valley, and is closely allied to it, though it usually does not grow so large by a pound or two. It has a smaller mouth, and has no teeth on the base of its tongue. Its color is brassy, olivaceous above, with seven very black stripes along its sides. The dorsal fins are somewhat connected at the base. First dorsal has nine spines ; second dorsal has one spine and twelve soft rays ; anal fin, three spines, nine soft rays. Any of the flies recommended for the black bass, though made smaller and tied on Sproat hooks, Nos. 4 to 6, will be found excellent for the white and yellow bass.

In the perch family (*Percidæ*) are several species that are excellent for the table, and not to be despised as game-fishes. The most commonly known is

The YELLOW PERCH (*Perca americana*), which inhabits most of the waters of the Northwest and East, being found in both fresh and brackish waters. In color it is dark olive with yellow sides, and some half-dozen dark vertical bars ; upper fins, dusky yellowish ; lower fins, reddish. Mouth moderate in size. First dorsal fin has thirteen spines ; second dorsal, one spine and thirteen soft rays ; anal, two spines, eight soft rays. It grows usually to a pound, though sometimes to double that weight. It rises pretty well at times, to a small gaudy fly, and on a five-ounce rod will give considerable sport to the angler.

The PIKE-PERCH (*Stizostedium vitreum*), likewise known as " Wall-eyed Pike," " Glass Eye," and in some waters called "Salmon," and in Canada known as " Pickerel," is a fine table fish, growing occasionally to fifteen or twenty, and even to forty pounds, though its usual weight is from four to six pounds. Its color is a greenish-olive, mottled with brassy yellow; it has a large black spot on the first dorsal fin. Eye large. First dorsal fin has thirteen spines; second dorsal, two spines and twenty soft rays; anal, two spines, twelve rays.

There is a much smaller variety of this species (var. *salmoneum*), which grows to but two or three pounds. It has a larger eye. Its color is bluer, or greener than the above, and not so brassy. First dorsal has fourteen spines; second dorsal, one spine, twenty soft rays; anal fin, two spines, thirteen soft rays.

Both of these fishes, together with the next-named, are hard-pulling, vigorous fishes on the rod, though they do not exhibit much dash or take much line. They swim away rather slowly, but are constantly jerking, tugging and pulling on the line in such a way as to compel the angler to handle them carefully to preserve his tackle intact. They are regarded with much favor by anglers in the West and Northwest. The same tackle is used as for black bass.

The SAUGER (*Stizostedium canadense*) is also called "Jack," "Sand-pike," "Gray-pike," and "Rattlesnake-pike." It is closely related to the foregoing species, though smaller, growing to a length of twelve to fifteen inches. It is longer and rounder in proportion than any of the pike-perches, with a more pointed head and smaller eye. Its color is paler, grayish above, with brassy sides, which are marked by several blackish blotches or patches. First dorsal fin has two or three rows of round black spots. First dorsal has twelve spines ; second dorsal, one spine, seventeen soft rays ; anal, two spines, twelve soft rays.

Both species of pike-perch are nocturnal (the last not so much so), and are very similar in their habits. Usually they rise best to the fly at sundown, continuing until late in the evening, especially on moonlight nights ; therefore at least one fly in the cast should be some light-colored fly, as the Coachman, White and Ibis, or Miller. Sometimes, however, darker flies are just as good after nightfall as during daylight. The flies for pike-perch should be as large or larger than bass flies, and should be tied on Sproat hooks, Nos. 1 to 3.

The angler who is so unfortunately situated as to be debarred from salmon, trout, or black bass fly-fishing, can always find in the small streams or ponds near him, one or more of the fishes described in the foregoing account, when, by the use of very light and suitable tackle, he can enjoy to a great degree the delights and pleasures of fly-fishing.

Even the despised pike or pickerel species (*Esocidæ*) and some of the catfishes will rise to a large and gaudy fly. In Florida I have taken catfish with the artificial fly until my arms ached and I was fain to cry quits. I have also taken many marine species with the fly, as red-fish, blue-fish, sea-trout, snappers, groupers, crevalle, bone-fish, snooks, etc., etc., and once, as a matter of experiment, a five-foot alligator. The 'gator was taken with a "fly" tied on a shark-hook, the hackled body being a squirrel's tail, with wings of a small seagull. The rod, used on that occasion only, was a light pine sprit (belonging to the sail of a small boat), fifteen feet in length, an inch and a half in diameter at the centre and tapering to an inch at each end.

Thus it will be seen that the opportunities and resources for fly-fishing are nearly as great as for bait-fishing, and that it only remains for the angler to take advantage of them, study the habits of the fishes, attain the necessary skill in casting, and practice due caution in fishing.

" All the charm of the angler's life would be lost but for these hours of thought and memory. All along a brook, all day on lake or river, while he takes his sport, he thinks. All the long evenings in camp, or cottage, or inn, he tells stories of his own life, hears stories of his friends' lives, and if alone calls up the magic of memory."— *W. C. Prime.*

"It is a mooted question among the very best 'fly-fishers,' whether an exact representation of the living insect is necessary to insure success in angling with the fly. The Scotch flies are not imitations of living insects ; and the best anglers in that country maintain the opinion that it is absolutely useless and unnecessary to imitate any insect either winged or otherwise."— *" Frank Forester."*

7. Henshall.	8. " Oconomowoc."
9. Oriole.	10. Polka.
11. Ondawa.	12. " W. T."

" Sometimes, of course, the loss of fish, or even fish and tackle, cannot be avoided : but good, careful work and the best materials will frequently obviate so annoying an ordeal. However, having struck your fish, the tackle and your own coolness are generally responsible for the issue, and woe betide you if careless knot or indifferent tying should have been made in constructing your leader or fly."—*Parker Gilmore.*

" It is well known that no person who regards his reputation will ever kill a trout with anything but a fly. It requires some training on the part of the trout to take to this method. The uncultivated, unsophisticated trout in unfrequented waters prefers the bait ; and the rural people, whose sole object in going a-fishing appears to be to catch fish, indulge them in their primitive taste for the worm. No sportsman, however, will use anything but a fly, except he happens to be alone."—*Charles Dudley Warner.*

"The true fly-fisher, who practises his art *con amore*, does not delight in big catches, nor revel in undue and cruel slaughter. He is ever satisfied with a moderate creel, and is content with the scientific and skilful capture of a few good fish. The beauties of nature, as revealed in his surroundings—the sparkling water, the shadow and sunshine, the rustling leaves, the song of birds and hum of insects, the health-giving breeze—make up to him a measure of true enjoyment, and peace, and thankfulness, that is totally unknown to the slaughterer of the innocents, whose sole ambition is to fill his creel and record his captures by the score."
—*James A. Henshall, M.D.*

"In the fly book the sportsman collects his treasures—the fairy imitations of the tiny nymphs of the water side—and it is the source of much delight in inspecting, replenishing and arranging during the season that the trout are safe from honorable pursuit."—*R. B. Roosevelt.*

"There have been caught in Walden, pickerel, one weighing seven pounds, to say nothing of another which carried off a reel with great velocity, which the fisherman safely set down at eight pounds, because he did not see him. I am thus particular, because the weight of a fish is commonly its only title to fame."— *Henry D. Thoreau.*

"Wet days in camp try 'grit.' 'Clear grit' brightens more crystalline the more it is rained upon ; sham grit dissolves into mud and water."—*Theodore Winthrop.*

"'I ain't got no objection to them fellers with the jinted poles. And I don't mind nuther their standin' off and throwin' their flies as far as they've a mind to. But what does rile me is the cheeky way in which they stand up and say there isn't no decent way of fishin' but their way. But if you feel tetchy about it you can send me *one of them poles in three pieces, a good strong one.*'"— *Frank R. Stockton.*

WINTER ANGLING.

BY

FRANK. S. PINCKNEY.

THE best winter angling is to be had in that charming interval between the hallowed old holidays and that
sloppy period which, of late years, heralds the slow
approach of spring in these our latitudes.

The practice of angling at this season of the year for
large trout, immense black bass and preternatural
mascalonge, has grown of late to proportions which
seem to warrant some special mention of so delightful,
if unseasonable, a sport, as well as some brief description of the tackle and paraphernalia required for its
fullest enjoyment.

To the winter angler a first-class outfit is of prime
importance. The poles should be of well-seasoned
hickory or hard maple, from eight to ten inches in
diameter, in sections about three feet in length. These
need not to be divested of their rich covering of bark,
curved, bronzed and lichened, but should be fitted,
fresh from the sheltered pile, with careful skill into an
old-fashioned open fire-place, about which, in years
agone, the angling forefathers of the angler of to-day
told marvellous tales of deeds of " derring do " with

"dipseys," bobs and poles; and about which now *his* children list with wonder, not unmingled with some tinge of incredulity, to his yet more wondrous recitals of brave contests and curious captures with dainty rods and delicate reels.

The winter angler's wading shoes may be made of any soft materiai that will protect his feet should they chance to slip from the old brass fender down upon the sombre painted brick hearth below, during some delicious drowse. Most anglers have lady friends— fair cousins and others, who make them nicely with substantially embroidered lily-pads and firm strong rosebuds and vigorous elastic daffadowndillys. These are a good protection—but the soles ?

Two dollars and a half, without hob nails, and no deduction for small feet ! Even winter angling has its drawbacks.

The winter angler's fishing coat should be warmly quilted to protect him from the cold, and may be of a color to suit his complexion if he has one. It should be given him by his wife or " ladye faire " as a sample of her skill in manipulating the needle and—the dressmaker.

As to the kind of lure required, much must depend upon the taste of the individual angler, but it certainly ought to be hot and not have *too* much water in it.

For protection against black flies, midgets and mosquitoes he may, if he likes, smear his face and hands with oils either of tar or of pennyroyal, or he may build a "smudge" on the library table, but the most successful winter anglers I know use for this purpose a hollow tube of convenient length with a bowl at one end and a set of teeth, either real or artificial, at the other. The bowl may be filled with any harmless weed capable of burning slowly as, for example, tobacco. As a rule, one of these will answer the purpose, but if the flies are especially troublesome, or the angler should chance to be bald-headed, he may be forced to ask a brother angler to come to his assistance with a contrivance of a similar nature. Together they will probably be able to defy all attacks of the black flies or even the blues.

As to creels (or baskets) the merest mention will suffice. At the nearest newspaper office will be found one of suitable size and fair proportions. It is called a "waste basket" and is specially constructed to hold the abnormal catches made by winter anglers.

Possibly the highest charm of winter angling (or as some call it "Fireside Fishing") is the grand wide ranging freedom of it. Three vast realms are at one's command. The realm of Memory, with its myriad streams of recollection filled with the fish and fancies of the Past. The realm of Anticipation bright with golden dreams of the coming open season, and lastly the realm of Pure Lying, wherein from the deep, dark pools of his own inner turpitude the angler at each cast hooks a speckled-sided Hallucination (*Salmo Hallucionidus*), a large-mouthed Prevarication (*Mi-*

cropterus Prevaricatrix), or a silver-gleaming False-hood (*Salmoides Falsus*), each more huge than the other, and all "beating the record" quite out of the field.*

What wonderful vistas, what remotely narrowing perspectives, stretch away into the vague distances of the first two of these grand realms! How far reachingly the life-lines of anglers uncoil in both directions from the reel of time—"playing" the hoarded treasures of memory at one end, and making tournament casts into the future with the other! Are not the time-worn rod-case and the well-thumbed fly-book and note-book on his table, side by side with the last daintily tapered product of his plane, rasp and scraper—his rod, just finished for the coming summer—which, perchance for him may never come?

Is he not at once revelling in the past and dreaming of the future?

There is no sport, when known in all its branches, that is so fully an all-the-year-round delight as is angling.

Many an idle hour of the long winter evenings may be pleasantly passed by the angler in "going over" his tackle, oiling his reels, airing his lines, and re-arranging his flies, freeing them from the moth and rust that do corrupt. He is but a slovenly worshipper at the

---

* NOTE—The writer respectfully submits this nomenclature to revision by Dr. Henshall, an unquestioned authority.

shrine of the good Saint Izaak, who casts aside his panoply after the last bout of autumn and gives no thought to it again till spring makes her annual jail-delivery of imprisoned life. Constant care of the belongings of his art, be he fly or bait fisher, is characteristic of the faithful angler, and only simple justice to the tackle maker. There is nothing sadder or more dejected-looking than a crippled rod and a neglected "kit" full of snarled lines, rusty hooks, and moth-eaten flies.

In the matter of winter angling, the fly-fisherman has a decided advantage over him who uses bait alone. The art for him has more side issues. He may, if he can, learn to tie flies or contrive and construct new-fangled fly-books. The effort to learn will probably ruin his temper and break up his domestic relations if he has any, but it is not for me to say that "*le jeu ne vaut pas la chandelle.*" If no domestic ties trend him toward caution as yet, and he dreads none in the future, he may even venture the attempt to make his own rods.

Let me say a word here of amateur tackle-making from the standpoint of personal experience. It is agreeable—it is even fascinating, but it does not *pay;* very few have the mechanical deftness, the patience, taste, and judgment combined to really excel in any of its branches. No young man with a career to make for himself by dint of constant toil or close application to a business or profession has any right to devote to these arts the time and attention they demand if even a fair degree of skill is to be attained. For the angler of "elegant leisure" this has no weight perhaps, but he too will, as a rule, find better tackle than he can make, readily at his command at a cost so inconsiderable as to quite justify me in saying that his amateur work will not *pay*—for, if he be young, out-of-door sports will far better serve to lay up in his still developing frame the treasures of health and vitality for future use. There are those, indeed, for whom it is a proper employment of time and who are endowed with the peculiar faculties required. To such it is a charming occupation, a delightful distraction, and a choice factor in the enjoyment of the winter angler by the fireside.

Every angler ought to keep a record or diary of his angling bouts. Most anglers do so, I think. Therein should be recorded not only the weight and size of daily catch, the number saved, and the number *thrown back*, (I look back with especial pride upon my record in this direction), but also some jottings of scenes, impressions, and incidents. Reading therefrom years after at the fireside he will detect a faint perfume of old forests in the winter air, and hear again in fancy the swirl of swift waters sweeping among mossy rocks.

I take up my own, quoting from it almost at random. Note, if you please, how, in untamed words, have expressed themselves the exhilaration of the stream—the tingling of healthy blood through ample veins—the joy

in nature's aspects, and the delightful sense of unre-
straint that comes only of fresh air, of wholesome exercise, of angling.

"*May* 20*th.*— * * * The streams hereabout lack
two important elements which are the charm of my
favorite —— kill, *to wit,* picturesqueness and the possibility of large trout—large, I mean, for our mountain
brooks where still found *au naturel.* I went over the
other day to Bright's Run. I don't know exactly
where it is, and I consider it (next to Bright's disease
of the kidneys) the very worst thing Bright has developed. It is a stream such as might properly empty
into the Dismal Swamp, and find itself quite at home
there. It is totally devoid of romantic beauty—and
nearly so of trout. I never worked so hard in my life
for twenty-two little ones, that put me to the blush as
I put them in the basket. I was perpetually in a row
with the overhanging thickets and the underlying logs,
and my thoughts were a monologue of exclamation
points. I would not angle in Bright's turgid waters
again for all the trout the most minute analysis might
discover in them.

" Yesterday I had a much more agreeable day without
a seven-mile ride on a pesky buck-board. I went quite
alone, up the Buckhill as far as the Fall. This is a
pleasant stream full of Nature—and sawdust—with
here and there a speckled trout and here and there a
black snake. (By special permission of Mr. Tennyson.)
There really are now and then cool little nooks which

make one envy the trout; and an occasional spring
dripping with a fresh *rat-tat-tat* over rocks and moss
and into one's whiskey in spite of all one can do. This
sort of thing is what makes a trout-stream after all.
You may catch a whale in a goose-pond but it isn't
angling. To me much depends upon surroundings. I
like to form a picturesque part of a picturesque whole.
Even when there is no audience in the gallery.

"Given, a dark glen fringed with pines that sigh and
pine high up aloft—a pool whose sweep is deep, around
which rocks in tiers, mossy as tombstones centuries
old, bow their heads in mourning—heads crowned
with weeds, and grave-mounds of mother earth, and
pallid flowers, pale plants and sapless vines that struggle
through shadows of a day in coma, laid in the hearse
of night, without a proper permit, and I am happy. I
don't know just why, but if I meet an undertaker I
mean to ask him. All these deep, dark hiding spots of
nature seem but so many foils to the keen sense of
life and thrills of vitality that fill me. My nervous
system sparkles against such sombre back-grounds.

"Then, too, the Fall was lovely. Next to Niagara,
the Kauterskill and Adams', this Buckhill Fall is one
of the most successful, in a small way, that I know of.
It might be bigger and higher and have twenty-five cents
worth more water coming over it out of a dam; but for
a mere casual Fall gotten up inadvertently by nature, it
is very good, in an amateurish sort of a way, you know!

"There is, I believe (hang it, there *always* is !) a romantic legend connected with—but stay !—you already guess it. Big Buck Indian—years ago—in love with mother-in-law—commits suicide — jumps over the ledge—ever since on moonlight nights, water the color of blood (probably tannery just above the Fall), Buck Kill, now corrupted into Buckhill. In the march of civilization the last *impedimenta* to be left by the way-side are the beautiful superstitions of ignorance.

"I am now quite alone here. A young music composer, hitherto my companion, left yesterday, so I am hand-cuffed to nature in solitary confinement.

"By the way, my composer was a voluntary exile from the domestic arena. He had but recently married—to formulate it by proportions—say about a ton of mother-in-law to about an ounce of wife, and when the contest waxed fiercer than became the endurance of a sensitive nature, he packed his bag and came a-fishing. He was a capital angler—a phenomenal musician and had an appetite and digestion like one or more of the valiant trencher men of England's merrie days, so he solaced his grief with Sonatas and buckwheat cakes in the mornings and tears and ginger-bread in the evenings. He was a born genius and as beautiful as a dream, so I advised him to go home, choke his m–in–l, kiss his wife and live happily all the days of his life. I think he has gone to try the plan.

"Speaking of buckwheat cakes, you can go out here most any time and catch a nice mess running about a half a pound and *game* all the way through. No ! No !

I'm thinking of the trout !   I mean they are light as a
feather, and taste to me just as did those I never had
half enough of when I was a lad with my good old
Presbyterian grandmother, who would not 'set' the
batter on Saturday night lest it should 'work' on the
Sabbath.

"Just here I wish to record an event which has happened to me while yet each detail is fresh in my memory.

" The day had been showery, yet the fishing had been
very poor, so I went at sunset to try my luck in the
stream near the house, ·where are some fair pools and a
semi-occasional trout.

" The darkness had begun to gather, indeed it was so
dark that I knew only by the instinct of habit where
my flies fell upon the water, for I could not fairly see
them.   I had just made a cast across a little rock which
protruded somewhat above the surface into a small pool
behind, and was slowly drawing my line toward me,
when I perceived a frog seated upon the rock, watching
the proceedings with some apparent anxiety.   Hardly
had I made out his frogship in the gloaming, when
pop ! he went into the water.   'Kerchung !'   At this
instant I felt a *strike* and returned the compliment
sharply, so as to set my hook well in and make sure of
my trout.   He was very *game*, and I was obliged to play
him with a five and a half ounce rod for some time, but
finally landed him in good form, only to discover that
instead of a trout I had taken froggy on a black hackle

fly, setting the hook firmly into the thin membrane
which connects the two hind legs and just where the
tail *ought* to be.   This left him the fullest freedom of
action and gave him so good a chance to fight me that
I never suspected him of being anything less than a
half-pounder.   He must have jumped from the rock
directly on to the fly trailing behind it and been thus
hooked by my 'strike.'   MEM.—This story is true as
gospel, but better not tell it where you enjoy an exceptional reputation for veracity.

"*July* 10*th*. * * * Nothing has happened!   Nothing
ever does happen here.   Delightful existence, free from
events !   I remember hearing Homer Martin once say that
it was the height of his artistic ambition to paint a picture
without objects.   The confounded objects, he said, always would get wrong and destroy his best effects.   How
far this was intended to be a humorous paradox and how
far the suggestion of an artistic ideal, I know not, but
I surely somewhere have seen a painting—from whose
brush I cannot say—which quite nearly fulfilled this
strange condition.   It represented an horizon, where
met a cloudless, moonless, starless summer sky and a
waveless, almost motionless sea—these and an atmosphere.   The effect was that one could hardly perceive
where the sea ceased and the sky began.   I wonder if
it would not be thus with a life quite devoid of events
—would one be able to distinguish such from Heaven ?

" The charm of it is that it leaves both the physical
and intellectual in one to develop freely.   When a cow,

grazing in a woodland pasture, comes at noonday to the
brook to drink and then calmly and not without a certain ungainly majesty of movement, crosses the deep
pool and climbs the steep bank on the other side, by no
apparent motive urged save of her own sweet will, she
always looks refreshed and filled in some sort with the
stolid bovine expression of great contentment.   Mark
how different it all is when the same cow crosses the
same brook driven by the barefooted urchin with a gad
and shrill cries and a possible small dog in the background.   How wearily and breathlessly she wades, and
with what distressful pantings she climbs, and how un-
happy and enduring and long-suffering she appears, as
you watch her shuffle away down the cow-path homeward !   It's the Must that hurts.   It's the barefooted
urchin Necessity with his infernal gad Ambition and his
ugly little cur dog Want, always chasing and shouting
after one, that makes it so tiresome to cross the stream.

"Then, too, as to the mind.   Shall not one gain better
intellectual growth when beyond the reach of the im-
perial ukase of daily custom which fixes the mind upon
and chains the tongue to some leading event of the
passing hour ?

"In swift and endless succession come foul murders,
robberies, revolutions, sickening disasters, nameless
crimes, and all the long list of events, and are as so
many manacles upon the mind.

"I hate Events.   They bore me.   *All except taking*
a pound trout.

"Alas! what a rent these last words make in the balloon I have been inflating! Logic (another troublesome nuisance, evolved, probably, at Hunter's Point) forces me from the clouds to earth and insists that I shall accept a trite aphorism: 'Little events fill little minds; great events for big ones.'

"Then if I take refuge in the cowardly device of saying I don't want a big mind, what becomes of my theory of intellectual development as the outgrowth of an eventless life!

"I decline to follow out more in detail this or any other line of argument. One can't argue in the face of such an event as the thermometer in the nineties away up here in the mountains.

"This chance allusion to logic reminds me that I have recently heard from a dear old angling friend. He writes incidentally that since his return to his active professional duties he has made money enough to pay many times over the expenses of his recent two weeks' fishing bout with me. I have written him that he might find it well to start at once upon another trip. I have no doubt there exists a certain correlation of forces whereby a week's fishing, with its resultant increase of oxygenation, and rebuilding of gray tissue, accurately represents a certain amount of possible mental labor and thus, indirectly, a fixed sum of money.

"It is then alarming to think how abnormally rich a man might become if he fished all the time."

If I have thus quoted somewhat at length vaporings

of other days from my note book it has been only to suggest to others, whose angling experiences are and have been wider and more varied than my own, how readily they can organize a " preserve " for winter angling. Believe me, no event, no feeling, no passing observation of your surroundings can be too trivial to record, and each written line will, in years to come, suggest a page of pleasant memories when as " Nessmuk " says—

> " The Winter streams are frozen
> And the Nor'west winds are out."

"Mr. Webster's sport of angling has given him many opportunities for composition, his famous address on Bunker Hill having been mostly planned out on Marshpee Brook ; and it is said that the following exclamation was first heard by a couple of huge trout immediately on their being transferred to his fishing-basket, as it subsequently was heard at Bunker Hill by many thousands of his fellow-citizens : ' Venerable men ! you have come down to us from a former generation. Heaven has bounteously lengthened out your lives that you might behold this joyous day.' "—*Lanman's Life of Webster.*

" Now, I love fishing dearly. There is no sport like it for me. but there is a vast deal in fishing besides catching fish."—*H. H. Thompson.*

    13. The Triumph.   **14. Alexandra.**
    15. Seth Green.   **16. Jungle Cock.**
    17. Fitz-Maurice.   **18. Caddis.**
             19. Davis.

" When fish are basking during the mid-day hours in the hot summer months, they are not always to be drawn to the surface. But the combination more suitable for this method is the dressing known as the ' Alexandra Fly.' "—*David Foster.*

" The exertion of crossing the Atlantic for fly-fishing will be amply repaid the sportsman by the quantity and weight of the fish he will capture ; for there the fish are not troubled with the fastidiousness of appetite which in Great Britain causes it always to be a source of doubt whether the water is in proper order, the wind in the east, or thunder overhead, either of which, or all combined, too frequently cause the most industrious to return, after a long and laborious day, with an empty basket."—*Parker Gilmore.*

"Of all places, commend me, in the still of the evening, to the long placid pool, shallow on one side, with deeper water and an abrupt overhanging bank opposite. Where the sun has shone all day, and legions of ephemera sported in its declining rays ; the bloom of the rye or clover scenting the air from the adjoining field ! Now light a fresh pipe, and put on a pale Ginger Hackle for your tail-fly, and a little white-winged Coachman for your dropper. Then wade in cautiously—move like a shadow—don't make a ripple. Cast, slowly, long, light ; let your stretcher sink a little. There, he has taken the Ginger—lead him around gently to the shallow side as you reel him in, but don't move from your position—let him tug awhile, put your net under him, break his neck, and slip him into your creel. Draw your line through the rings—cast again ; another and another—keep on until you can see only the ripple made by your fly ; or know when it falls, by the slight tremor it imparts through the whole line down to your hand—until the whip-poor-will begins his evening song, and the little water-frog tweets in the grass close by ; –not till then is it time to go home."—*Thaddeus Norris.*

"You may always know a large trout when feeding in the evening. He rises continuously, or at small intervals—in a still water almost always in the same place, and makes little noise— barely elevating his mouth to suck in the fly, and sometimes showing his back-fin and tail. A large circle spreads around him, but there are seldom any bubbles when he breaks the water, which usually indicates the coarser fish."—*Sir Humphry Davy*

"It is not difficult to learn how to cast ; but it is difficult to learn not to snap the flies off at every throw."—*Charles Dudley Warner.*

"I esteem the color of the fly's body of far greater importance than that of the wings."—*Hewett Wheatley.*

NOT ALL OF FISHING TO FISH.

BY

A. NELSON CHENEY.

" We cast our flies on many waters, where memories and fancies and facts rise, and we take them and show them to each
other, and, small or large, we are content with our catch."— *W.
C. Prime.*

The commonly accepted definition of fly-fishing is
the casting—with a light, strong, elastic, pliant rod—
of two, three or four artificial flies, on a delicate leader
attached to a fine tapered silk line, over the surface of
waters inhabited by the lordly, silver-coated salmon;
that aristocratic beauty, the speckled trout, or the
more sombre-colored but gamy black bass.

This, in truth, is called the acme of fishing, the
highest degree attainable in the school of the angler.
But of what a small portion, comparatively, of the
pleasure of angling does the mere casting of the fly,
however artistic, and the creeling of the fish, however
large, consist.

If it were all of fishing to fish ; if fish were only to
be obtained in pools in a desert waste that never reflected leaf or twig ; from walled-in reservoirs, where
fish are fattened like a bullock for the shambles ; from

sluggish, muddy streams within the hearing of great towns, redolent of odors that are bred and disseminated where humanity is massed between walls of brick and mortar, or even from a perfect fish preserve, where everything is artificial except the water ; or if the beginning of fishing was making the first cast and the end the creeling of the last fish, would the gentle art under such conditions have been a theme for the poet's pen, a subject for the artist's brush, or a topic for the interesting story during the centuries that have passed since the first line was written, or the first words sung ? *I* think not.

Fishing for the fish alone would not have inspired Dame Juliana Berners, Izaak Walton, Charles Cotton, Sir Humphry Davy, John Bunyan, Sir Walter Scott, "Christopher North," and other and more modern writers to tell of the peace, the quiet, the health and the pleasure to be gained in the pursuit of this pastime.

The skill exercised and the delicate tackle used by a past master of the art would have been unnecessary to cultivate or fashion, solely to supply the brain with food through the alimentary canal.

An angler's brain is fed by absorption as well as by assimilation.

There might be reason in calling a fisherman with an eye simply to the catching of fish, a "lover of cruel sport," but the cruelty would be of the same kind, but in a less degree, as that displayed by the butcher who supplies our tables with beef and mutton.

To an angler the pleasures of the rod and reel are far-reaching and have no boundary save when the mind ceases to anticipate and the brain to remember. I have had the grandest sport on a midwinter's night with the snow piled high outside and the north wind roaring down the chimney, while I sat with my feet to the blaze on the hearth, holding in my hand an old fly-book. The smoke from my lighted pipe, aided by imagination, contained rod, fish, creel, odorous balsam, drooping hemlock and purling brook or ruffled lake. I seemed to hear the twittering birds, leaves rustled by the wind and the music of running water, while the incense of wild flowers saluted my nostrils. The heat of the fire was but the warm rays of the sun and the crackle of the burning wood the noise of the forest. Thus streams that I have fished once or twice have been fished a score of times.

I had nothing to show for the later fishings, but I could feel that God was good and my memory unimpaired. The fish in the pipe-smoke has been as active as was the fish in the water, and afforded as fine play. My reel has clicked as merrily in the half-dream as on the rod in the long ago, and my rod has bent to the play of the fish as though it were in my hand instead of lying flat on a shelf in a cool room up-stairs. I have had in my musings all the pleasure of actual fishing, everything but the fish in the flesh.

When Winter comes and the ravages in tackle have been repaired and all is in perfect order for another season, I put my rods where they will not be injured by the modern furnace heat, each joint of each rod placed flat on a shelf. But the tackle trunk, securely locked that no vandal hand may get to its treasures, is where my eye rests upon it daily, and my fly books are in one of the drawers of my writing desk where I can easily reach them. When I take one of the books out of an evening, or at any time during my waking hours in early winter, I generally seek out some tattered fly that is wrapped carefully in a paper and placed in one of its pockets. The book may be full of flies, sombre or gorgeous in all the freshness of untried silk, mohair, feathers and tinsel ; but take for instance this one with the legend written on its wrapper :

"Puffer Pond, June, 1867.—Thirty-five pounds of trout in two hours. The last of the gentlemen that did the deed."

This, to me, tells the story of a very pleasant week spent in the Adirondacks. I remember, as I hold the ragged, faded fly in my hand and see that it still retains something of the dark blue of its mohair body and the sheen of its cock-feather wings, that it was one of six flies that I had in my fly-book that June day that stands out from other June days, in my memory, like a Titan amongst pygmies. The fly had no name, but the trout liked it for all that, and rose to it with as much avidity as though they had been properly introduced to some real bug of which this was an excellent counterfeit.

That glorious two hours' time—with its excitement of

catching and landing without a net some of the most
beautiful and gamy fish that ever moved fin—comes
back to me as vividly as though at this moment the
four walls of my room were the forest-circled shores of
that far-away pond, and I stand in that leaky boat,
almost ankle deep in the water that Frank, the guide,
has no time to bail, occupied as he is in watching my
casts and admiring my whip-like rod during the play
of a fish, or fishes, and in turning the boat's gunwale
to the water's edge to let my trout in when they are exhausted. It is sharp, quick work, and the blue-bodied
fly is always first of all the flies composing the cast to
get a rise, until I take off all but the one kind, and
then one after another I see them torn, mutilated and
destroyed. Later they will be put away as warriors gone
to rest and the epitaph written on their wrappings :

" Thy work was well done ; thy rest well earned."

Now there is no time to mantle the fallen or sing
pæans to the victors ; the action is at its height. I put
my last blue fly on my leader and cast it again and
again with success, before those dark open jaws, that
come out of the water every time it falls on the surface,
have destroyed its beauty forever. Frank says the time
is up and we must go.

The boat, propelled with broken oars, is headed for
the landing-place, and I sit back in the stern admiring
those sleek beauties that lie in the bottom, and that have
fought so well and so vainly. My rod is inclined over
my shoulder and the blue fly is trailing on the water

\stern. Suddenly I feel a twitch and hear a splash,
and turning around find I am fast to a fish, the noblest
Roman of that day's struggle. Once, twice, thrice he
shows himself in all his fair proportions.

" Two pounds and a half, if an ounce," says Frank.

I get down on my knees in the water of the cranky
boat, as the reel sings the merriest tune that ever
delighted the ear of an angler. Two or three mad
dashes, and I think the trout is tiring. I reel him
slowly in, but the sight of the boat gives him new life
and he darts under it in spite of my efforts to swing
him around the stern. The rod tip is passed clear of
the boat and the fight continues.

Exhausted ? The fight is only begun.

The unwieldy boat is far too slow to follow the fish,
and I see my line growing rapidly less on my reel with
no sign of weakness on the part of the fish. I am compelled to advance the butt of the rod and the tip droops
nearer and, hesitatingly, still nearer to it, as though
the tip would whisperingly confess that the strain is
greater than it can bear, while the stout nature of the
wood rebels at the confession. Involuntarily I raise
myself by a muscular action as though the cords and
sinews of my body could relieve the pressure on the
lancewood and save the rod.

" You'll smash your pole ! " is the warning Frank
utters.

I care not now, for the fight has been a glorious one,
but the " pole " survives to fight many another fight ;

the trout is turned and, at last comes, side up, to the boat, vanquished but not subdued.

Here, in another paper, are three flies fastened together. A Chicken Red Palmer Hackle, a Grizzly King and a fly with black body, brown wings, red tail and tip. They are large trout flies and won honorable retirement by catching three small-mouthed black bass at one and the same time. Fishing from a boat in the Hudson River, above a long rough rapid, I cast inshore and saw the stretcher fly taken by a small bass; immediately after the two droppers were taken by other bass that did not show themselves when taking the lures. My rod was the same that I have already mentioned, an ash and lancewood of eight ounces—scale weight—and my entire attention was directed to it and the fish, that were bending it like a willow wand; when, suddenly, I discovered that the boatman had also been interested in the play of the fish and allowed the boat to drift into the swift water at the head of the rapids. The boatman made an effort to row up stream at the same time the fish decided to go down, and I found I must either smash my tackle and lose the fish—at this time I had seen but the one bass that took the stretcher fly—or run the rapids at the risk of an upset. I was very anxious to see the size of the fish that were struggling on my leader in that swift running water, and every angler will know the decision that was instantly made, to " shoot the rapids."

The sight of these old tinseled lures brings back to

me the wild excitement of that driving, whirling ride through the racing, seething waters. Hatless I crouch down in the boat, one hand clutching the gunwale of the broad river craft, and the other holding aloft my rod. I give no thought to the possible fate of the occupants of the boat. My anxiety is for the fish. When the curved line is straight again, will I feel the bass at the end or only the bare flies ? These very flies !

Very soon the boat is rocking in the lumpy water at the foot of the chute, and I stand up, fill my lungs, and find my fish are still fast. Here in the broad water I bring to net three small-mouthed bass that together weigh four and one-quarter pounds, only one of which, at any time, showed himself above water. As I put the faded flies back into their paper coverings I find that my pulse has quickened and my pipe no longer burns.

I must not exhibit all my treasures here, to the public. These old souvenirs are only for the eyes of sympathizing angling friends when we meet to blow a cloud and talk of other days.

A little brown-eyed maiden once, looking into my fly-book, asked why I had the old frayed flies tied up in separate papers and marked, while the nice new flies did not show this care. Had she been of maturer years I might have quoted Alonzo of Aragon's commendation of old friends, but instead, I merely said :

" The nice new flies I can easily buy, but no one sells such old flies, therefore I take the greater care of them because of their rarity."

The new flies will not be slighted, for they, also, have their season of admiration and caressing touch. When their day has come the old veterans of many a fight will not be forgotten either, but while maturing plans for augmenting their numbers, the recruits in their new, bright dress will be inspected to see what claims they may have for future honors.

The lengthening days and diminishing snowbanks naturally turn the angler's thoughts forward, and he sniffs the south wind as though he would discover some slight remaining odor of fragrant apple blossoms borne to him from the far southland as the forerunner of warm air, blue sky, bursting buds, open streams, green grass, "gentle spring," and time to go a-fishing. Then the untried flies are examined and speculation is rife as to their excellence, each for its own particular kind of fish.

Day dreams and evening musings give place to an activity of mind and body when fishing is under consideration. The lessons of the last season and other seasons are brought to bear to perfect all arrangements for a fresh campaign. Consultations with brother anglers are frequent, and plans many and various are weighed and discussed. The tackle box is overhauled again and again, notwithstanding the attention paid to it at the close of the last season, to be sure that nothing is wanting or left undone. Lines are tested ; leaders are subjected to the closest scrutiny to see that no flaws or chafed places exist to give way at a critical moment during some future contest, when a trifle will turn the scales; reels are taken apart and carefully oiled; rods sent to the maker for a new coat of varnish, and, perhaps, a few new whippings for the guide rings; fishing shoes, although they have a row of holes just above the soles, get an extra dressing of oil to keep the leather soft; and an inventory of the wardrobe is taken and old garments are selected that appear for the time, considering the use they are to serve, far more faultless than when first sent home by the tailor. "About these days" your business letters, if written to people into whose souls the love of angling has entered, may terminate as follows:

"*P. S.*—What are the prospects for the spring fishing in your neighborhood? Did the late freshets of last fall destroy the trout eggs deposited in the streams about you?" or, "Did the unusual severity of the winter cause destruction to the trout spawn in the headwaters of your brooks?"

Some evening when the "fever is on" you will write to a guide up in the North Woods, some honest, faithful fellow that you have known in all weathers for many seasons:

"Be sure and take a boat over to Mahogany Pond, (that is not the name of it, for its title is taken from a domestic wood that grows on its shores), before the snow goes off and keep me informed as to the condition of things, for I wish to start and be with you as soon as the water is free from ice. I shall bring a friend with me, the gentleman I told you about last summer, who knows the name of every plant that grows in the woods, as well as the name of every fish that swims in the water. The old camp, with a few repairs, will answer, as Mr. —— is an old woodsman and angler of the first order, and requires no more than the few simples that you usually take to camp. He, like myself, goes into the woods to fish and fill his lungs with the pure mountain air that you live in."

When Dick reads the letter he smiles, for it contains nothing unknown to him before. It is his own idea to carry a boat to the pond on the snow, for there is no road, path or trail, but he only says to himself :

"He's got it just as bad this spring as ever. The medicine will be ready for him."

The angler does all this and more; mind, I say the *angler*, for the other fellow that goes a-fishing because it is the thing to do, or because he has heard some one dilate upon the pleasure to be found in practising the art, will do nothing of the sort. It is too much trouble, or, more likely, these things never occur to him.

Now the man of severe aspect who, if he smiles, looks as though he wore a petrified smile that he had bought at a bargain, and whose sole ambition and pleasure is to make money, live as long as he can in doing so, and die as rich as possible; this man, if he could know, and comprehend, what is passing through the angler's mind at this season, would say such vagabonds are the cumberers of the earth; but he could not find a "cumberer" in all the land who would change places with him, take his joyless life, sapless heart, frozen visage, narrow views and great wealth, and give in return the angler's light heart, happy disposition, love of God, his fellow-man and Nature; his resources within himself, engendered by his fondness for the wild woods, to enjoy the past and anticipate the future, whatever betide; his desire to see good in every thing, his clear conscience and his fishing tackle.

Bear in mind that the pleasure of angling is not alone the consummation of your hopes for a large score. Hear what Sir Humphrey Davy says on this subject:

"From the savage in his rudest and most primitive state, who destroys a piece of game, or a fish, with a club or spear, to man in the most cultivated state of society, who employs artifice, machinery, and the resources of various other animals, to secure his object, the origin of the pleasure is similar, and its object the same: but that kind of it requiring most art may be said to characterize man in his highest or intellectual state; and the fisher for salmon and trout with the fly employs not only machinery to assist his physical powers, but applies sagacity to conquer difficulties; and the pleasure derived from ingenious resources and devices, as well as from active pursuits, belongs to this amusement. Then, as to its philosophical tendency, it is a pursuit of moral discipline, requiring patience, forbearance, and command of temper.

"As connected with natural science, it may be vaunted as demanding a knowledge of the habits of a considerable tribe of created beings — fishes, and the animals that they prey upon, and an acquaintance with the signs and tokens of the weather, and its changes, the nature of waters, and of the atmosphere.   As to its poetical relations, it carries us into the most wild and beautiful scenery of nature, amongst the mountain lakes, and the clear and lovely streams that gush from the higher ranges of elevated hills, or that make their way through the cavities of calcareous strata.   How delightful in the early spring, after the dull and tedious time of winter, when the frosts disappear and the sunshine warms the earth and waters, to wander forth by some clear stream, to see the leaf bursting from the purple bud, to scent the odors of the bank perfumed by the violet, and enamelled as it were with the primrose and the daisy ; to wander upon the fresh turf below the shade of trees, whose bright blossoms are filled with the music of the bee ; and on the surface of the waters to view the gaudy flies sparkling like animated gems in the sunbeams, whilst the bright and beautiful trout is watching them from below ; to hear the twittering of the water-birds, who, alarmed at your approach, rapidly hide themselves beneath the flowers and leaves of the water-lily ; and, as the season advances, to find all these objects changed for others of the same kind, but better and brighter, till the swallow and the trout contend as it were for the gaudy May-fly, and till in pursuing your amusement in the calm and balmy evening, you are serenaded by the songs of the cheerful thrush and melodious nightingale, performing the office of paternal love, in thickets ornamented with the rose and woodbine."

While it is not all of fishing to fish, it does not consist entirely of preparation, and it must have something substantial as a basis for the day dream or fireside musing. You must catch some fish, as capital stock, to talk about. I never knew an angler that was satisfied to do all the listening.

In my native State the law makes it legally possible to wet a hook for speckled trout, for the first time each year on April first, and this day has come to be called " Opening Day," and is spoken of in such glowing language that one might think it the opening of some vast commercial enterprise instead of the opening of the fishing season. As the result of an angler's hopes and preparations, as I have tried, imperfectly, to sketch them, I will quote from my fishing diary what is there set down as one consummation:

"*April* 1*st*, 1878.—Opening day. Fished Halfway brook from Morgan brook to, and through the woods ; then fished Ogden brook from Van Husen's road to Gleason's. Banks more than full of roily snow water ; weather decidedly cold ; strong wind from the Northwest ; cloudy sky. Caught one small trout that I returned to his native element to grow ; discovered from my single specimen of the *Salvelinus fontinalis* that they have the same bright spots that they have always had; look the same, smell the same, *feel* the same ; other peculiarities lacking. Warm sun and rain required to develop the characteristics we so much admire in our leaping friend. Managed to fall into the Ogden brook—in fact, went in without the slightest difficulty, amid applause from the bank ; discovered from my involuntary plunge that the water is just as wet as last year, and if memory serves, a trifle colder. Reached home in the evening, cold, wet, tired and hungry. Nevertheless, had a most *glorious time.*"

" If skilful, as he ought to be, the angler need fix no quivering life on his hook, but with feather and silk and downy dubbing, he makes a bait far more winning, that drops upon the curling water, or plays among the whirlpools, as though it were born for the frolic."—*G. W. Bethune, D.D.*

" The subject-matter of angling is necessarily of a somewhat limited range ; and there must, of course, be some similarity in the works of those writers who treat mainly of it in its purely practical aspects, and especially in reference to the more common branches of the art. Bearing this in mind, we should be inclined, notwithstanding the multitude of angling works which have been published during the present century, to consider the diversity of style and matter as a marked feature in the angling literature of that period."—*Rev. J. J. Manley.*

" When a fly is said to be in season it does not follow that it is abroad on every day of its existence."—*Alfred Ronalds.*

'' The amusing study of entomology is necessary to a skilful fly-fisher, who ought to be acquainted with all the various insects and flies applicable to his art, and be able to produce a close imitation of them."—*T. C. Hofland.*

" After a rain fish usually feed ; perhaps there is a little wash of mud and some worms into the river ; perhaps the rain-water raises the temperature of the stream slightly, and so hatches out flies that otherwise would have remained in their pupa cases until another day."—*Fred Mather.*

" In days when the natural flies are most numerous, the trout will not take the artificial fly so freely ; on the contrary, when these insects are rarely to be seen, if the angler can find the color that is then prevailing, and imitate it, his success will be considerably increased."—*William Blacker.*

" Much fishing, besides to a certain extent thinning the trout, operates against the angler's killing large takes, by making the remaining trout more wary, and it is more from this cause than the scarcity of trout that so many anglers return unsuccessful from much-fished streams."—*W. C. Stewart.*

" These flies, I am sure, would kill fish."—*Charles Cotton.*

" I would advise all experts to keep a well-filled fly-book. It is a pleasure to experiment, and the educated eye takes delight in looking at the varieties of colors, shapes and forms which the skilled workman in fly-art has provided as lures for the speckled beauties."—*George Dawson.*

" Fly-fishing and bait-fishing are co-ordinate branches of the same study, and each must be thoroughly learned to qualify the aspirant to honors for the sublime degree of Master of the Art."
—*Charles Hallock.*

" Americans have reason to be proud of the black bass, for its game qualities endear it to the fisherman, and its nutty, sweet flavor to the *gourmand.*"—*Parker Gilmore.*

20. Black Maria.	21. Tipperlinn.
22. Premier.	23. Grizzly King.
24. Ferguson. 2d.	25. Californian.

" 'What flies do you most affect here ?' 'Any, at times, and almost all. In some weather I have killed well with middle-sized gaudy lake-flies ; but my favorites, on the whole, are all the red, brown, orange and yellow hackles, and the blue and yellow duns.' "—*Henry Wm. Herbert.*

" The real enjoyment of camping and tramping in the woods lies in a return to primitive conditions of lodging, dress and food, in as total an escape as may be from the requirements of civilization. And it remains to be explained why this is enjoyed most by those whose are most highly civilized."—*Charles Dudley Warner.*

" Fish will frequently, although breaking freely, refuse the fly, but generally a few will be misled, and occasionally one will be caught."—*R. B. Roosevelt.*

" The *natural* and acquired skill actually necessary before any man can throw a ' neat fly,' is only known to those who have made this method of angling their study and amusement."— *" Frank Forester."*

" Luck has little to do with the size of an angling score ; for skill in handling, a knowledge of the haunts of the fish, of the conditions of wind, weather and water, character of baits to be used, of the changes and drift of tideways, sun-rays and shadows, and a familiar acquaintance with the natural history of the family pisces, their habits, habitat, and idiosyncrasies (for no other animal is so erratic as these scaly fins), all go to make up the complete angler, known as such from the days and writings of Izaak Walton, in the seventeenth, up to this great nineteenth century."— *Wm. C. Harris.*

" What is the use of my telling you what manœuvres that trout will perform before he comes to the landing-net, gently as a lamb ? I don't know what he will do ; never saw two of them act alike."— *Oliver Gibbs, Jr.*

" Probably the secret of the infatuation of this amusement to most or many of the brothers of the angle, is to be found in the close and quiet communion and sympathy with nature essential to the pursuit of the spoil of the water."— *John Lyle King.*

" The principle of the rod is in reality only this, that it is the home end of the line, stiffened and made springy, so that you can guide and manage it—cast and draw it, keep a gentle pressure with it on the hook, so that the fish shall not rid himself of it, and finally lift him to the landing net."— *W. C. Prime.*

" The Palmer hackle is never totally out of season."— *Alfred Ronalds.*

" Hold him tight, O'Shaughnessy ; you are the greatest hook ever invented."— *Thaddeus Norris.*

FLY-FISHING IN FLORIDA.

BY

DR. J. C. KENWORTHY.

THE votaries of the rod and reel have overlooked an important field for sport, for, in my opinion, no portion of the United States offers such advantages for fly-fishing as portions of Florida during the winter months. The health of the State is beyond cavil or dispute ; the climate is all the most fastidious can ask ; there is an almost total absence of insect pests, and last though not least, a greater variety of fish that will take the fly than in any other section of the Union. My own experience is mainly based on opportunities for observation on the south-west coast, and it is possible that points on the eastern coast, as the Indian River inlet and the outlet of Lake Worth, may offer advantages over the section referred to.

As far as my knowledge extends, fly-fishers are indebted to my friend, Geo. C. Johnson, of Bridgeport, Conn., for the development of fly-fishing in Florida. Some years since I met Mr. Johnson on his arrival in this city *en route* to Homosassa. He remarked that he had brought his fly-rod with him, and I suggested that a heavy bass rod would prove more serviceable.

On the evening of his arrival at Homosassa he visited the dock in front of Jones' house, and noticed fish breaking water near the shore. He proceeded to the house, rigged his rod, and was followed to the dock by a number of laughing sceptics, who ridiculed the "spindly rod and feather baits." In compliance with Mr. Johnson's request, Dr. Ferber rowed him a short distance from the dock, and the fun commenced with large-mouthed bass and red trout ; and from that evening fly-fishing became an established institution on the south-west coast of Florida. For a number of years Dr. Ferber has devoted his winters to fly-fishing on the south-west coast, and it is to be regretted that he was not requested to give his ripe and ample experience, instead of one who is far beneath him in experience and ability to wield the split bamboo or pen.

The next season after Mr. Johnson's visit to Homosassa Mr. Francis Endicott, of New York, visited the locality and indulged in fly-fishing. He informed me that he had captured with the fly eight distinct species of fish on the Homosassa River ; and I will ask where else in the United States can the devotee of the gentle art capture eight distinct species of fish with the fly on a river but ten miles in length ?

My friend, Dr. Ferber, on his return from the south-west coast in April last, visited me, and stated that he had caught on that coast, with artificial flies, eleven distinct species of fish. Among the number I may mention large-mouthed bass (trout of the South), channel bass, cavalli, ravallia, skip jacks, sea trout, brown snappers, roach, and three species of bream.

Instead of wading icy-cold and over-fished brooks, tearing clothes and flesh in creeping through briers and brush, and being subjected to the sanguinary attention of mosquitoes and black flies in bringing to creel a few fingerlings, in Florida the angler can cast his fly from a sandy beach or boat, inhale an invigorating atmosphere, bask in the sunshine, and capture specimens of the finny tribe, the weight of which can be determined by pounds instead of ounces.

Sea trout of the South are closely allied to the weak fish of the North, and frequent rapid waters, oyster beds and weedy flats. They range from one to five pounds, are good biters and make a noble resistance to avoid the landing net.

Large-mouthed black bass (trout of the South) exist in great numbers in the lakes and streams of the State. In very clear lakes and streams they are not disposed to indulge in artificial baits. As fighters they are unworthy of the notice of experts. It has been my lot to capture them in many localities, and I have found that after the first few struggles they open their mouths and come to gaff like a grain bag.

Brown snappers exist in countless numbers in some of the streams of the State—as in the Homosassa. They range from six ounces to one pound, and cannot resist the temptation to capture a hook decorated with feathers. They are good biters and full of game. Owing to the presence of a number of rat-like teeth, they play sad havoc with flies ; and we would advise those who propose engaging in the capture of this fish to provide an ample supply of feathery lures.

Skip-jacks (or bone-fish) visit the streams in schools. They range from two to six pounds. They readily take a fly and die game. Owing to their build, size of fins, and muscular devolopment, they are worthy of notice. On one occasion I was camped at Little Gasparilla pass, and at the bay side of the inlet there existed an eddy in which I could see hundreds of skip-jacks. For some time I amused myself by casting, and the moment the bait would touch the water the surface would be in a boil. I would strike and the next instant a bone-fish would be two or three feet in the air. As a rule they enter the streams with the flood tide, and as they are constantly breaking the water they can be followed in a boat. By following the fish on the flood and ebb the rodster may enjoy a number of hours of exciting sport. Between Esteno and Marco passes I have seen them for hours at a time feeding on minnows near the beach.

The Ravallia is a fish with which I am unacquainted, although I have reason to believe that it exists in quantity at certain points on the south-west coast. My friend Dr. Ferber, informed me that in one of his cruises he entered Billy Bow Legs Creek and noticed a deep pool. He made a cast and landed a ravallia. Nearly every cast he would land one or two ranging from one to three pounds, unless a ravenous cavalli interfered.

The cavalli of large size would seem to tire of the flouncing and floundering of their neighbors, and would join in the fray, when the doctor would part with a fly or leader. The doctor assured me that the sport was kept up until he was surfeited. He describes the fish as resembling a pike perch of the North, and is loud in its praise as a game fish. Friends have informed me that they have captured specimens of this fish, with cut bait, weighing thirty pounds. My impression is, that if pools and inlets south of Punta Rassa were thoroughly tried with the fly that the piscator would be rewarded with large-sized specimens.

Bream of several species exist in great numbers in many of the streams and lakes of the State. They range from four ounces to one pound, and afford considerable sport on a light rod. Roach are not plentiful, but where they exist they will not refuse a brown hackle.

In many of the streams of the State war-mouthed perch exist in numbers, ranging from one to three pounds. When the streams are low, they readily take a fly, and give the angler all he can attend to.

In some of the creeks tributary to the St. Johns' and in some of the interior lakes, pickerel exercise their snapping propensities, and do not object to appropriate a gaudy fly in the early morn or at the close of the day.

On the Eastern Coast, more especially at Indian River inlet, small blue fish congregate in numbers during the winter months, and at times will not refuse a fly. They are fair fighters, and as the piscator can fish from a sandy beach, much enjoyment can be secured.

In Florida cat fish will take a fly, and I may also add a spinner. In this State we have a number of species of this fish, and one is a surface feeder. In the evening, when they are feeding on the surface, they will not reject a large and gaudy fly. To those who have been accustomed to capture with a stout rod diminutive specimens of catties, I will say, hook on to a catty weighing from six to twelve pounds and there will be "music in the air," and unless skill is exercised on the part of the fisherman the leader will go to where the " woodbine twineth."

In Florida, as everywhere else, the best fishing is near where A., B. or C. run a hotel or keep a boarding house, or where certain steamboats make a terminal landing. But in my experience the best places to fish, as a rule, are where there are no hotels or specimens of the colored persuasion with their cast nets. When "I go a-fishing" I leave civilization, hotels, and boarding-houses in the rear.

The best points for fly-fishing for large-mouthed bass are on the upper St. Johns, the tributaries of Indian river, the Kessimmee and the streams and lagoons on the south-west coast. For pickerel and bream the best points are the tributaries of the St. Johns between Mandarin and Lake Monroe. For war-mouthed perch, the best streams will be found in Alachua County.

From all that I can glean from gentlemen who have

fished the locality, the lower Indian River and its tributaries will furnish a fine field for the fly-caster. West of Cedar Keys to St. Marks is a shoal coast covered with marine algæ ; and the coast line is cut up with a number of small streams stocked—nay, swarming—with fish. This section is uninhabited, the streams have not been fished, and a fine field for sport awaits the fisherman. In addition, hand line or bass rod fishing can be enjoyed for sheepshead and channel bass. The woods abound with deer, the hummocks contain plenty of turkeys, and the bays and grassy flats during the winter are alive with ducks, and in certain localities geese and brant will be found. Beech birds, as snipe and curlews, can be bagged in quantity.

The first stream worthy of notice on the southwest coast is the Homosassa River, forty miles south of Cedar Keys. But this beautiful river has lost its greatest attraction, " Mother Jones." I have been informed that she left Homosassa, and, as a sequence, there will be wanting the clean rooms and beds, the stewed and scalloped oysters, the aromatic coffee, the delicious breakfast bacon, and the luscious sheepshead done to a turn. With " Mother Jones" will depart many of the attractions of the place, more particularly the cusine. I write feelingly, for I was the first to make known the attractions of my favorite Homosassa.

According to my friend, Dr. Ferber, Billy Bow Legs Creek, a tributary of Sarasota Bay, presents many attractions to the fly-fisher, more especially in the capture of cavalli and ravallia. Long Boat Inlet, an entrance to this bay, must not be overlooked.

Many points in Charlotte Harbor offer inducements to the fly-fisher. If he tires of using the split bamboo, he can troll with a spinner and land large channel bass and cavalli ; for divertisement he can seat himself in an arm chair on the dock at Punta Rassa and imitate my friend Matthew Quay (late Secretary of State of Pennsylvania), who landed fifty-six large sheepshead in one hour. If dissatisfied with this description of sport the piscator can indulge in the capture of Jew-fish, weighing from one to three hundred pounds. On the Calloosahatchee, above the islands, the fly caster can be satiated with sport in landing large-sized cavalli. From Charlotte Harbor southward every entrance, bay, pass and lagoon will afford royal sport.

Delicate mist-colored leaders are not a necessity, for Florida fish have not been educated or posted with regard to the tricks of the craft. They seem to recognize but little difference between a single strand of gut and a clothes-line. The main things requisite are strong leaders and large-sized hooks, for when fish are so plentiful and valueless the fisherman is apt to try and see how many he can land within a given period. With regard to flies, almost any of the more common ones will answer a good purpose. My choice for channel bass, cavalli, sea trout and bone fish is a large-sized gaudy fly with a large-sized hook.

To reach the south-west coast persons can go direct

from Savannah or Fernandina, or visit Jacksonville *en route*. At Cedar Keys, Tampa, or Manatee they can charter a sloop or schooner of from four to six tons for five or six dollars per day. This amount will cover captain, boy, small boat, bedding, stove and cooking utensils. Fish, beach birds, oysters and clams are plentiful, and the expense of the culinary department will be from fifty cents to five dollars per capita per diem, according to the dietetic proclivities of the persons comprising the party.

The coast is shallow, the ten-fathom line ranging from thirty to forty miles from shore, and as a consequence there is no undertow, rollers or heavy seas. The passage from Cedar Keys to Bay Biscayne can be made in a small boat at almost any time. On one occasion the writer made the trip from Key West to Cedar Keys in a boat sixteen feet in length.

Fly-fishing in Florida is a recent development, and it offers a large field for experiment and investigation ; and I trust that the period is not far distant when the sport will be indulged in by the many. By the first of January, 1884, Tampa will be reached from this city in twenty-four hours via Sanford and Kissimmee. From what we know of railroads in this State we feel assured that one will be completed to Punta Rassa within two years ; when Charlotte Harbor and Estero Bay, the greatest of fishing points, will be rendered accessible to all.

In preparing this article we have used the common

names of fish, and the reason for so doing will be obvious to all. In passing through this city, if fly-fishers will call upon me between 12 M. and 2 P.M., I will endeavor to smooth the road for them.

JACKSONVILLE, FLA.

FLY-FISHING.

BY

COL. E. Z. C. JUDSON.—"Ned Buntline."

FISHERMEN are *born* such—not made ! That is my private opinion, publicly expressed. It is founded upon the experience of full half a century on ocean, lake, river, and brook. I have taken a mature man with me on a fishing trip, who had never cast "a line in pleasant places," lent him rod and tackle, made a few casts in his presence, caught perhaps a half a dozen trout, and then watched his imitative power combined with the tact *born* in him. If he was one of the right sort he would go right on improving every hour, and in a little while begin to fill his creel with the best of us.

My personal knowledge of fish and fishing began early. My father had few superiors as an angler, and trouting was his specialty. He made his own rods, lines and flies. The first was a tapering ashen pole—generally about ten feet long—scraped, oiled and varnished till it was as smooth and bright as glass. The line was made from horse-hair and braided with a care and patience that used to be a wonder to me.

The blue-jay, the red-headed woodpecker, the pheasant and wood-duck were shot for fly-feathers. When I was a wee toddler in skirts I used to hold hooks and snells and play at "helping papa."

All this was done here at the head of the Delaware, where both my father and myself were born. But a change came. When I was about six years old my father bought a large tract of wild land in the wildest part of Wayne County, Pennsylvania, and settled on it. The Lackawaxen Creek ran right through it, and that then lovely stream was literally alive with speckled trout. From the day we entered our log house there I was a *fisher-boy*. I caught trout every day in the summer, for a big spring rose within a rod of the house and from it ran a lively brook to the main stream, ten rods away, and even a pin-hook and linen thread would draw them out.

As I grew older I would go with my father to the big eddies and deep holes, where he would lure the largest to his fly and I was only too—too utterly happy when allowed to wade waist deep in the water to carry or float his string of trout toward home.

Since then never a summer has passed, except when actively engaged in naval or military service for my country, that has not found me fishing somewhere. I have covered the best waters in Maine, New Hampshire and Vermont ; Canada and the British Provinces know me of old ; California, Oregon and British Columbia— all along the Big Rockies—have seen me testing flies and bait, the former often tied rudely on the spur of necessity, but generally very effectively. For where trout are *very* plenty, food is scarce, and they will bite at anything. I speak of trout mostly, for that is my *favorite* fish. Salmon next, although the work comes in when you strike anything over eight or ten pounds, and sport degenerates when it becomes *labor*. I have heard of " labors of love," but I never took stock in anything of the kind.

In all this active piscatorial life, I have studied *Fishermen* as well as fish. And I have come to the conclusion which opens this article—that fishermen are *born* for it and can't be manufactured out of *raw* material !

I have felt thankful to our Father above that nine out of ten of the *tourists* who take to the streams in easy reach, are indifferent fishermen. For thereby the streams still contain fish. Were all who fish in them skillful and hoggish, in a little while there would be no fishing except in far-away places, difficult to reach.

I do not claim to hold a Master's Degree as a fly-fisherman. I do delight in the art, for one of the arts and sciences it surely is. I have bowed my head in reverence before the skilled hand of my dear friend, George Dawson—now beside the bright waters of the Happy Land above. I have stood silent and pleased while Seth Green deftly made casts which I could only feebly imitate.

Yet those who know me best say that I *can* use a fly-rod and catch trout and salmon therewith, so I essay a few words on the subject, speaking only from my own experience. I have never been observant enough to see a trout strike a fly with his tail, drown it and then eat it. I always take a trout in the mouth on my fly—generally hooked in the upper lip, showing that he does *his* part of the business in a straightforward way and does not come tail first to the lure.

I own to be a little particular about my rod, the middle joint not too limber, but with back-bone as well as spring; it suits me if it tapers so as to describe a perfect arc when the tip is brought near to the butt. I specify no makers—though I own to favorites in that line. I wish to make no petty jealousies here.

A rod as near ten feet long as may be, for trout fishing, weight from seven to eight ounces, never over ten, with the reel close to and *under* the butt; an easy running click-reel; a line of braided hair and silk, strong and weighty enough for a cast against the wind as well as with it; a clear, strong, looped leader for a quick change of flies; a book well supplied with the latter to give the speckled beauties a choice, and I am ready for work.

The idea of special flies for special seasons of the year I have found to be a humbug. Trout are exceedingly whimsical about flies. Watch those that are on the stream, see which the trout leap for and get as near the like of them as your book will allow.

Always, if possible, fish down stream. It is easier. You can detect swirls, eddies, shaded pools, coverts of rock, mossy-banks and overhanging branches, from above, better than below. Trout do not scare so easily

that a cast of fifteen or twenty feet will not find them
ready to rise if they are hungry. You have also the
aid of the current in guiding your fly to each coveted
spot after it touches the water.

Enter a stream, say its average width is seventy-five
or one hundred feet, few of our mountain streams
are so much, and a skilled rodster can cover it with
ease—for wading down he chooses his water, makes his
casts, seldom over twenty or twenty-five feet of line to
a cast, much oftener less, and in "good waters" fills
his creel.

For a forward cast, with your line as far out as may
be necessary for the distance, throw your rod sharply
back to an angle of not over fifteen degrees, and then
bring it forward quickly till, as your line and flies are extended, the tip is on a level with your breast, never
lower so as to dip water. With a line "taut," so to speak,
if a trout rises as your fly or flies touch the stream, a
sharp, quick turn of the wrist will strike the hook home
and secure him. Your strike must be firm and decisive ;
give the trout one second to understand and he *spits*
the fly out. Laugh if you will, but that is what he does.

When hooked, if not too large for your tackle, *draw*
the trout swiftly to you, *lift* him out, and break his
neck, by bending back the head where it joins the
back-bone. Thus he is out of pain, and does not bruise
and flop himself soft, while dying, in your creel.
"Playing" a trout for the mere fun of the thing, is
unnecessary torture ; besides, you frighten more than

you secure, in the process. A very large trout, of course, must be weakened in the water, but many fishermen think there is no sport without they "play" a fish, no matter how small he is.

Never cast a foot more line than you need. You cannot gather slack half as easy as you can pay it out.

In regard to flies—I have found the brighter the day, as a general thing, the darker fly do trout want. At early dawn, or in the soft twilight of evening, a very light fly—a Coachman, is best. Next, Gray Miller, and especially the Stone fly. I use more Coachmen, Black Gnats and Stone flies in *one* season, than I do of all other flies put together in three summers.

Be sure, of all things, that your line runs easy through the standing guides, or guide-rings. I like the former best.

In casting right or left, to reach under bushy or over-hanging limbs, the same sharp, or quick action which makes an over-cast successful, is required, and great care not to draw any slack line when your fly drops where you want it.

Many fly-fishermen are considered adepts according to the *length* rather than the grace and certainty of their casts. I do not think in actual stream fishing an average of a day's casting, would reach over fifteen feet to a cast. I never made but one *very* long cast in actual angling in my life.

Once, on the bank of a mill-pond in the upper part of Alder Brook, in Ulster County, N. Y., I saw a trout in shoal water, the largest I ever caught in that vicinity. To reach him without alarm, I cast seventy-two feet, *measured* afterward from a knot on my line near my reel, and got my fish.

He weighed two and a quarter pounds, and I had to play him some to save him.

And now, with a word to young fishermen and old *beginners*, I will close.

Learn first to cast a line and take a trout with bait before you try a fly. You will thereby gain confidence, learn to hook your fish at the instant he strikes, and gain the supple use of arm and wrist which makes the fly-fisherman skillful.

My dear wife, by whose sick bed I pen these words, for one long joyous summer in camp, fished by my side, using bait while she saw me casting no lure but flies.

The next time we went on the stream she had a six-ounce fly-rod, and fifty beautiful trout in two hours to her basket proved how apt a pupil she had been.

With many words of cheer to all who love the glorious pastime, I remain, as of yore—Uncle Ned—*a born fisherman.*

" Eagle's Nest," Delaware Co., N. Y.

"In casting against the wind you must lift your line from the water so that it extends behind you at about an angle of forty-five degrees, and then bring your rod down sharply right onto the water, and straight against the wind; this makes the line cut through it, and extend out straight onto the water. The secret is to keep the line well up behind, and then continue the forward impetus sharply until the rod tip touches, or nearly touches the water."—*Reuben Wood.*

"It is impossible to lay down inflexible rules for stream fishing, which is the most artistic of all fishing, and requires more knowledge of the habits of fish and changes of tactics to meet the varying moods of the weather."—*Fred Mather.*

"A little horse sense goes a great way in all things, trouting not excepted; it is an indispensable foundation to success."—"*Bourgeois.*"

"Summarizing some facts from the journal of the club we add the opinions of its members. Good flies for black bass trolling are 'Montreal,' 'scarlet ibis,' 'brown hackle,' 'Cheney,' and 'grizzly king.'"—*M. M. Backus.*

"The trout rose freely, and we had good sport, until the fog lifted, when the fishing ceased."—*Fitz James Fitch.*

"You can't help now and then giving a vicious little tug to feel sure your hook is well set in, or a sharp twist of the wrist when you find the 'enemy' heading for a stump; but once he's landed and lies on the mossy bank or lichened rock, his spangled armor gleaming in the sunshine, his little life drifting painlessly away in spasmodic sobs, Lord! how you love him!"—*Frank. S. Pinckney.*

"There is not a sign of fear about the speckled trout, he is pluck personified, from his keen lustrous eyes to the swirl and dash of his square tail that waves in defiance."—*W. David Tomlin.*

"At the commencement of the open season, and until the young maple leaves are half grown, bait will be found more successful than the fly."—"*Nessmuk.*"

" There are two peculiarities of all sorts of fish, which are frequently unnoticed ; that they are largely attracted to their food by scent, and that they feed at night."—*Seth Green.*

" The first and last object of the fly-fisher is to show as much of the fly to the fish as possible, and as little of anything else."—*Francis Francis.*

" The notion of the main mass of anglers would appear to be, that if an unusually cunning fish takes up an impregnable-looking position he is to be religiously left unassailed. ' Breakers ahead !' seem to be scented by the over-cautious pliers of the rod, when the chances of conquest are really ' as even ' as in less dangerous localities ; and even supposing this were not so, the greater the difficulties the more exciting the sport, and the keener the pleasure."—*David Foster.*

26. Manchester.	27. Blue Jay.
28. Imperial.	29. McLeod.
30. Black and Gold.	31. White and Jungle Cock.

" Many men of fame, even equal to Dr. Johnson's, have been eminent as anglers, and have redeemed and disculpated angling from his surly and foolish sneer."—*John Lyle King.*

" I invariably endeavor, when dressing a fly, to imitate the living insect; still I have seen nondescript flies beat all the palmer hackles and the most *life-like* flies that ever graced a casting-line."—" *Frank Forester.*"

" If we are content with an ungainly fly, we will be satisfied with inferiority of rod and tackle ; and although the fish may not see the difference, the angler may become, from neglecting one point, slovenly in all. A well-made fly is a beautiful object, an ill-made one an eye-sore and annoyance ; and it is a great satisfaction both to exhibit and examine a well-filled book of handsomely tied flies."—*R. B. Roosevelt.*

"What is life, after all, but just going a-fishing all the time, casting flies on many rivers and lakes, and going quietly home as the day is ending ?"—*W. C. Prime.*

" This fishing story is at an end ; not for want of material, for there are other scenes and other times of equal pleasure that crowd my memory as I write these lines.   And so it will ever be to you, my friend, should you, even in your later years, take up the angler's art : it grows with its growth, and strengthens with its strength, and, if uncurbed, may perchance, with many of us, become a passion.

" But, for all that, it will fill the storehouse of our memories with many a scene of unalloyed pleasure, which in the sunset of life we may look back upon with fondest satisfaction.

"If in the minds of any one of you who as yet are ignorant of the charm of fishing, as it has here been revealed, I have induced the desire for a test, ' Stand not upon the order of your going, but go at once,' provided it be the season, and, the word of an old fisherman for it, you will thank me for these random pages."— *Charles W. Stevens.*